THE ART OF ENTERTAINING

LECTOR HOUSE PUBLIC DOMAIN WORKS

THE ART OF ENTERTAINING

MARY ELIZABETH WILSON SHERWOOD

ISBN: 978-93-90215-05-8

Published: 1893

THE ART OF ENTERTAINING

BY

M. E. W. SHERWOOD

This night
Beneath my roof my dearest friends I entertain

Homer

1893

PREFACE.

In America the art of entertaining as compared with the same art in England, in France, in Italy and in Germany may be said to be in its infancy. But if it is, it is a very vigorous infant, perhaps a little overfed. There is no such prodigality of food anywhere nor a more genuinely hospitable people in the world than those descendants of the Pilgrims and the Cavaliers who peopled the North and South of what we are privileged to call the United States. Exiles from Fatherland taught the Indians the words "Welcome!" and "What Cheer?" —a beautiful and a noble prophecy. Well might it be the motto for our national shield. We, who welcome to our broad garden-lands the hungry and the needy of an overcrowded old world, can well appropriate the legend.

No stories of that old Biblical world of the patriarchs who lived in tents have been forgotten in the New World. The Western settler who placed before his hungry guest the last morsel of jerked meat, or whose pale, overworked wife broiled the fish or the bird which had just fallen before his unerring gun, —these people had mastered in their way the first principle in the art of entertaining. They have the hospitality of the heart. From that meal to a Newport dinner what an infinite series of gradations!

Perhaps we may help those on the lower rungs of the ladder to mount from one to the other. Perhaps we may hint at the poetry, the romance, the history, the literature of entertaining; perhaps with practical hints of how to feed our guests we may suggest where meat faileth to feed the soul, and where intellect, wit, and taste come in.

American dinners are pronounced by foreign critics as overdone. The great *too much* is urged against us. We are a wasteful people as to food; we should learn an elegant and a wise economy. In a French family, eggs and lumps of sugar are counted. Economy is a part of the art of entertaining; if judiciously studied it is far from niggardliness. Such economy leads to judicious selection.

One has but to read the Odes of Horace to learn how much of the mind can be appropriately devoted to the art of entertaining. Milton does not disdain, in Paradise Lost, to give us the *menu* of Eve's dinner to the Angel. We find in all great poets and historians stories of great feasts. And with us in the nineteenth century, dinner is not alone a thing of twelve courses, it is the bright consummate flower of the day, which brings us all together from our various fields of work. It is the open sesame of the soul, the hour of repose, of amusement, of innocent hilarity, —the hour which knits up the ravelled sleeve of care. The body is carefully apparelled, the mind swept and garnished, the brain prepared for fresh impress. It is said that no important political movement was ever inaugurated without a dinner, and we may fancifully state that no great poem, no novel, no philosophical treatise, but has been made or marred by a dinner.

There is much entertaining, however, which is not eating. We do not gorge ourselves, as in the days of Dr. Johnson, until the veins in the forehead swell to bursting, but perhaps we are just as far from those banquets which Horace describes,—a glass of Falernian, a kid roasted, a bunch of grapes, and a rose, with good talk afterward. We have not mingled enough of the honey of Hymettus with our cookery.

Lady Morgan described years ago a dinner at Baron Rothschild's in Paris where the fineness of the napery, the beauty of the porcelain and china, the light, digestible French dishes, seemed to her a great improvement on the heaviness of an English dinner. That one paper is said to have altered the whole fabric of English dinner-giving. English dinners of to-day are superlatively good and agreeable in the best houses, and although national English cookery is not equal to that on the other side of the Channel, perhaps we could not have a better model to follow. We can compass an "all round" mastery of the art of entertaining if we choose.

It is not alone the wealth of America which can assist us, although wealth is a good thing. It is our boundless resource, and the capability, spirit, and generosity of our people. Venice alone at one imperial moment of her success had such a chance as we have; she was free, she was industrious, she was commercial, she was rich, she was artistic. All the world paid her tribute. And we see on her walls to-day, fixed there by the pencils of Tintoretto and Titian, what was her idea of the art of entertaining. Poetry, painting, and music were the hand-maidens of plenty; they wait upon those Godlike men and those beautiful women. It is a saturnalia of colour, an apotheosis of plenty with no vulgar excess, with no slumberous repletion. "'Tis but the fool who loves excess," says our American Horace in his "Ode to an Old Punch Bowl."

When we read Charles Lamb's "Essay on Roast Pig," Brillat Savarin's grave and witty "Physiologie du Gout," Thackeray's "Fitz Boodle's Professions," Sydney Smith's poetical recipe for a salad; when we read Disraeli's description of dinners, or the immortal recipes for good cheer which Dickens has scattered through his books, we learn how much the better part of dinner is that which we do not eat, but only think about. What a liberal education to hear the late Samuel Ward talk about good dinners! Variety not vegetables, manners not meat, was his motto. He invested the whole subject with a sort of classic elegance and a humorous sense of responsibility. Anacreon and Charles Delmonico seemed to mingle in his brain, and one would gladly now be able to dine with him and Longfellow at their yearly Christmas dinner.

Cookery books, receipts, and *menus* are apt to be of little use to young housekeepers before they have mastered the great art of entertaining. Then they are like the system of logarithms to the mariner. Almost all young housekeepers are at sea without a chart. A great, turbulent ocean of butchers, bakers and Irish servants swim before their eyes. How grapple with that important question, "How shall I give a dinner?" Who can help them? Shall we try?

CONTENTS

THE ART OF ENTERTAINING.

OUR AMERICAN RESOURCES, AND FOREIGN ALLIES.

"Let observation, with extensive view,
Survey mankind from China to Peru."

The amount of game and fish which our great country and extent of sea-coast give us, the variety of climate from Florida to Maine, from San Francisco to Boston, which the remarkable net-work of our railway communication allows us to enjoy,—all this makes the American market in any great city almost fabulously profuse. Then our steamships bring us fresh artichokes from Algiers in mid-winter, and figs from the Mediterranean, while the remarkable climate of California gives us four crops of delicate fruits a year.

There are those, however, who find the fruits of California less finely flavoured than those of the Eastern States. The peaches of the past are almost a lost flavour, even at the North. The peach of Europe is a different and far inferior fruit. It lacks that essential flavour which to the American palate tells of the best of fruits.

It may be well, for the purposes of gastronomical history, to narrate the variety of the larder in the height of the season, of a certain sea-side club-house, a few years ago:

"The season lasted one hundred and eighty days, during which time from eighty thousand to ninety thousand game-birds, and eighteen thousand pounds of fish were consumed, exclusive of domestic poultry, steaks and chops. On busy days twenty-four kinds of fish, all fit for epicures, embracing turbot, Spanish mackerel, sea trout; the various kinds of bass, including that gamest of fish the black bass, bonito from the Gulf of Mexico, the purple mullet, the weakfish, chicken halibut, sole, plaice, the frog, the soft crab from the Chesapeake, were served. Here, packed tier upon tier in glistening ice, were some thirty kinds of birds in the very ecstasy of prime condition, and all ready prepared for the cook. Let us enumerate 'this royal fellowship of game.' There were owls from the North (we might call them by some more enticing name), chicken grouse from Illinois, chicken partridge, Lake Erie black and summer ducks and teal, woodcock, upland plover (by many esteemed as the choicest of morsels), dough-birds, brant, New Jersey millet, godwit, jack curlew, jacksnipe, sandsnipe, rocksnipe, humming-birds daintily served in nut-shells, golden plover, beetle-headed plover, redbreast plover, chicken plover, seckle-bill curlew, summer and winter yellow-legs, reed-birds and rail from Delaware (the latter most highly esteemed in Europe, where it is known as the ortolan), ring-neck snipe, brown backs, grass-bird, and peeps."

Is not this a list to make "the rash gazer wipe his eye"?

And to show our riches and their poverty in the matter of game, let us give the game statistics of France for one September. There are thirty thousand communes in France, and in each commune there were killed on the average on September 1, ten hares,—total, three hundred thousand; seventeen partridges,—total, five hundred and ten thousand; fourteen quail,—total, four hundred and twenty thousand; one rail in each commune,—thirty thousand total as to rails. That was all France could do for the furnishing of the larder; of course she imports game from Savoy, Germany, Norway, and England. And oh, how she can cook them!

Woodcock, it is said, should be cooked the day it is shot, or certainly when fresh. Birds that feed on or near the water should be eaten fresh; so should snipe and some kinds of duck. The canvasback alone bears keeping, the others get fishy.

Snipe should be picked by hand, on no account drawn; that is a practice worthy of an Esquimaux. Nor should any condiment be cooked with woodcock, save butter or pork. A piece of toast under him, to catch his fragrant gravy, and the delicious trail should alone be eaten with the snipe; but a bottle of Chambertin may be drunk to wash him down.

The plover should be roasted quickly before a hot fire; nor should even a pork jacket be applied if one wishes the delicious juices of the bird alone. This bird should be served with water-cresses.

Red wine should be drunk with game,—Chambertin, Clos de Vougeot, or a sound Lafitte or La Tour claret. Champagne is not the wine to serve with game; that belongs to the filet. With beef *braisé* a glass of good golden sherry is allowable, but not champagne. The deep purple, full-bodied, velvety wines of the Côte d'Or,—the generous vintages of Burgundy,—are in order. Indeed these wines always have been in high renown. They are passed as presents from one royal personage to another, like a *cordon d'honneur*. Burgundy was the wine of nobles and churchmen, who always have had enviable palates.

Chambertin is a lighter kind of Volnay and the *vin velouté par excellence* of the Côte d'Or. It was a great favourite with Napoleon I. To considerable body it unites a fine flavour and a *suave bouquet* of great *finesse*, and does not become thin with age like other Burgundies. As for the Clos de Vougeot, its characteristics are a rich ruby colour, velvety softness, a delicate bouquet, which has a slight suggestion of the raspberry. It is a strong wine, less refined in flavour than the Chambertin, and with a suggestion of bitterness. It was so much admired by a certain military commander that while marching his regiment to the Rhine he commanded his men to halt before the vineyard and salute it. They presented arms in its honour.

Château Lafitte, renowned for its magnificent colour, exquisite softness, delicate flavour, and fragrant bouquet, recalling almonds and violets, is one of the wines of the Gironde, and is supposed of late to have deteriorated in quality; but it is quite good enough to command a high price and the attention of *connoisseurs*.

Château La Tour, a grand Médoc claret, derives its name from an existing ancient, massive, round tower, which the English assailed and defended by turns during the wars in Guienne. It has a pronounced flavour, and a powerful bouquet, common to all wines of the Gironde. It reminds one of the odour of almonds, and of Noyau cordials.

These vineyards were in great repute five centuries ago; and it would be delightful to pursue the history of the various *crûs*, did time permit. The Cos d'Estoumet of the famous St. Estephe *crûs* is still made by the peasants treading out the grapes, *foule à pied*, to the accompaniment of pipes and fiddles as in the days of Louis XIV.

We will mention the two *premiers grands crûs* of the Gironde, the growth of the ancient vineyards of Leoville and the St. Julian wines, distinguished by their odour of violets.

Thackeray praises Chambertin in verse more than once:—

"'Oui, oui, Monsieur,' 's the waiter's answer;
'Quel vin Monsieur desire-t-il?'
'Tell me a good one.'—'That I can, sir:
The Chambertin, with yellow seal.'"

Then again he speaks of dipping his gray beard in the Gascon wine 'ere Time catches him at it and Death knocks the crimson goblet from his lips.

In countries where wine is grown there is little or no drunkenness. It is to be feared that drunkenness is increased by impure wines. It is shocking to read of the adulterations which first-class wines are subjected to, or rather the adulterations which are called first-class wines.

Wilkie Collins has a hit at this in his "No Name," where he makes the famous Captain Wragge say, "We were engaged at the time in making, in a small back parlour in Brompton, a fine first-class sherry, sound in the mouth, tonic in character, and a great favourite with the Court of Spain."

Our golden sherry, our Chambertin, our Château Lafitte is said often to come from the vineyards of Jersey City and the generous hillsides of Brooklyn; and we might perhaps quote from the famous song of "The Canal":—

"The tradesmen who in liquor deal,
Of our Canal good use can make;
And when they mean their casks to fill,
They oft its water freely take.
By this device they render less
The ills that spring from drunkenness;
For harmless is the wine, you'll own,
From vines that in canals is grown."

A large proportion of the so-called foreign wines sold in America are of American manufacture. The medium grade clarets and so-called Sauternes are made in California, in great quantities. Our Senator, Leland Stanford, makes excellent wines. On the islands of Lake Erie, the lake region of Central New York, and along the banks of the Ohio and Missouri Rivers, are vineyards producing excellent wines. An honest American wine is an excellent thing to drink; and yet it disgusted Commodore McVicker, who was entertained in London as President of our Yacht Club, to be asked to drink American wines. Yet the Catawbas, "dulcet, delicious and creamy," are not to be despised; neither are the sweet and dry California growths.

The indigenous wines which come from Ohio, Iowa, Missouri and Mississippi are likely to be musty and foxy, and are not pleasant to an American taste. The Catawbas are pleasant, and are of three colours,—rose colour, straw colour, and colourless, if that be a colour. In taste they are like sparkling Moselle, but fuller to the palate.

The wine produced from the Isabella grape is of a decided raspberry flavour. The finest American wines are those produced from the vines known as Norton's Virginia and the Cynthiana. The former produces a well-blended, full-bodied, deep-coloured, aromatic, and almost astringent wine; the second,—probably the finer of the two,—is a darker, less astringent, and more delicate product.

Among the American red wines may be mentioned the product of the Schuylkill Muscadel, which was the only esteemed growth in the country previous to the cultivation of the Catawba grape, being in fact ambitiously compared to the *crûs* of the Gironde. It was a bitter, acidulous wine, little suited to the American palate, and invariably requiring an addition of either sugar or alcohol.

Longfellow sings of the wine of the Mustang grape of Texas and New Mexico:—

> "The fiery flood
> Of whose purple blood
> Has a dash of Spanish bravado."

The Carolina Scuppernong is detestable, reminding us of the sweet and bitter medicines of childhood. The Herbemont, a rose-tinted wine is very like Spanish Manganilla.

Longfellow says of sparkling Catawba, that it "fills the room with a benison on the giver." It has, indeed, a charming bouquet, as says the poet.

The name of Nicholas Longworth is intimately connected with the subject of American wines. To him will ever be given all honour, as being the father of this industry in the New World; but the superior excellence of the California wines has driven the New York and Ohio wines, it is said, to a second place in the market.

In the expositions of 1889 at Paris, and in Melbourne, silver medals were awarded to the Inglenook wines, which are of the red claret, burgundy and Médoc type; also white wines,—Sauterne Chasselas, and Hock, Chablis, Riesling, etc.

The right soil for the cultivation of the grape is a hard thing to find; but Captain Niebaum, a rich California grower, has hit the key-note, when he says, "I have no wish to make any money out of my vineyard by producing a large quantity of wine at a cheap or moderate price. I am going to make a California wine which, if it can be made, will be worthily sought for by *connoisseurs*; and I am prepared to spend all the money needed to accomplish that result." He says frankly that he has not yet produced the best wine of which California is capable, but that he has succeeded in producing a better wine than many of the foreign wines sold in America. He might have added that hogsheads of California grape-juice are sent annually to Bordeaux to be doctored, and returned to America as French claret.

The misfortunes of the vine-grower in Europe, the ruin of acres of grape-producing country by the phyloxera, should be the opportunity for these new vine-growers in the United States. It is only by travel, experiment, and by a close study of the methods of the foreign wine-growers that a Californian can possibly make himself a vineyard which shall be successful. He must induce Nature to sweeten his wines, and he can then laugh at the chemist.

Of vegetables we have not only all that Europe can boast, excepting perhaps the artichoke, but we have some in constant use and of great excellence which they have not. For instance, sweet corn boiled or roasted and eaten from the cob with butter and salt is unknown in Europe. They have not the sweet potato, so delicious when baked. They have not the pumpkin-pie although they have the pumpkin. They have egg-plant and cauliflower and beans and peas, but so have we. They have bananas, but never fried, which is a negro dish, and excellent. They have not the plantain, good baked, nor the avocado or alligator pear, which fried in butter or oil is so admirable. They have not the ochra, of which the negro cooks make such excellent gumbo soup. They have all the salads, and use sorrel much more than we do. They do not cook summer squash as we do, nor have they anything to equal it. They use vegetables always as an *entrée*, not served with the meat, unless the vegetable is cooked with the meat, like beef stewed in carrots, turnips, and onions, veal and green peas, veal with spinach, and so on. The peas are passed as an *entrée*, so is the cauliflower, the beet-root, and the turnips. They treat all vegetables as we do corn and asparagus, as a separate course. For asparagus we must give the French the palm, particularly when they serve it with Hollandaise sauce; and the Italians cook cauliflower with cheese, *à ravir*.

THE HOSTESS.

"A creature not too bright or good
For human nature's daily food;
For transient sorrow, simple wiles,
Praise, blame, love, kisses, tears, and smiles."

The "house-mother," — the mistress of servants, the wife, the mother, the hostess, — is the first person in the art of entertaining; and considering how busy, how hard worked, how occupied, are American men, she is generally the first person singular. In nine cases out of ten, American men neither know nor care much about the conduct of the house if the wife will assume it; they only like to be made comfortable, and to find a warm, clean home, with a good dinner awaiting them. It is the wife who must struggle with the problems of domestic defeat or victory.

When Washington Irving was presented at the Court of Dresden his Saxon Majesty remarked, "Mr. Irving, with a republic so liberal, you can have no servants in America."

"Yes, Sire, we have servants, such as they are," said the amiable author of the "Sketchbook;" "but we do not call them servants, we call them help."

"I cannot understand that," said the king.

The king's mental position was not illogical; for, with his experience of the servile position of the domestic in Europe, he could not reconcile to his mind the declaration of social equality in America.

The American hostess must, it would seem, for many centuries if not forever, have to struggle against this difficulty. As some writer said twenty years ago, of this question: "Rich as we are in money, profuse in spending it to heighten the enjoyment of life, the good servant, that essential of comfort and luxury, seems beyond our reach. Superfine houses we have, and superfine furniture, and superfine ladies, and all the other superfineties to excess, but the skilful cook, the handy maid, and the trusty nurse we rarely possess."

Thus, afar from the great cities and even in them, we must forge the instruments with which we work, instead of finding them ready to hand, as in other countries. That is to say, the mistress of a household must teach her cook to cook, her waiter to wait, her laundress to get up fine linen. She is happy if she can get honest people and willing hands, but trained servants she durst not expect away from the great centres of life.

Considering what has been expected of the American woman, has she not done rather well? That she must be first servant-trainer, then housekeeper, wife, mother, and conversationist, that she must keep up with the always advancing spirit of the times, read, write, and cipher, be beautifully dressed, play the piano, make the wilderness to blossom as the rose, be charitable, thoughtful, and good, put the mind at its ease, strive to learn how to do all things in the best way, be a student of good taste and good manners, make a house luxurious, ornamental, cheerful, and restful, have an inspired sense of the fitness of things, dress and entertain in perfect accord with her station, her means, and her husband's ambition, master, unassisted, all the ins and outs of the noble art of entertaining,—has not this been something of the nature of a large contract?

She must go to the cooking-lecture, come home and visit the kitchen, go to the intelligence office, keeping her hand on all three. She must be the mind, while the Maggies and Bridgets furnish the hands. She must never be fussy, never grotesque; she must steer her ship through stormy seas, and she must also learn to enjoy Wagner's music. There is proverbially no sea so dangerous to swim in as that tumultuous one of a new and illy regulated prosperity; and in the changeful, uncertain nature of American fortunes an American woman must be ready to meet any fate.

Judging from many specimens which we have seen, may we not claim that the American woman must be stamped with an especial distinction? Has she not conquered her fate?

Curiously enough, fashion and good taste seem to lackey to the American woman, no matter where she was born or where educated. In spite of all drawbacks, and the counter-currents of destiny, she is a well bred and tasteful woman. No matter what the American woman has to fight against, poverty or lack of opportunities, she is likely, if she is called upon to do so, to administer gracefully the hospitalities of the White House or to fill the difficult *rôle* of an ambassadress.

Some of them have bad taste perhaps. "What is good taste but an instantaneous, ready appreciation of the fitness of things?" To most of us who observe it in others, it seems to be an instinct. We envy those few who are always well dressed, who never buy unbecoming stuffs, who have the gift to make their clothes look as if they had simply blossomed out of their inner consciousness, as a rose blossoms out of its calyx. Some women always dress their hair becomingly; others, even if handsome, look like beautiful frights. Some wear their clothes as if they had been hurled at them by a tornado, and remind one of the poor husband's remark, "I feel as if I had married a hurricane." The same exceptions, which only prove the rule, because you notice them, may extend to the housewives who aim at more than they can accomplish, who make their house an anguish to look at, pretentious without beauty, overloaded or incorrect, who have not tact, who say the awkward thing. Such people exist sometimes, sinning from ignorance, but they are decidedly in the minority. The American woman is generally a success. She has fought a hard battle, but she has won. She has had her defeats, however.

Who does not remember the failure of that first dinner-party?—when the baby began to cry so loud; when the hostess was not dressed when the bell rang; when the cook spilled the soup all over the range and filled the house with a bad odour;

when the waitress, usually so cool, lost all her presence of mind and fell on the basement stairs, breaking all the plates; when one failure succeeded another until the husband looked reproachfully at his wife, who, poor creature, had been working day and night to get up this dinner, who was responsible for none of the failures, and who had an attack of neuralgia afterward which lasted all winter.

Who has not read Thackeray's witty descriptions of the dinners, poor and pretentious, ordered in from the green-grocer's, and uneatable,—in London? "If they would have a leg of mutton and an apple pudding and a glass of sherry, they could do well; but they must shine, they must outdo their neighbours." And that is the first mistake. People with three thousand a year should not try to emulate those who have fifty thousand a year.

And Thackeray says again: "But there is no harm done, not as regards the dinner-givers, though the dinner-eaters may have to suffer. It only shows that the former are hospitably inclined, and wish to do the very best in their power. If they do badly, how can they help it? They know no better."

The first thing at which a young housekeeper must aim is to live well every day. Her tablecloth must be fresh, her glass and silver clean; a few flowers must be on her table to make it dainty, a few dishes well cooked,—such a table as will be well for her children and acceptable to her husband; and then she has but to add a little more and it is fit for any guest, and any guest will be glad to join such a dinner-party.

But here I am met by the almost unanswerable argument that the simplest dinner is the most difficult to find. Who knows how to cook a beefsteak, to roast a piece of mutton so that its natural juices are retained,—to roast it so that the blood shall follow the knife; to mash potatoes and brown them; to make a perfect rice-pudding that is said to "deserve that *cordon bleu* which Vatel, Ude, and Bechamel craved"?

The young housekeeper of to-day with very modest means has, however, now to meet a condition of prosperity which even twenty-five years ago was unknown. All extremes of luxury and every element of profusion is now fashionable,—one may say expected.

But agreeable young people will be entertained by the man who is worth fifty thousand dollars a day, and they will wish to return the civility. Herein lie the difficulties in the art of entertaining; but let them remember that there is one simple dinner which covers the whole ground, which the poor gentleman may aspire to give, and to which he might invite a prince. The essentials of a comfortable dinner are but few. The beauty of a Grecian vase without ornament is perfect. You may add cameo and intaglio, vine, acanthus leaf, satyrs, and fauns, handles of ram's horns and circlet of gems to your vase if you wish, and are rich enough, but unless the outline is perfect the splendour and the arabesque but render the vase vulgar. So with the simple dinner; it is the Grecian vase unadorned.

Remember that rich people, stifled with luxury at home, like to be asked to these dinners. A lady in England, very much admired for her witty conversation, said she intended to devote herself to the amelioration of the condition of the upper classes, as she thought them the most bored and altogether the least attended to of any people; and we have heard of the rich man in New York who complained that he was no longer asked to the little dinners. There is too much worship and fear of money in our country. In England and on the Continent there is no shame in acknowledging, "I cannot afford it." I have been asked to a luncheon in England where a cold joint of mutton, a few potatoes, and a plate of peaches constituted the whole repast; and I have heard more delightful conversation and have met more agreeable people than at more expensive feasts. Who in America would dare to give such a lunch?

The simple dinner might be characterized, giving the essentials, as a soup, a fish, a roast, one *entrée*, and a salad, an ice and fruit (simply the fruit in season), a cup of coffee afterward, with a glass of sherry, claret, or champagne. Such a dinner is good enough for anybody, and is possible to the person of moderate means.

From this up to the splendid dinners of millionnaires, served on gold and silver and priceless Sèvres, Dresden, Japanese, and Chinese porcelain, with flagons of ruby glass bound in gold, with Benvenuto Cellini vases, and silver candelabra, the ascent may be gradual. In the one the tablecloth is of spotless damask; in the other it may be of duchesse lace over red. The very mats are mirrors, the crystal drops of the epergne flash like diamonds. It may be served in a picture-gallery. Each lady has a bouquet, a fan, a ribbon painted with her name, a basket or *bonbonnière* to take home with her. The courses are often sixteen in number, the wines are of fabulous value, antiquity, and age. Each drop is like the River Pactolus, whose sands were of gold. The viands may come from Algiers or St. Petersburg; strawberries and peaches in January, the roses of June in February, fruit from the Pacific, from the Gulf, artichokes from Marseilles, oranges and strawberries from Florida, game from Arizona and Chesapeake Bay, mutton and pheasants from Scotland, luxury from everywhere. The primal condition of this banquet is, that everything should be unusual.

But remember that, after all, it is only the Grecian vase heavily ornamented. No one person can taste half the dishes; it takes a long time, and the room may be too hot. The limitations of a dinner should be considered. It is a splendid picture, no doubt, but it need not appall the young hostess who desires to return the civility.

A vase of flowers or a basket of growing plants can replace the epergne. Some pretty dinner-cards may be etched by herself, with a Shakspearean quotation showing a personal thought of each guest. Her spotless glass and silver, her good soup, her fresh fish, the haunch of venison roasted before a wood fire, the salad mixed by her own fair hands, perhaps a dessert over which she has lingered, a bit of cheese, a cup of coffee, a smiling host, a composed hostess, a congenial company, and wit withal,—who shall say that the little dinner is not as amusing as the big dinner? To be composed: yes, that is the first thing to be remembered on the part of a young hostess. She may be essentially nervous and anxious, particularly if she is just beginning to entertain, but here she must resolutely put on a mask of composure, and assume a virtue if she have it not. Nothing is of much importance, excepting her own demeanor. A fussy hostess who scolds the servants, wrinkles her brow, or even forgets to listen to the man who is talking to her is the ruin of a dinner. The author of "Cecil" tells his niece that if stewed puppy-dog is brought to the table she must not notice it. Few hostesses are subjected to so severe an ordeal as this, but the remark contains a goodly hint.

As, however, it is a great intellectual feat to achieve a perfect little dinner with a small household and small means, perhaps that form of entertaining may be postponed a few years. Never attempt anything which cannot be well done. There is the afternoon tea, the musical evening, the reception, the luncheon; they are all easier to give than the dinner. The young hostess ambitious to excel in the art of entertaining can choose a thousand ways. Let her alone avoid attempting the impossible; and let her remember that no success which is not honestly gained is worth a pin. If it is money, it stings; if it is place and position, it becomes the shirt of Nessus.

But for the well mannered and well behaved American woman what a noble success, what a perfect present, what a delightful future there is! She is the founder of the American nobility. All men bow down to her. She is the queen of the man who loves her; he treats her with every respect. She is to teach the future citizen honour, loyalty, duty, respect, politeness, kindness, the law of love. Such a man could read his Philip Sidney and yet not blush to find himself a follower. An American woman wields the only rod of empire to which American men will bow. She should try to be an empress in the best sense of the word; and to a young woman entering society we should recommend a certain exclusiveness. Not snobbish exclusiveness; but it is always well to choose one's friends slowly and with due consideration. We are not the most perfect beings in all the world; we do not wish to be intimate with too much imperfection. A broken friendship is a very painful thing. We should think twice before we give an intimate friendship to any one. No woman who essays to entertain should ask everybody to her house. The respect she owes to herself should prevent this; her house becomes a camp unless she has herself the power of putting a coarse sieve outside the door.

We have no such inviolable virtue that we can as yet rate Dives and Lazarus before they are dead. Very rich people are apt to be very good people; and in the realms of the highest fashion we find the simplest, best, and purest of characters. It is therefore of no consequence as to the shade of fashion and the amount of the rent-roll. It must not be supposed because some leaders of fashion are insolent that all are. A young hostess must try to find the good, true, honourable, generous, well bred, well educated member of society, no matter in what conditions of life. Read character first, and hesitate before drawing general deductions.

A hostess is the slave of her guests after she has invited them; she must be all attention, and all suavity. If she has nothing to offer them but a small house, a cup of tea, and a smile, she is just as much a hostess as if she were a queen. If she offers them every luxury and is not polite, she is a snob and a vulgarian. There is no such detestable use of one's privileges as to be rude on one's ground. "The man who eats your salt is sacred." To patronize is a great necessity to some natures. There is little opportunity for it in free, brave America, but some mistaken hostesses have gone that way. Every one feels pleasantly toward the woman who invites one to her house; there is something gracious in the act. But if, after opening her doors, the hostess refuses the welcome, or treats her guests with various degrees of cordiality, why did she ask at all? Every young American can become a model hostess; she can master etiquette, and create for herself a polite and cordial manner. She should be as serene as a summer's day; she should keep all her domestic troubles out of sight. If she entertains, let her do it in her own individual way, — a small way if necessary. There was much in Touchstone's philosophy, — "a poor thing, but mine own." She must have the instinct of hospitality, which is to give pleasure to all one's guests; and it seems unnecessary to say to any young American hostess, *Noblesse oblige*. She should be more polite to the shy, ill-dressed visitor from the country — if indeed there is such a thing left in America, where, as Bret Harte says, "The fashions travel by telegraph" — than to the sweeping city dame, that can take care of herself. A kindly greeting to a gawky youth will never be forgotten; and it is to the humblest that a hostess should address her kindest attentions.

There are born hostesses, like poets, but a hostess can also be made, in which she has the advantage of the poets; and to the very wealthy hostess we should quote this inestimable advice: —

Si tibi deficiant medici, medici tibi fiant
Hæc tria: mens hilaris, requies, moderata diæta.

HORACE.

Do not over-feed people. Who is it that says, "If simplicity is admirable in manners and in literary style, in the matter of dinners it becomes exalted into one of the cardinal virtues"?

The ambitious housewife would do well to remember this when she cumbers herself, and thinks too much about her forthcoming banquet. If she ignores this principle of simplicity and falls into the opposite extreme of ostentation and pretentiousness, she may bore her guests rather than entertain them.

It is an incontestable fact that dinners are made elaborate only at a considerable risk; as they increase in size and importance, their character is likely to deteriorate. This is true not only with regard to the number of guests, but with reference to the number of dishes that go to make up a bill-of-fare.

In fact we, as Americans, generally err on the side of having too much rather than too little. The terror of running short is agony to the mind of the conscientious housewife. How much will be enough and no more? It stands to reason that the fewer the dishes, the more the cook can concentrate her attention upon them; and here is reason for reducing the *menu* to its lowest terms. Then to consult the proper gradation.

Brillat Savarin recounts a rather cruel joke perpetrated on a man who was a well-known gourmand. The idea was that he should be induced to satisfy himself with the more ordinary viands, and that then the choicest dishes should be presented in vain before his jaded appetite. This treacherous feast began with a sirloin of beef, a fricandeau of veal, and a stewed carp with stuffing. Then came a magnificent turkey, a pike, six *entremets*, and an ample dish of macaroni and Parmesan cheese. Nor was this all. Another course appeared, composed of sweetbread, sur-rounded with shrimps in jelly, soft roes, and partridge wings, with a thick sauce or *purée* of mushrooms. Last of all came the delicacies, — snipes by the dozen, a pheas-ant in perfect order, and with them a slice of tunny fish, quite fresh. Naturally, the gourmand was *hors du combat*. As a joke, it was successful; as an act of hospitality, it was a cruelty; as pointing a moral and adorning a tale, it may be useful.

This anecdote has its historical value as showing us that the present proces-sion of soup, fish, roast, *entrée*, game, and dessert was not observed one hundred years ago, as a fish was served after beef and after turkey.

Dr. Johnson describes a dinner at Mrs. Thrales which shows us what was con-sidered luxurious a hundred years ago. "The dinner was excellent. First course: soups at head and foot, removed by fish and a saddle of mutton. Second course: a fowl they call galenan at head, a capon larger than our Irish turkeys at foot. Third course: four different ices, — pineapple, grape, raspberry, and a fourth. In each re-move four dishes; the first two courses served on massive plate."

These "gentlemen of England who live at home at ease," these earls by the king's grace, viceroys of India, clerks and rich commoners, would laugh at this dinner to-day; so would our clubmen, our diners at Delmonico's, our million-naires. Imagine the feelings of that *chef* who received ten thousand a year, with absolute power of life or death, with a wine-cellar which is a fortress of which he alone knows the weakest spot, — what would he say to such a dinner?

But there are dinners where the gradation is perfect, where luxury stimulates the brain as Château Yquem bathes the throat. It would seem as if the Golden Age, the age of Leo X. had come back; and our nineteenth century shows all the virtues of the art of entertaining since the days of Lucullus, purified of the enormities, including dining at eleven in the morning, of the intermediate ages.

It must not be forgotten that this simplicity which is so commended can only be obtained by the most studied, artful care. As Gray's Elegy reads as the most consummately easy and plain poetry in the world, so that we feel that we have but to sit down at the writing-desk and indite one exactly like it, we learn in giving a little, simple, perfect dinner that its combinations must be faultless. Gray wrote ev-ery verse of his immortal poem over many times. The hostess who learns enough art to conceal art in her simple dinner has achieved that perfection in her art which Gray reached. Perfect and simple cookery are, like perfect beauty, very rare.

However, if the art of entertaining makes hostesses, hostesses must make the art of entertaining. It is for them to decide the *juste milieu* between the *not enough* and the great *too much*.

BREAKFAST.

Before breakfast a man feels but queasily,
And a sinking at the lower abdomen
Begins the day with indifferent omen.

Browning. — The Flight of the Duchess.

And then to breakfast with what appetite you have.

Shakspeare.

Breakfast is a hard thing to manage in America, particularly in a country-house, as people have different ideas about eating a hearty meal at nine o'clock or earlier. All who have lived much in Europe are apt to prefer the Continental fashion of a cup of tea or coffee in one's room, with perhaps an egg and a roll; then to do one's work or pleasure, as the case may be, and to take the *déjeûner à la fourchette* at eleven or twelve. To most brain-workers this is a blessed boon, for the heavy American breakfast of chops, steaks, eggs, forcemeat balls, sausages, broiled chicken, stewed potatoes, baked beans, and hot cakes, good as it is, is apt to render a person stupid.

It would be better if this meal could be rendered less heavy, and that a visitor should always be given the alternative of taking a cup of tea in her room, and not appearing until luncheon.

The breakfast dishes most to be commended may begin with the omelet. This the French make to perfection. Indeed, Gustav Droz wrote a story once for the purpose of giving its recipe. The story is of a young couple lost in a forest, who take refuge in a wood-cutter's hut. They ask for food, and are told that they can have an omelet:

"The old woman had gone to fetch a frying-pan, and was then throwing a handful of shavings on the fire.

"In the midst of this strange and rude interior Louise seemed to me so fine and delicate, so elegant, with her long *gants de Suède*, her little boots, and her tucked-up skirts. With her two hands stretched out she sheltered her face from the flames, and from the corner of her eye, while I was talking with the splitters, she watched the butter that began to sing in the frying-pan.

"Suddenly she rose, and taking the handle of the frying-pan from the old woman's hand, 'Let me help you make the omelet,' she said. The good woman let go the pan with a smile, and Louise found herself alone in the position of a fisherman at the moment when his float begins to bob. The fire hardly threw any light; her eyes were fixed on the liquid butter, her arms outstretched, and she was biting her lips a little, doubtless to increase her strength.

"'It is a bit heavy for Madame's little hands,' said the old man. 'I bet that it is the first time you ever made an omelet in a wood-cutter's hut, is it not, my little lady?'

"Louise made a sign of assent without removing her eyes from the frying-pan.

"'The eggs! the eggs!' she cried all at once, with such an expression of alarm that we all burst out laughing. 'The eggs! the butter is bubbling! quick, quick!'

"The old woman was beating the eggs with animation. 'And the herbs!' cried the old man. 'And the bacon, and the salt,' said the young man. Then we all set to work, chopping the herbs and cutting the bacon, while Louise cried, 'Quick! quick!'

"At last there was a big splash in the frying-pan, and the great act began. We all stood around the fire watching anxiously, for each having had a finger in the pie, the result interested us all. The good old woman, kneeling down by the dish, lifted up with her knife the corners of the omelet, which was beginning to brown.

"'Now Madame has only to turn it,' said the old woman.

"'A little sharp jerk,' said the old man.

"'Not too strong,' said the young man.

"'One jerk! houp! my dear,' said I.

"'If you all speak at once I shall never dare; besides, it is very heavy, you know—'

"'One little sharp jerk—'

"'But I cannot—it will all go into the fire—oh!'

"In the heat of the action her hood had fallen; she was red as a peach, her eyes glistened, and in spite of her anxiety, she burst out laughing. At last, after a supreme effort, the frying-pan executed a rapid movement and the omelette rolled, a little heavily I must confess, on the large plate which the old woman held.

"Never was there a finer-looking omelet."

This is an excellent description of the dish which is made for you at every little *cabaret* in France, as well as at the best hotels. That dexterous turn of the wrist by which the omelet is turned over is, however, hard to reach. Let any lady try it. I have been taken into the kitchen in a hotel in the Riviera to see a cook who was so dexterous as to turn the frying-pan over entirely, without spilling the omelet.

However, they are innumerable, the omelet family, plain, and with parsley, the fancy omelet, and the creamy omelet. Learn to make every sort from any cooking-book, and your family will never starve.

Conquer the art of toasting bacon with a fork; it is a fine relish for your egg, no matter how cooked. To fry good English bacon in a pan until it is hard, is to disfigure one of Fortune's best gifts.

Study above all things to learn how to produce good toast; not all the cooks in the great kingdom or empire or republic of France (whatever it may be at this minute) can produce a good slice of toast. They call it *pain rôti*, and well they may; for after the poor bread has been burned they put it in the oven and roast it. No human being can eat it. It is taken away and grated up for sawdust.

They make delicious toast in England, and in a few houses in America. The bread should be a little stale, the slice cut thin, the fire perfect, a toasting-fork should hold it before coals, which are as bright as Juno's eyes. It should be a delicate brown, dropped on a hot plate, fresh butter put on at once, and then, ah! 't would tempt the dying anchorite to eat. Then conquer cream toast; and there is an exalted substance called Boston brown bread which is delicious, toasted and boiled in milk.

Muffins are generally failures in these United States. Why, after conquering the English, we cannot conquer their muffins, I do not know. They are well worth repeated efforts. We make up on our hot biscuits and rolls; and as for our waffles, griddle-cakes, and Sally Lunns, we distance competition. Do not believe that they are unhealthy! Nothing that is well cooked is unhealthy to everybody; and all things which are good are unhealthy to somebody. Every one must determine for himself what is healthy and unhealthy.

A foreign breakfast in France consists of eggs in some form,—frequently *au beurre noir*, which is butter melted in a little vinegar and allowed to brown,—a stew of vegetables and meat, a little cold meat (tongue, ham, or cold roast beef,) a very good salad, a small dish of stewed fruit or a little pastry, cheese, fruit, and coffee, and always red wine.

Or perhaps an omelet or egg *au plat* (simply dropped on a hot plate), mutton cutlets, and fried potatoes, perhaps stewed pigeons, with spinach or green peas, or trout from the lake, followed by a beefsteak, with highly flavoured Alpine strawberries or fresh apricots or figs, then all eating is done for the day, until seven o'clock dinner. This is of course the mid-day *déjeûner à la fourchette*. At the earlier breakfast a Swiss hotel offers only coffee, rolls, butter, and honey.

All sorts of stews—kidney, liver, chicken, veal, and beef—are good, and every sort of little pan-fish. In our happy country we can add the oyster stew, or the lobster in cream, the familiar sausage, and the hereditary hash; if any one knows how to make good corned-beef hash she need not fear to entertain the king.

There are those who know how to broil a chicken, but they are few,—"Amongst the few, the immortal names which are not born to die." There are others, also few, who know how to broil ham so that it will not be hard, and on it to drop the egg so that it be like Saturn,—a golden ball in a ring of silver.

Amongst the good dishes and cheap dishes which I have seen served in France for a breakfast I recommend lambs' feet in a white sauce, with a suspicion of onion.

All sorts of fricassees and warmed over things can be made most deliciously for breakfast. Many people like a salt mackerel or a broiled herring for breakfast; these are good *avant goûts*, stimulating the appetite. The Danes and Swedes have every form of dried fish, and even some strange fowl served in this way. Dried beef served up with eggs is comforting to some stomachs. Smoked salmon appeals to others; and people with an ostrich digestion like toasted cheese or Welsh rarebits. The fishball of our forefathers is a supreme delicacy if well made, as is creamed codfish; but warmed over pie, or warmed over mutton or beef, are detestable. The appetite is in a parlous state at nine o'clock and needs to be tempted; a bit of breakfast bacon, a bit of toast, an egg, and a fresh slice of melon or a cold sliced tomato in summer, *voilà tout!* as the French say. Begin with the melon or a plate of strawberries. These early breakfasts at nine o'clock may be followed by the hot cake, but later on the *déjeûner à la fourchette*, which with us becomes luncheon, demands another order of meal, as we have seen, more like a plain dinner.

It is a great comfort to the housekeeper, or to the lady who has been imprisoned behind the tea and coffee pot that she may serve thence a large family, to sometimes escape and have both tea and coffee served from the side tables. Of course, for a small and intimate breakfast there is nothing like the "steaming urn," and the tea made by the lady at the table; and the Hon. Thomas H. Benton declared that he "liked to drink his tea from a cup which had been washed by a lady." Woman is the genius of the tea-kettle.

To make a good cup of coffee is a rare accomplishment. Perhaps the old method is as good as any: a small cupful of roasted and ground coffee, one third Mocha and two thirds Java, a small egg, shell and all, broken into the pot with the dry coffee. Stir well with a spoon and then pour on three pints of boiling water; let it boil from five to ten minutes, counting from the time it begins to boil. Then pour in a cupful of cold water, and turn a little of the coffee into a cup to see that the nozzle of the pot is not filled with grounds. Turn this back, and let the coffee stand a few minutes to settle, taking care that it does not boil again. The advantages of boiled egg with coffee is, that the yolk gives a rich flavour and good colour; also the shells and the white keep the grounds in order, settling them at the bottom of the pot.

But the most economical and the easiest way of making coffee is by filtering. The French coffee biggin should be used. It consists of two cylindrical tin vessels, one fitting into the other, the bottom of the upper being a fine strainer. Another coarser strainer, with a rod coming from the centre, is placed on this. Then the coffee, which must be finely ground, is put in, and another strainer is placed on the top of the rod. The boiling water is poured on, and the pot set where it will keep hot, but not boil, until the water has gone through. This will make a clear, strong coffee with a rich, smooth flavour.

The advantage of the two strainers is, that the one coming next to the fine strainer prevents the grounds from filling up the fine holes, and so the coffee is clear,—a grand desideratum. Boiled milk should be served with coffee for an early breakfast. Clear coffee, *café noir*, is served after dinner, and in France, always after the twelve o'clock breakfast.

For a nine o'clock breakfast the hostess should also serve tea, and perhaps chocolate, if she has a large family of guests, as all cannot drink coffee for breakfast.

Pigs' feet *à la poulette* find favour in Paris, and are delicious as prepared there;

also calf's liver *à l'Alsacienne*. Chicken livers are very nice, and cod's tongues with black butter cannot be surpassed. Mutton kidneys with bacon are desirable, and all the livers and kidneys *en brochette* with bacon, empaled on a spit, are excellent. Hashed lamb *à la Zingara* is highly peppered and very good.

Broiled fish, broiled chicken, broiled ham, broiled steak and chops are always good for breakfast. The gridiron made Saint Lawrence fit for heaven, and its qualities have been elevating and refining ever since.

The summer breakfast can be very nice. Crab, clam, lobster,—all are admirable. Fresh fish should be served whenever one can get it. Devilled kidneys and broiled bones do for supper, but fresh fish and easily digested food should replace these heavier dainties for breakfast.

Stewed fruit is much used on the Continent at an early breakfast. It is thought to avert dyspepsia. Americans prefer to eat fruit fresh, and therefore have not learned to stew it. Stewing is, however, a branch of cookery well worth the attention of a first-class housekeeper. It makes canned fruit much better to stew it with sugar. Stewed cherries are delicious and very healthy; and all the berries, even if a little stale, can be stewed into a good dish, as can the dried fruits, like prunes, etc.

Stewed pears make an elegant dessert served with whipped cream; but this is too rich for breakfast. Baked pears with cream are sometimes offered, and eggs in every form,—scrambled, dropped, boiled, stuffed, and even boiled hard, sliced and dressed as a salad. "What is so good as an egg salad for a hungry person?" asked a hostess in the Adirondacks who had nothing else to offer! Eggs are the staple for breakfast.

Ham omelet with a little parsley, lamb chops with green peas, tripe *à la Bourdelaise*, hashed turkey, hashed chicken with cream, and breaded veal with tomato sauce, calf's brains with a black butter, stewed veal *à la Chasseur*, broiled shad's roe, broiled soft-shell clams, minced tenderloin with Lyonnaise potatoes, blue-fish *au gratin*, broiled steak with water-cress, picked-up codfish, and smoked beef in cream are of the thousand and one delicacies for the early breakfast,—if one can eat them.

It is better to eat a saucer of oatmeal and cream at nine o'clock, take a cup of tea, and do one's work; then at twelve to sit down to as good a breakfast as possible,—a regular *déjeuner à la fourchette*. The digestion is then active; the brain after several hours work needs repose, and at one or two o'clock can go to work again like a giant refreshed.

An early breakfast with meat is thought by foreign doctors not to be good for children. But in France they give children wine at a very early age, which is rarely done in this country. At all boarding-schools and hospitals wine is given to young children. Certainly there are fewer drunkards and fewer dyspeptics in France than in America.

Brillat Savarin says of coffee, "It is beyond doubt that coffee acts upon the functions of the brain as an excitant." Voltaire and Buffon drank a great deal of coffee. If it deprives persons of sleep it should never be taken. It is to many a poison;

and hospitals are full of men made cripples by the immoderate stimulus of coffee. The Spanish people live and flourish on chocolate; introduced into Spain during the seventeenth century, it crossed the Pyrenees with Anne of Austria, daughter of Philip II. and wife of Louis XIII., and at the commencement of the Regency was more in vogue than coffee.

Many modern writers advise a good cup of chocolate at breakfast as wholesome and easily digested, and it is good for clergymen, lawyers, and travellers. In America it is considered heavy and headachy; and doubtless the climate has something to do with this. Cocoa and the lighter preparations of chocolate are good at sea, and very comforting to those who find their nerves too much on the alert to stand coffee or tea. Every one must consult his own health and taste in this as in all matters.

The boldest attempts to increase the enjoyments of the palate, or to tell people what they shall eat or drink, are constantly overthrown by some subtle enemy in the stomach; and breakfasts should especially be so light that they can tickle the palate without disturbing the brain. A red herring is a good appetizer.

> "Meet me at breakfast alone,
> And then I will give you a dish
> Which really deserves to be known,
> Though 'tis not the genteelest of fish.
> You must promise to come, for I said
> A splendid red herring I'd buy.
> Nay, turn not aside your proud head;
> You'll like it, I know, when you try.
>
> "If moisture the herring betray,
> Drain till from the moisture 'tis free.
> Warm it through in the usual way,
> Then serve it for you and for me.
> A piece of cold butter prepare,
> To rub it when ready it lies;
> Egg sauce and potatoes don't spare,
> And the flavour will cause you surprise."

It is not only the man who has eaten a heavy supper the night before; it is not only the heavy drinker, although brandy and soda are not the best of appetite provokers, so they say; but it is also the brainworker who finds it impossible to eat in the morning. For sleep has the effect of eating. Who sleeps, eats, says the French proverb; and we often find healthy children unwilling to eat an early breakfast. Appetites vary both in individuals and at various seasons of the year. Nothing can be more unwise than to make children eat when they do not wish to do so. During the summer months we are all of us less inclined for food than when sharp set by hard exercise in the frosty air; and we loathe in July what we like in winter.

The heavy domestic breakfast of steak and mutton-chops in summer is often repellent to a delicate child. The perfection of good living is to have what you want exactly when you want it. A slice of fresh melon, a plate of strawberries, a thin slice of bread and butter may be much better for breakfast in summer than the baked beans and stewed codfish of a later season. Do not force a child to eat even a baked potato if he does not like it.

It is maintained by some that a strong will can keep off sea-sickness or any other malady. This is a fallacy. No strong will can make a delicate stomach digest a heavy breakfast at nine o'clock. Therefore we begin and end with the same idea,— breakfast is a hard thing to manage in America.

In England, however, it is a very happy-go-lucky meal; and although the essentials are on the table, people are privileged to rise and help themselves from the sideboard. I may say that I have never seen a fashionable English hostess at a nine o'clock breakfast, although the meal is always ready for those who wish it.

For sending breakfasts to rooms, trays are prepared with teapot, sugar, and cream, a plate of toast, eggs boiled, with cup, spoon, salt and pepper, a little pat of butter, and if desired a plate of chops or chicken, plates, knives, forks, and napkins. For an English country-house the supply of breakfast trays is like that of a hotel. The pretty little Satsuma sets of small teapot, cream jug, and sugar-bowl, are favourites.

When breakfast is served in the dining-room, a white cloth is generally laid, although some ladies prefer variously coloured linen, with napkins to match. A vase of flowers or a dish of fruit should be placed in the centre. The table is then set as for dinner, with smaller plates and all sorts of pretty china, like an egg dish with a hen sitting contentedly, a butter plate with a recumbent cow, a sardine dish with fishes in Majolica,—in fact, any suggestive fancy. Hot plates for a winter breakfast in a plate-warmer near the table add much to the comfort.

Finger bowls with napkins under them should be placed on the sideboard and handed to the guest with the fruit. It is a matter of taste as to whether fruit precedes or finishes the breakfast; and the servant must watch the decision of the guest.

A grand breakfast to a distinguished foreigner, or some great home celebrity at Delmonico's for instance, would be,—

A table loaded with flowers.

Oysters on the half-shell.   Chablis.

Eggs stuffed.   Eggs in black butter, (*au beurre noir*).

Chops and green peas.   Champagne.

Lyonnaise potatoes.

Sweetbreads.   Spinach.

Woodcock.   Partridges.

Salad of lettuce.   Claret.

Cheese *fondu.*

Dessert:

Charlotte Russe.	Fruit Jelly.	Ices.
	Liqueurs.	
Grapes.	Peaches.	Pears.
	Coffee.	

A breakfast even at twelve o'clock is thus made noticeably lighter than the meal called lunch. It may be introduced by clam juice in cups, or bouillon, but is often served without either. These breakfasts are generally prefaced by a short reception, where all the guests are presented to the foreigner of distinction. There is no formality about leaving. Indeed, these breakfasts are given in order to avoid that.

For an ordinary breakfast at nine o'clock in a family of ten, we should say that the *menu* should be something as follows: The host and hostess being present, the lady makes the tea. Oatmeal and cream would then be offered; after that a broiled chicken would be placed before the host, which he carves if he can. An omelet is placed before the lady or passed; stewed potatoes are passed, and toast or muffins. Hot cakes finish this breakfast, unless fruit is also added. It is considered a very healthful thing to eat an orange before breakfast. But who can eat an orange well? One must go to Spain to see that done. The señorita cuts off the rind with her silver knife. Then putting her fork into the peeled fruit, she gently detaches small slices from the pulp, leaving the core and seeds untouched; passing the fork upward, she detaches every morsel with her pearly teeth, looking very pretty the while, and contrives to eat the whole orange without losing a drop of the juice, and lays down the core with the fork still in it.

It seems hardly necessary to say to an American lady that she should be neatly dressed at breakfast. The pretty white morning dresses which are worn in America are rarely seen in Europe, perhaps because of the difference of climate. In England elderly ladies and young married women sometimes appear in very smart tea gowns of dark silk over a colour; but almost always the young ladies come in the yachting or tennis dresses which they will wear until dinner-time, and almost always in summer, in hats. In America the variety of morning dresses is endless, of which the dark jacket over a white vest, the serviceable merino, the flannel, the dark foulards, are favourites.

In summer, thin lawns, percales, Marseilles suits, calicos, and ginghams can be so prettily made as to rival all the other costumes for coquetry and grace.

> "Still to be neat, still to be drest
> As she were going to a feast,"

such should be the breakfast dress of the young matron. It need not be fine; it need not be expensive; but it should be neat and becoming. The hair should be carefully arranged, and the feet either in good, stout shoes for the subsequent walk, or in the natty stocking and well fitting slipper, which has moved the poet to such feeling verses.

THE LUNCH.

"A Gothic window, where a damask curtain
Made the blank daylight shadowy and uncertain;
A slab of agate on four eagle-talons
Held trimly up and neatly taught to balance;
A porcelain dish, o'er which in many a cluster
Plump grapes hung down, dead ripe, and without lustre;
A melon cut in thin, delicious slices,
A cake, that seemed mosaic-work in spices;
Two china cups, with golden tulips sunny,
And rich inside, with chocolate like honey;
And she and I the banquet scene completing
With dreamy words, and very pleasant eating."

If all lunches could be as poetic and as simple and as luxurious as this, the hostess would have little trouble in giving a lunch. But, alas! from the slice of cold ham, or chicken, and bread and butter, has grown the grand hunt breakfast, and the ladies' lunch, most delicious of luxurious time-killers. The lunch, therefore, has become in the house of the opulent as elaborate as the dinner.

Twenty years ago in England I had the pleasure of lunching with Lord Houghton, and I well remember the simplicity of that meal. A cup of bouillon, a joint of mutton, roasted, and carved by the host, a tart, some peaches, very fine hot-house fruit, and a glass of sherry was all that was served on a very plain table to twenty guests. But what a company of wits, belles, and beauties we had to eat it! I once lunched with Browning on a much simpler bill of fare. I have lunched at the beautiful house of Sir John Millais on what might have been a good family dinner with us. And I have lunched in Hampton Court, in the apartments of Mr. Beresford, now dead, who was a friend of George the Fourth and an old Tory whipper-in, on a slice of cold meat, a cutlet, a gooseberry tart, and some strawberries as large as tomatoes from the garden which was once Anne Boleyn's.

What a great difference between these lunches and a ladies' lunch in New York, which, laid for twenty-eight people, offers every kind of wine, every luxury of fish, flesh, and fowl, flowers which exhibit the most overwhelming luxury of an extravagant period, fruits and bonbons and *bonbonnières*, painted fans to carry home, with ribbons on which is painted one's monogram, etc.

I have seen summer wild-flowers in winter at a ladies' lunch, as the last concession to a fancy for what is unusual. The order having been given in September, the facile gardener raised these flowers for this especial lunch. Far more expensive than roses at a dollar apiece is this bringing of May into January. It is impossible to say where luxury should stop; and, if people can afford it, there is no necessity for its stopping. It is only to be regretted that luxury frightens those who might like to give simple lunches.

A lunch-party of ladies should not be crowded, as handsome gowns take up a great deal of room; and therefore a lunch for ten ladies in a moderate house is better than a larger number. As ladies always wear their bonnets the room should not be too hot.

The menu is very much the same as a dinner, excepting the soup. In its place cups of bouillon or of clam juice, boiled with cream and a bit of sherry, are placed before each plate. There follows presumably a plate of lobster croquettes with a rich sauce, *filet de bœuf* with truffles and mushrooms, sweetbread and green peas, perhaps asparagus or cauliflower.

Then comes *sorbet*, or Roman punch, much needed to cool the palate and to invigorate the appetite for further delicacies. The Roman punch is now often served in very fanciful frozen shapes of ice, resembling roses, or fruit of various kinds. If a lady is not near a confectioner she should learn to make this herself. It is very easy, if one only compounds it at first with care, Maraschino cordial or fine old Jamaica rum being mixed with water and sugar as for a punch, and well frozen.

The game follows, and the salad. These two are often served together. After that the ices and fruit. Cheese is rarely offered at a lady's lunch, excepting in the form of cheese straws. Château Yquem, champagne, and claret are the favourite wines. Cordial is offered afterward with the coffee. A lady's lunch-party is supposed to begin at one o'clock and end at three.

It is a delightful way of showing all one's pretty things. At a luncheon in New York I have seen a tablecloth of linen into which has been inserted duchesse lace worth, doubtless, several hundred dollars, the napkins all trimmed with duchesse, worth at least twenty dollars apiece. This elegant drapery was thrown over a woollen broadcloth underpiece of a pale lilac.

In the middle of the table was a grand epergne of the time of Louis Seize; the glass and china were superb. At the proper angle stood silver and gold cups, ornamental pitchers, and claret jugs. At every lady's plate stood a splendid bouquet tied with a long satin ribbon, and various small favours, as fans and fanciful *menus* were given.

As the lunch went on we were treated to new surprises of napery and of Sèvres plates. The napkins became Russian, embroidered with gold thread, as the spoons and forks were also of Russian silver and gold, beautifully enamelled. Then came those embroidered with heraldic animals, — the lion and the two-headed eagle and griffin, — the monogram gracefully intertwined.

Plates were used, apparently of solid gold and beautiful workmanship. The Roman punch was hidden in the heart of a water lily, which looked uncommonly innocent with its heart of fire. The service of this lunch was so perfect that we did not see how we were served; it all moved as if to music. Pleasant chat was the only addition which our hostess left for us to add to her hospitality. I have lunched at many great houses all over the world, but I have never seen so luxurious a picture as this lunch was.

It has been a question whether oysters on the half-shell should be served at a lady's lunch. For my part I think that they should, although many ladies prefer to begin with the bouillon. All sorts of *hors d'œuvres*, like olives, anchovies, and other relishes, are in order.

In summer, ladies sometimes serve a cold luncheon, beginning with iced bouillon, salmon covered with a green sauce, cold birds and salads, ices and strawberries, or peaches frozen in cream. Cold asparagus dressed as a salad is very good at this meal.

In English country-houses the luncheon is a very solid meal, beginning with a stout roast with hot vegetables, while chicken salad, a cold ham, and various meat pies stand on the sideboard. The gentlemen get up and help the ladies; the servants, after going about once or twice, often leave the room that conversation may be more free.

It might well improve the young housekeeper to study the question of potted meats, the preparation of Melton veal, the various egg salads, as well as those of potato, of lobster and chicken, so that she may be prepared with dishes for an improvised lunch. Particularly in the country should this be done.

The etiquette of invitations for a ladies' lunch is the same as that of a dinner. They are sent out a fortnight before; they are carefully engraved, or they are written on note paper.

Mrs. Somerville
Requests the pleasure of
Mrs. Montgomery's
Company at lunch on Thursday, 15th,
at 1 o'clock.

R. S. V. P.

This should be answered at once, and the whole engagement treated with the gravity of a dinner engagement.

These lunch-parties are very convenient for ladies who, from illness or indisposition to society, cannot go out in the evening. It is also very convenient if the lady of the house has a husband who does not like society and who finds a dinner-party a bore.

The usual custom is for ladies to dress in dark street dresses, and their very best. That with an American lady means much, for an American husband stops at no expense. Worth says that American women are the best customers he has,—far better than queens. The latter ask the price, and occasionally haggle; American women may ask the price, but the order is, the very best you can do.

Luncheons are very fashionable in England, especially on Sunday. These lunches, although luxurious, are by no means the costly spreads which American women indulge in. They are attended by gentlemen as well as ladies, for in a land where a man does not go to the House of Commons until five in the afternoon he may well lunch with his family. What time did our forefathers lunch? In the reign of Francis the First the polite French rose at five, dined at nine, supped at five, and went to bed at nine. Froissart speaks of "waiting upon the Duke of Lancaster at five in the afternoon after he had supped." If our ancestors dined at nine, when did they lunch?

After some centuries the dinner hour grew to be ten in the morning, by which time they had besieged a town and burned up a dozen heretics, probably to give them a good appetite, a sort of *avant goût*. The later hours now in vogue did not prevail until after the Restoration.

Lunch has remained fastened at one o'clock, for a number of years at least. In England, curiously enough, they give you no napkins at this meal, which certainly requires them.

A hunt breakfast in America is, of course, a hearty meal, to which the men and women are asked who have an idea of riding to hounds. It is usually served at little tables, and the meal begins with hot bouillon. It is a heartier meal than a lady's lunch, and as luxurious as the hostess pleases; but it does not wind up with ices and fruits, although it may begin with an orange. Much more wine is drunk than at a lady's lunch, and yet some hunters prefer to begin the day with tea only. Everything should be offered, and what is not liked can be refused.

"What is hit, is History,
And what is missed is Mystery."

There are famous breakfasts in London which are not the early morning meal, neither are they called luncheons. It is the constant habit of the literary world of London to have reunions of scientific and agreeable people early in the day, and what would be called a party in the evening, is called a breakfast. We should call it a reception, except that one is asked at eleven o'clock. But the greatest misnomer of all is the habit in London of giving a dinner, a ball, and a supper out of doors at five o'clock, and calling that a "breakfast." Except that the gentlemen are in morning dress and the ladies in bonnets this has no resemblance to what we call breakfast.

Breakfast at nine, or earlier, is a solemn process. It has no great meaning for us, who have our children to send to school, our husbands to prepare for business, ourselves for a busy day or a long journey. For the very luxurious it no longer exists.

Luncheon on the contrary is apt to be a lively and exhilarating occasion. It is the best moment in the day to some people. A thousand dollars is not an unusual sum to expend on a lady's lunch in New York for eighteen or twenty-five guests, counting the favours, the flowers, the wines, and the viands, and even then we have not entered into the cost of the china, the glass, porcelain, *cloisonné*, Dresden, Sèvres, and silver, which make the table a picture. The jewelled goblets from Carlsbad, the knives and forks with crystal handles, set in silver, from Bohemia, and the endless succession of beautiful plates, — who shall estimate the cost of all this?

As to the precedence of plates, it is meet that China, oldest of nations, should suffice for the soup. The oysters have already been served on shell-like Majolica. England, a maritime nation surrounded by ocean, must furnish the plates for the fish. For the roast, too, what plates so good as Doulton, real English, substantial *faïence*?

For the *Bouchers à la Reine* and all the *entrées* we must have Sèvres again.

Japanese will do for the *filet aux champignons*, the venison, the *pièces de resistance*, as well as English. Japanese plates are strong. But here we are running into dinner; indeed, these two feasts do run into each other.

One should not have a roast at ladies' lunch, unless it be a roast pheasant.

Dresden china plates painted with fruits and flowers should be used for the dessert. On these choice plates, with perforated edges marked "A R" on the back, should lie the ices frozen as natural fruits. We can scarcely tell the frozen banana or peach before us, from the painted banana on our plate.

For the candied fruit, we must again have Sèvres. Then a gold dish filled with rose-water must be passed. We dip a bit of the napkin in it, for in this country we do have napkins with our luncheon, and wipe our lips and fingers. This is called a *trempoir*.

The cordials at the end of the dinner must be served in cups of Russian gold filagree supporting glass. There is an analogy between the rival, luscious richness of the cordial and the cup.

The coffee-cups must be thin as egg-shells, of the most delicate French or American china. We make most delicate china and porcelain cups ourselves nowadays, at Newark, Trenton, and a dozen other places.

There is a vast deal of waste in offering so much wine at a ladies' lunch. American women cannot drink much wine; the climate forbids it. We have not been brought up on beer, or on anything more stimulating than ice-water. Foreign physicians say that this is the cause of all our woes, our dyspepsia, our nervous exhaustion, our rheumatism and hysteria. I believe that climate and constitution decide these things for us. We are not prone to over-eat ourselves, to drink too much wine; and if the absence of these grosser tastes is visible in pale cheeks and thin arms, is not that better than the other extreme?

All entertaining can go on perfectly well without wine, if people so decide. It would be impossible, however, to make many poetical quotations without an allusion to the "ruby," as Dick Swiveller called it. Since Cleopatra dissolved the pearl, the wine-cup has held the gems of human fancy.

> *Champagne Cup*: One pint bottle of soda water, one quart dry champagne, one wine-glass of brandy, a few fresh strawberries, a peach quartered, sugar to taste; cracked ice.

> *Another recipe*: One quart dry champagne, one pint bottle of Rhine wine, fruit and ice as above; cracked ice. Mix in a large

pitcher.

Claret Cup: One bottle of claret, one pint bottle of soda water, one wine-glass brandy, half a wine-glass of lemon-juice, half a pound of lump sugar, a few slices of fresh cucumber; mix in cracked ice.

Mint Julep: Fresh mint, a few drops of orange bitters and Maraschino, a small glass of liqueur, brandy or whiskey, put in a tumbler half full of broken ice; shake well, and serve with fruit on top with straws.

Another recipe for Mint Julep: Half a glass of port wine, a few drops of Maraschino, mint, sugar, a thin slice of lemon, shake the cracked ice from glass to glass, add strawberry or pineapple.

Turkish Sherbets: Extract by pressure or infusion the rich juice and fine perfume of any of the odouriferous flowers or fruits; mix them in any number or quantity to taste. When these essences, extracts, or infusions are prepared they may be immediately used by adding a proper proportion of sugar or syrup; and water. Some acid fruits, such as lemon or pomegranate, are used to raise the flavour, but not to overpower the chief perfume. Fill the cup with cracked ice and add what wine or spirit is preferred.

Claret Cobbler: One bottle wine, one bottle Apollinaris or Seltzer, one lemon, half a pound of sugar; serve with ice.

Champagne Cobbler: One bottle of champagne, one half bottle of white wine, much cracked ice, strawberries, peaches or sliced oranges.

Sherry Cobbler: Full wine-glass of sherry, very little brandy, sugar, sliced lemon, cracked ice. This is but one tumblerful.

Kümmel: This liqueur is very good served with shaved ice in small green claret-cups.

Punch: One bottle Arrack, one bottle brandy, two quart bottles dry champagne, one tumblerful of orange curaçoa, one pound of cracked sugar, half a dozen lemons sliced, half a dozen oranges sliced. Fill the bowl with large lump of ice and add one quart of water.

Shandygaff: London porter and ginger ale, half and half.

AFTERNOON TEA.

"And while the bubbling and loud-hissing urn
Throws up a steamy column, and the cups
That cheer but not inebriate wait on each,
So let us welcome peaceful evening in."

Whatever objections can be urged against all other systems of entertaining, including the expense, the bore it is to a gentleman to have his house turned inside out, the fatigue to the lady, the disorganization of domestic service, nothing can be said against afternoon tea, unless that it may lead to a new disease, the *delirium teamens*. There is danger to nervous women in our climate in too great indulgence in this delicious beverage. It sometimes murders sleep and impairs digestion. We cannot claim that it is always safer than opium. It was very much abused in England in 1678, ten years after Lords Arlington and Ossory brought it over from the meditative Dutchman, who was the first European to appreciate it. It was then called a "black water with an acrid taste." It cost, however, in England sixty shillings a pound, so that it must have been fashionable. Pepys in his diary records that he sent for a cup of tea, a "China drink which he had not used before." He did not like it, but then he did not like the "Midsummer Night's Dream." "The most insipid, ridiculous play I ever saw in my life," he writes; so we do not care what he thought about a blessed cup of tea.

In the middle of the sixteenth century, with pasties and ale for breakfast, with sugared cakes and spiced wines at various hours of the day, with solid "noonings," and suppers with strong potations of sack and such possets as were the ordinary refreshments, it is not probable that tea would have been appreciated. The Dutch were crafty, however; they saw that there was a common need of a hot, rather stimulating beverage, which had no intoxicating effects. They exported sage enough to pay for the tea, and got the better of even the wily Chinaman, who avowed some time after, in their trade with America, "That spent tea-leaves, dried again, were good enough for second-chop Englishmen."

Jonas Haunay wrote a treatise against tea-drinking in Johnson's time, and that vast, insatiable, and shameless tea-drinker took up the cudgels for tea, settling it as a brain-inspirer for all time, and wrote Rasselas on the strength of it. Cobbett wrote against its use by the labouring classes, and the "Edinburgh Review" endorsed his arguments, stating that a "prohibition absolute and uncompromising of the noxious beverage was the first step toward insuring health and strength for the poor," and asserting that when a labourer fancied himself refreshed with a mess of this stuff, sweetened with the coarsest brown sugar and diluted by azure-blue milk, it was only the warmth of the water which consoled him for the moment. Cobbett claimed that the tea-table cost more to support than would keep two children at nurse.

The "Quarterly Review" in an article written perhaps by the most famous chemist of the day, said, however, that "tea relieves the pains of hunger rather by mechanical distention than by supplying the waste of nature by adequate sustenance," but claimed for it the power of calm, placid, and benignant exhilaration, greatly stimulating the stomach, when fatigued by digestive exertion, and acting as an appropriate diluent of the chyle. More recent inquiries into the qualities of the peculiar power of tea have tended to raise it in popular esteem, although no one has satisfactorily explained *why* it has become so universally necessary to the human race.

An agreeable little book called "The Beverages We Indulge In," "The Herbs Which We Infuse," or some such title, had a great deal to do with the adoption of tea as a drink for young men who were training for a boat-race, or who desired to economize their strength for a mountain climb. But every one, from the tired washerwoman to the student, the wrestler, the fine lady, and the strong man, demands a cup of tea.

To the invalid it is the dearest solace, dangerous though it may be. Tannin, the astringent element in tea, is bad for delicate stomachs and seems to ruin appetite. Tea, therefore, should never be allowed to stand. Hot water poured on the leaves and poured off into a cup can hardly afford the tannin time to get out. Some tea-drinkers even put the grounds in a silver ball, perforated, and swing this through a cup of boiling water, and in this way is produced the most delicate cup of tea.

The famous Chinese lyric which is painted on almost all the teapots of the Empire is highly poetical. "On a slow fire set a tripod; fill it with clear rain-water. Boil it as long as it would be needed to turn fish white and lobsters red. Throw this upon the delicate leaves of choice tea; let it remain as long as the vapour rises in a cloud. At your ease drink the pure liquor, which will chase away the five causes of trouble."

The "tea of the cells of the Dragons," the purest Pekoe from the leaf-buds of three-year-old plants, no one ever sees in Europe; but we have secured many brands of tea which are sufficiently good, and the famous Indian tea brought in by the great Exposition in Paris in 1889 is fast gaining an enviable reputation. It has a perfect bouquet and flavour. Green tea, beloved by our grandmothers and still a favourite with some connoisseurs, has proved to have so much theine, the element of intoxication in tea, that it is forbidden to nervous people. Tea saves food by its action in preventing various wastes to the system. It is thus peculiarly acceptable to elderly persons, and to the tired labouring-woman. Doubtless Mrs. Gamp's famous teapot with which she entertained Betsy Prig contained green tea.

There is an unusually large amount of nitrogen in theine, and green tea possesses so large a proportion of it as to be positively dangerous. In the process of drying and roasting, this volatile oil is engendered. The Chinese dare not use it for a year after the leaf has been prepared, and the packer and unpacker of the tea suffer much from paralysis. The tasters of tea become frequently great invalids, unable to eat; therefore our favourite herb has its dangers.

More consoling is the legend of the origin of the plant. A drowsy hermit, after long wrestling with sleep, cut off his eyelids and cast them on the ground. From them sprang a shrub whose leaves, shaped like eyelids and bordered with a fringe of lashes, possessed the power of warding off sleep. This was in the third century, and the plant was tea.

But what has all this to do with that pleasant visage of a steaming kettle boiling over a blazing alcohol lamp, the silver tea-caddy, the padded cozy to keep the teapot warm, the basket of cake, the thin bread and butter, the pretty girl presiding over the cups, the delicate china, the more delicate infusion? All these elements go to make up the afternoon tea. From one or two ladies who stayed at home one day in the week and offered this refreshment, to the many who came to find that it was a very easy method of entertaining, grew the present party in the daytime. The original five o'clock tea arose in England from the fact that ladies and gentlemen after hunting required some slight refreshment before dressing for dinner, and liked to meet for a little chat. It now is used as the method of introducing a daughter, and an ordinary way of entertaining.

The primal idea was a good one. People who had no money for grand spreads were enabled to show to their more opulent neighbours that they too had the spirit of hospitality. The doctors discovered that tea was healthy. English breakfast tea would keep nobody awake. The cup of tea and the sandwich at five would spoil nobody's dinner. The ladies who began these entertainments, receiving modestly in plain dresses, were not out of tone with their guests who came in walking-dress.

But then the other side was this, — ladies had to go to nine teas of an afternoon, perhaps taste something everywhere. Hence the new disease, *delirium teamens*. It was uncomfortable to assist at a large party in a heavy winter garment of velvet and fur. The afternoon tea lost its primitive character and became an evening party in the daytime, with the hostess and her daughters in full dress, and her guests in walking-costume.

The sipping of so much tea produces the nervous prostration, the sleeplessness, the nameless misery of our overwrought women; and thus a healthful, inexpensive and most agreeable adjunct to the art of entertaining grew into a thing without a name, and became the large, gas-lighted ball at five o'clock, where half the ladies were in *decolleté* dresses, the others in fur tippets. It was pronounced a breeder of influenzas, and the high road to a headache.

If a lady can be at home every Thursday during the season, and always at her position behind the blazing urn, and will have the firmness to continue this practice, she may create a *salon* out of her teacups.

In giving a large afternoon tea for which cards have been sent out, the hostess should stand by the drawing-room door and greet each guest, who, after a few words, passes on. In the adjoining room, usually the dining-room, a large table is spread with a white cloth; and at one end is a tea service with a kettle of water boiling over an alcohol lamp, while at the other end is a service for chocolate. There should be flowers on the table, and dishes containing bread and butter cut as thin as a shaving. Cake and strawberries are always permissible. One or two servants should be in attendance to carry away soiled cups and saucers, and to keep the table looking fresh; but for the pouring of the tea and chocolate there should always be a lady, who like the hostess should wear a gown closed to the throat; for nothing is worse form now-a-days than full dress before dinner. The ladies of the house should not wear bonnets.

When tea is served every afternoon at five o'clock, whether or no there are visitors, as is often the case in many houses, the servant—who, if a woman, should always in the afternoon wear a plain black gown, with a white cap and apron—should place a small, low table before the lady of the house, and lay over it a pretty white cloth. She should then bring in a large tray, upon which are the tea service, and a plate of bread and butter, or cake, or both, place it upon the table, and retire,—remaining within call, though out of sight, in case she should be needed. The best rule for making tea is the old-fashioned one: "one teaspoonful for each person and one for the pot." The pot should first be rinsed with hot water, then the tea put in, and upon it should be poured enough water, actually boiling, to cover the leaves. This decoction should stand for five minutes, then fill up the pot with more boiling water, and pour it immediately. Some persons prefer lemon in their tea to cream, and it is a good plan to have some thin slices, cut for the purpose, placed in a pretty little dish on the tray. A bowl of cracked ice is also a pleasant addition in summer, iced tea being a most refreshing drink in hot weather. Neither plates nor napkins need appear at this informal and cosey meal. A guest arriving at this time in the afternoon should always be offered a cup of tea.

Afternoon tea, in small cities or in the country, in villages and academic towns, can well be made a most agreeable and ideal entertainment, for the official presentation of a daughter or for the means of seeing one's friends. In the busy winter season of a large city it should not be made the excuse for giving up the evening party, or the dinner, lunch, or ball. It is not all these, it is simply itself, and it should be a refuge for those women who are tired of balls, of over dressing, dancing, visiting, and shopping. It is also very dear to the young who find the convenient tea-table a good arena for flirtation. It is a form of entertainment which allows one to dispense with etiquette and to save time.

Five-o'clock teas should be true to their name, nor should any other refreshment be offered than tea, bread and butter, and little cakes. If other eatables are offered the tea becomes a reception.

There is a high tea which takes the place of dinner on Sunday evenings in cities, which is a very pretty entertainment; in small rural cities, in the country, they take the place of dinners. They were formerly very fashionable in Philadelphia. It gave an opportunity to offer hot rolls and butter, escalloped oysters, fried chicken, delicately sliced cold ham, waffles and hot cakes, preserves—alas! since the days of canning, who offers the delicious preserves of the past? The hostess sits behind her silver urn and pours the hot tea or coffee or chocolate, and presses the guest to take another waffle. It is a delightful meal, and has no prototype in any country but our own.

It is doubtful, however, whether the high tea will ever be popular in America, in large cities at least, where the custom of seven-o'clock dinners prevails. People find in them a violent change of living, which is always a challenge to indigestion. Some wit has said that he always liked to eat hot mince-pie just before he went to bed, for then he always knew what hurt him. If anyone wishes to know what hurts him, he can take high tea on Sunday evening, after having dined all the week at seven o'clock. A pain in his chest will tell him that the hot waffle, the cold tongue, the peach preserve, and that "last cup of tea" meant mischief.

Oliver Cromwell is said to have been an early tea-drinker; so is Queen Elizabeth, — elaborate old teapots are sold in London with the cipher of both; but the report lacks confirmation. We cannot imagine Oliver drinking anything but verjuice, nor the lion woman as sipping anything less strong than brown stout. Literature owes much to tea. From Cowper to Austin Dobson, the poets have had their fling at it. And what could the modern English novelist do without it? It has been in politics, as all remember who have seen Boston Harbor, and it goes into all the battles, and climbs Mt. Blanc and the Matterhorn. The French, who despised it, are beginning to make a good cup of tea, and Russia bathes in it. The Samovar cheers the long journeys across those dreary steppes, and forms again the most luxurious ornament of the palace. On all the high roads of Europe one can get a cup of tea, except in Spain. There it is next to impossible; the universal chocolate supersedes it. If one gets a cup of tea in Spain, there is no cream to put in it; and to many tea drinkers, tea is ruined without milk or cream.

In fact, the poor tea drinker is hard to please anywhere. There are to the critic only one or two houses of one's acquaintance where five o'clock tea is perfect.

THE INTELLECTUAL COMPONENTS OF DINNER.

"Lend me your ears."

"It has often perplexed me to imagine," writes Nathaniel Hawthorne, "how an Englishman will be able to reconcile himself to any future state of existence from which the earthly institution of dinner is excluded. The idea of dinner has so imbedded itself among his highest and deepest characteristics, so illuminated itself with intellect, and softened itself with the kindest emotions of his heart, so linked itself with Church and State, and grown so majestic with long hereditary custom and ceremonies, that by taking it utterly away, Death, instead of putting the final touch to his perfection, would leave him infinitely less complete than we have already known him. He could not be roundly happy. Paradise among all its enjoyments would lack one daily felicity in greater measure than London in the season."

No dinner would be worth the giving that had not one witty man or one witty woman to lift the conversation out of the commonplace. As many more agreeable people as one pleases, but one leader is absolutely necessary.

Not alone the funny man whom the *enfant terrible* silenced by asking, "Mamma would like to know when you are going to begin to be funny," but those men who have the rare art of being leaders without seeming to be, who amuse without your suspecting that you are being amused; for there never should be anything professional in dinner-table wit.

The dinner giver has often to feel that something has been left out of the group about the table; they will not talk! She has furnished them with food and wine, but can she amuse them? Her witty man and her witty woman are both engaged elsewhere,—they are apt to be,—and her room is too warm, perhaps. She determines that at the next dinner she will have some mechanical adjuncts, even an empirical remedy against dulness. She tries a dinner card with poetical quotations, conundrums, and so on. The Shakspeare Club of Philadelphia inaugurated this custom, and some very witty results followed:—

"Enter Froth" (before champagne).
"What is thine age?" (*Romeo and Juliet*) brings in the Madeira.
LOBSTER SALAD.
"Who hath created this indigest?"

Pray you bid these unknown friends welcome, for it is a way to make us better friends. — *Winter's Tale.*

ROAST TURKEY.
See, here he comes swelling like a turkey cock. — *Henry IV.*

YORK HAMS.
Sweet stem from York's great stock. — *Henry VI.*

TONGUE.
Silence is only commendable in a neat's tongue dried — *Merchant of Venice.*

BRAISED LAMB AND BEEF.
What say you to a piece of lamb and mustard? — a dish that I do love to feed upon. — *Taming of the Shrew.*

LOBSTER SALAD.
Sallat was born to do me good. — *Henry IV.*

And so on. The Bible affords others, well worth quoting: —

OYSTERS.
He brought them up out of the sea. — *Isaiah.*
And his mouth was opened immediately. — *Luke* i. 64.

BEAN SOUP.
"Jacob gave Esau bread and pottage of lentils."

FISH, STRIPED BASS.
We remember the fish we did eat freely. — *Numbers.*
These with many stripes. — *Deuteronomy.*

STEINBERGER CABINET.
Thou hast kept the good wine until now. — *John* ii. 10.

BOILED CAPON.
Accept it always and in all places. — Acts xxiv. 3.

PIGEON BRAISE.
Pigeons such as he could get. — *Leviticus.*

SUCCOTASH.
They brought corn and beans. — *Samuel.*

QUAIL LARDED.
Even quail came. — *Exodus.*
Abundantly moistened with fat. — *Isaiah.*

LETTUCE SALAD.
A pleasant plant, green before the sun. — *Isaiah.*
Pour oil upon it, pure oil, olive. — *Leviticus.*
Oil and salt, without prescribing how much. — *Ezra* vii. 22.

ICE CREAM.
Ice like morsels. — *Psalms.*

CHEESE.

Carry these ten cheeses unto the captain.—*Samuel.*

FRUITS

All kind of fruits.—*Eccles.*

COFFEE

Last of all.—*Matthew* xxi. 37.

They had made an end of eating.—*Amos* vii. 2.

CIGARS.

Am become like dust and ashes.—*Job* xxx. 19.

And so on. Written conundrums are good stimulants to conversation, and dinner cards might be greatly historical, not too learned. A legend of the day, as Lady Day, or Michaelmas, is not a bad promoter of talk. Or one might allude to the calendar of dead kings and queens, or other celebrities, or ask your preferences, or quote something from a memoir, to find out that it is a birthday of Rossini or Goethe. All these might be written on a dinner card, and will open the flood gates of a frozen conversation.

Let each dinner giver weave a net out of the gossamer threads of her own thoughts. It will be the web of the Lady of Shalott, and will bid the shadows of pleasant memory to remain, not float "forever adown the river," even toward "towered Camelot" where they may be lost.

Some opulent dinner giver once made the dinner card the vehicle of a present, but this became rather burdensome. It was trying and embarrassing to carry the gifts home, and the poorer entertainer hesitated at the expense. The outlay had better come out of one's brain, and the piquing of curiosity with a contradiction like this take its place:—

"A lady gave me a gift which she had not,
And I received the gift, which I took not,
And if she take it back I grieve not."

But there is something more required to form the intellectual components of a dinner than these instruments to stimulate curiosity and give a fillip to thought. We must have variety.

Mrs. Jameson, the accomplished author of the "Legends of the Madonna" gives the following description of an out-of-door dinner, which should embolden the young American hostess to go and do likewise:—

"Yesterday we dined *al fresco* in the Pamfili Gardens, in Rome, and although our party was rather too large, it was well assorted, and the day went off admirably. The queen of our feast was in high good humour and irresistibly charming, Frattino very fascinating, T. caustic and witty, W. lively and clever, J. mild, intelligent and elegant, V. as usual quiet, sensible, and self-complacent, L. as absurd and assiduous as ever.

"Everybody played their part well, each by a tacit convention sacrificing to the *amour propre* of his neighbour, each individual really occupied with his own peculiar *rôle*, but all apparently happy and mutually pleased. Vanity and selfishness, indifference and *ennui* were veiled under a general mask of good humour and good breeding, and the flowery bonds of politeness and gallantry held together those who knew no common tie of thought or interest.

"Our luxurious dinner, washed down by a competent proportion of Malvoisie and champagne, was spread upon the grass, which was literally the flowery turf, being covered with violets, iris, and anemones of every dye.

"For my own peculiar taste there were too many servants, too many luxuries, too much fuss; but considering the style and number of our party, it was all consistently and admirably managed. The grouping of the company, picturesque because unpremeditated, the scenery around, the arcades and bowers and columns and fountains had an air altogether poetical and romantic, and put me in mind of some of Watteau's beautiful garden pieces."

Now in this exquisite description Mrs. Jameson seems to me to have given the intellectual components of a dinner. "The hostess, good-humoured and charming, Frattino very fascinating, T. caustic and witty, W. lively and clever, J. mild, intelligent, and elegant, V. as usual quiet, sensible, and self-complacent, L. as absurd and as assiduous as ever."

There was variety for you, and the three last were undoubtedly listeners. In the next paragraph she covers more ground, and this is most important:—

"Each by a tacit convention sacrificing to the *amour propre* of his neighbour."

That is an immortal phrase, for there can be no pleasant dinner when this unselfishness is not shown. It was said by a witty Boston hostess that she could never invite two well-known diners-out to the same dinner, for each always silenced the other. You must not have too many good talkers. The listeners, the receptive listeners, should outnumber the talkers.

In England, the land of dinners, they have, of course, no end of public, semi-official, and annual dinners,—as those of the Royal Literary Fund, the Old Rugbians, the Artists Benevolent Fund, the Regimental dinners, the banquets at the Liberal and the Cobden Club, and the nice little dinners at the Star and Garter, winding up with the annual fish dinner.

Now of all these the most popular and sought after is the annual dinner of the Royal Academy. Few gratifications are more desired by mortals than an invitation to this dinner. The president, Sir Frederic Leighton, is handsome and popular. The dinner is representative in character; one or more members of the Royal Family are present; the Church, the Senate, the Bar, Medicine, Literature and Science, the Army, the Navy, the City,—all these have their representatives in the company.

Who would not say that this would be the most amusing dinner in London? Intellect at its highest water mark is present. The *menu* is splendid. But I have heard one distinguished guest say that the thing is over-freighted, the ship is too full, and the crowd of good things makes a surfeit.

Dinners at the Lord Mayor's are said to be pleasant and fine specimens of civic cheer, but the grand nights at the Middle Temple and others of the Inns of Court are occasions of pleasant festivity.

We have nothing to do with these, however, except to read of them, and to draw our conclusions. I know of no better use to which we can put them than the same rereading which we gave Mrs. Jameson's well-considered *menu*: "Each individual really occupied with his own *rôle*, but all apparently happy and mutually pleased. Variety and selfishness or indifference or *ennui* well veiled under a general mask of good humour and good breeding, and the flowery bands of politeness and gallantry holding together those who knew no common tie of thought and interest." It requires very civilized people to veil their indifference and *ennui* under a general mask of good humour.

To have unity, one must first have units; and to make an agreeable dinner-party the hostess should invite agreeable people, and her husband should be a good host; and here we must again compliment England. An Englishman is churlish and distant, self-conscious and prejudiced everywhere else but at his own table. He is a model host, and a most agreeable guest. He is the most genial of creatures after the soup and sherry. Indeed the English dinner is the keynote to all that is best in the English character. An Englishman wishes to eat in company.

How unlike the Spaniard, who never asks you to dinner. However courtly and hospitable he may be at other times and other hours of the day, he likes to drag his bone into a corner and gnaw it by himself.

The Frenchman, elegant, *soigné*, and economical, invites you to the best-cooked dinner in the world, but there is not much of it. He prefers to entertain you at a café. Country life in France is delightful, but there is not that luxurious, open-handed entertaining which obtains in England.

In Italy one is seldom admitted to the privacy of the family dinner. It is a patriarchal affair. But when one is admitted one finds much that is *simpatica*. The cookery is good, the service is perfect, the dinner is short, the conversation gay and easy.

In making up a dinner with a view to its intellectual components, avoid those tedious talkers who, having a theme, a system, or a fad to air, always contrive to drag the conversation around to their view, with the intention of concentrating the whole attention upon themselves. One such man, called appropriately the Bore Constrictor of conversation in a certain city, really drove people away from every house to which he was invited; for they grew tired of hearing him talk of that particular science in which he was an expert. Such a talker could make the planet Jupiter a bore, and if the talker were of the feminine gender how one would shun her verbosity.

"I called on Mrs. Marjoribanks yesterday," said a free lance once, "and we had a little gossip about Copernicus." We do not care to have anything quite so erudite, for if people are really very intimate with Copernicus they do not mention it at dinner.

It is as impossible to say what makes the model diner-out as to describe the soil which shall grow the best grapes. We feel it and we enjoy it, but we can give no receipt for the production of the same.

As history, with exemplary truthfulness, has always painted man as throwing off all the trouble of giving a dinner on his wife, why have not our clever women appreciated the power of dinner-giving in politics? Why are not our women greater politicians? Where is our Lady Jersey, our Lady Palmerston, our Princess Belgioso? The Princess Lieven, wife of the Russian Ambassador in London, was said to have held the peace of Europe in the conduct of her *entrées*; and a country-woman of our own is to-day supposed to influence the policy of Germany largely by her dinners. From the polished and versatile memoirs of the Grammonts, Walpoles, D'Azelios, Sydney Smith, and Lord Houghton, how many an anecdote hinges on the efficacy of a dinner in reconciling foes, and in the making of friends. How many a conspiracy was hatched, no doubt, behind an aspic of plover's eggs or a *vol au vent de volaille*. How many a budding ministry, according to Lord Lammington, was brought to full power over a well-ordered table-cloth. How many a war cloud dispelled by the proper temperature of the Burgundy. It is related of Lord Lyndhurst that when somebody asked him how to succeed in life, he answered, "Give good wine." A French statesman would have answered, "Give good dinners." Talleyrand kept the most renowned table of his day, quite as much for political as hygienic reasons. At eighty years of age he still spent an hour every morning with his *chef*, discussing the dishes to be served at dinner. The Emperor Napoleon, who was no epicure, nor even a connoisseur, was nevertheless pleased with Talleyrand's luxurious and refined hospitality, in consequence of the impression it made on those who were so fortunate as to partake of it. On the other hand, one hesitates to contemplate the indigestions and bad English cooking which must have hatched an Oliver Cromwell, or still earlier that decadence of Italian cookery which made a Borgia possible.

Social leaders in all ages and countries have thus studied the tastes and the intellectual aptitudes and capabilities of those whom they have gathered about their boards; and Mythology would suggest that the *petits soupers* on high Olympus, enlivened by the "inextinguishable laughter of the gods," had much to do with the politics of the Greek heaven under Jupiter. Reading the Northern Saga in the same connection, may not the vague and awful conceptions of cookery which seem to have filled the Northern mind have had something to do with the opera of Siegfried? Even the music of Wagner seems to have been inspired by a draught from the skull of his enemy. It has the fascination of clanging steel, and the mighty rustling of armour. The wind sighs through the forest, and the ice-blast freezes the hearer. The chasms of earth seem to open before us. But it has also the terror of an indigestion, and the brooding horror of a nightmare from drinking metheglia and eating half-roasted kid. The political aspect of a Scandinavian heaven was always stormy. Listen to the Trilogy.

In America a hostess sure of her soups and her *entrées*, with such talkers as she could command, could influence American political movements—she might influence its music—by her dinners, and become an enviable Lady Palmerston.

Old people are apt to say that there is a decay in the art of conversation, that it is one of the lost arts. No doubt this is in a measure true all over the world. A French *salon* would be to-day an impossibility for that very reason. It is no longer the fashion to tell anecdotes, to try to be amusing. A person is considered a prig who sits up to amuse the company. All this is bad; it is reactionary after the drone of the Bore Constrictor. It is going on all over the world. It is part of that hurry which has made us talk slang, the jelly of speech, speech condensed and boiled down, easily transported, and warranted to keep in all climates.

But there is a very pleasant *juste milieu* between the stately, perhaps starchy, anecdotist of the past and the easy and witty talker of to-day, who may occasionally drop into slang, and what is more, may permit a certain slovenliness of speech. There are certain mistakes in English, made soberly, advisedly, and without fear of Lindley Murray, which make one sigh for the proprieties of the past. The trouble is we have no standard. Writers are always at work at the English language, and yet many people say that it is at present the most irregular and least understood of all languages.

The intellectual components of a successful dinner, should, if we may quote Hawthorne, be illuminated with intellect, and softened by the kindest emotions of the heart. To quote Mrs. Jameson, they must combine the caustic and the witty, the lively and the clever, and even the absurd, and the assiduous above all. Everybody must be unselfish enough not to yawn, and never seem bored. They must be self-sacrificing, but all apparently well-pleased. The intellectual components of a dinner, like the condiments of a salad, must be of the best; and it is for the hostess to mix them with the unerring tact and fine discrimination of an American woman.

CONSCIENTIOUS DINERS.

It is chiefly men of intellect who hold good eating in honour. The head is not capable of a mental operation which consists in a long sequence of appreciations, and many severe decisions of the judgment, which has not a well-fed brain.

BRILLAT SAVARIN.

A good dinner and a pretty hostess,—for there are terms on which beauty and beef can meet much to the benefit of both,—one wit, several good talkers, and as many good listeners, or more of the latter, are said to make a combination which even our greatest statesmen do not despise. Man wants good dinners. It is woman's province to provide them; but nature and education must make the conscientious diner.

It is to be feared that we are too much in a hurry to be truly conscientious diners. Our men have too many school-tasks yet,—politics, money-making, science, mental improvement, charities, psychical research, building railroads, steam monitors, colleges, and such like gauds,—too many such distractions to devote themselves as they ought to the question of *entrées* and *entremets*. They should endeavour to give the dinner a fitting place. Just see how the noble language of France, which Racine dignified and Molière amplified, respectfully puts on its robes of state which are lined with ermine when it approaches the great subject of dinner!

It is to be feared that we are far off from the fine art of dining, although many visits to Paris and much patronage of Le Doyon's, the Café Anglais, and the Café des Ambassadeurs, may have prepared us for the *entremet* and the *pièce de résistance*. We are improving in this respect and no longer bolt our dinners. The improvement is already manifest in the better tempers and complexions of our people.

But are we as conscientious as the gentleman in "Punch" who rebuked the giddy girl who would talk to him at dinner? "Do you remember, my dear, that you are in the house of the best *entrées* in London? I wish to eat my dinner."

That was a man to cook for! He had his appropriate calm reserve of appreciation, for the *suprême de volaille*. He knew how to watch and wait for the sweetbreads, and green peas. Not thrown away upon him was that last turn which makes the breast of the partridge become of a delicate Vandyck brown. How respectful was he to that immortal art for which the great French cook died, a suicide for a belated turbot.

"Ah," said Parke Godwin once, when in one of his most brilliant Brillat Savarin moods, "how it ennobles a supper to think that all these oysters will become ideas!"

But if a dinner is not a cookery book, neither is it a matter of expense alone, nor a payment of social debts. It is a question of temperature, of the selection of guests, of the fitness of things, of a proper variety, and of time. The French make their exquisite dinners light and short. The English make theirs a trifle long and heavy.

The young hostess, to strike the *juste milieu*, must travel, reflect, and go to a cooking-school. She must buy and read a library of cooking-books. And when all is done and said, she must realize that a cookery-book is not a dinner. There are some natures which can absorb nothing from a cookery-book. As Lady Galway said that she had put all her wits into Bradshaw's "Railway Guide" and had never got them out again, so some amateur cook remarked that she had tested her recipes with the "cook-book in one hand and the cooking-stove in the other," yet the wit had stayed away. All young housekeepers must go through the discipline—in a land where cooks are as yet scarce—of trying and failing, of trying and at length succeeding. They must go to *La Belle France* to learn how to make a soup, for instance. That is to say, they must study the best French authorities.

The mere question of sustenance is easy of solution. We can stand by a cow and drink her milk, or we can put some bread in our pockets and nibble it as we go along; but dinner as represented by our complicated civilization is a matter of interest which must always stand high amongst the questions which belong to social life. It is a very strange attendant circumstance that having been a matter of profound concern to mankind for so many years, it is now almost as easy to find a bad dinner as a good one, even in Paris, that headquarters of cookery.

There would be no sense in telling a young American housekeeper to learn to make sauces and to cook like a French *chef,* for it is a profession requiring years of study and great natural taste and aptitude. A French *chef* commands a higher salary than a secretary of state or than a civil engineer. As well tell a young lady that she could suddenly be inspired with a knowledge of the art of war or of navigation. She would only perhaps learn to do very badly what they in ten years learn to do so well. She would say in her heart, "For my part I am surfeited with cookery. I cry, something *raw* if you please for me,—something that has never been touched by hand except the one that pulled it off the blooming tree or uprooted it from the honest ground. Let me be a Timon if you will, and eat green radishes and cabbages, or a Beau Brummel, asphyxiated in the consumption of a green pea; but no *ragoût, côtelette, compote, crème,* or any hint or cooking till the remembrance of all that I have seen has faded and the smell of it has passed away!"

Thus said one who attended a cooking-school, had gone through the mysteries of soup-making, had learned what *sauté* means; had mastered *entremets,* and *entrées,* and *plats,* and *hors d'œuvres;* had learned that *boudins de veau* are simply veal puddings, something a little better than a veal croquette made into a little pie; and had found that all meats if badly cooked are much alike. There is a great deal of nonsense talked about making good dishes out of nothing. A French cook is very economical, he uses up odds and ends, but he must have something to cook with.

Stone broth does not go down with a hungry man, nor bad food, however disguised with learned sauces. A little learning is a dangerous thing, and one who attempts too much will fail. But one can read, and reflect, and get the general outlines of cultivated cookery. As to cultivated cookery being necessarily extravagant, that is a mistake. A great, heavy, ill-considered dinner is no doubt costly. Almost all American housekeeping is wasteful in the extreme, but the modern vanities which depend on the skill of the cook and the arranging mind of the housekeeper, all these are the triumphs of the present age, and worthy of deep thought and consideration. Let the young housekeeper remember that the pretty *entrées* made out of yesterday's roast chicken or turkey will be a great saving as well as a great luxury, and she will learn to make them.

Amongst a busy people like ourselves, from poorest to the richest, dinners are intended to be recreations, and recreations of inestimable value. The delightful contrast which they offer to the labours of the day, the pleasant, innocent triumph they afford to the hostess, in which all may partake without jealousy, the holiday air of guests and of the dining-room, which should be fresh, well aired, filled with flowers, made bright with glass and silver,—all this refreshes the tired man of affairs and invigorates every creature. As far as possible, the discussion of all disagreeable subjects should be kept from the dinner-table. All that is unpleasant lowers the pulse and retards digestion. All that is cheerful invigorates the pulse and helps the human being to live a more brave and useful life. No one should bring an unbecoming grumpiness to the dinner-table. Be grumpy next day if you choose, when the terrapin may have disagreed with you, but not at the feast. Bring the best bit of news and gossip, not scandal, the choicest critique of the last novel, the cream of your correspondence. Be sympathetic, amiable, and agreeable at a feast, else it were better you had stayed away. The last lesson of luxury is the advice to contribute of our very best to the dinners of our friends, while we form our own dinners on the plane of the highest luxury which we can afford, and avoid the great *too much*. Remember that in all countries the American lavish prodigality of feasting, and the expensive garniture of hothouse flowers, are always spoken of as vulgar. How well it will be for us when our splendid array of fish, flesh, and fowl shall have reached the benediction of good cookery; when we know how to serve it, not with barbaric magnificence and repletion, but with a delicate sense of fitness.

Mr. Webster, himself an admirable dinner giver, said of a codfish salad that it was "fit to eat." He afterwards remarked, more gravely,—and it made him unpopular,—that a certain nomination was "not fit to be made."

That led to a discussion of the word "fit." The fitness of things, the right amount, the thing in the right place, whether it be the condiment of a salad or the nomination to the presidency,—this is the thing to consult, to think of in a dinner; let it be "fit to be made."

An American dinner resolves itself into the following formula:—

The oyster is offered first. What can equal the American oyster in all his salt-sea freshness, raw, on the half-shell, a perpetual stimulant to appetite,—with a slice of lemon, and a bit of salt and pepper, added to his own luscious juices, his perfect flavor? The jaded palate, worn with much abuse, revives, and stands, like Oliver, asking for more.

The soup follows. To this great subject we might devote a chapter. What visions of white and brown, clear and thick, fresh beef stock or the maritime delicacies of cray fish and prawn rise before us,—in every colour, from pink or cream to the heavy Venetian red of the mulligatawny or the deep smoke-tints of mock turtle and terrapin! The subject grows too large for mere mention; we must give a chapter to soup.

When we speak of fish we realize that the ocean even is inadequate to hold them all. Have we not trout, salmon, the great fellows from the Great Lakes, and the exclusive ownership of the Spanish mackerel? Have we not the fee simple of terrapin and the exclusive excellence of shad? This subject, again, requires a volume.

The roast! Ah! here we once bowed to our great Mother England, and thought her roast beef better than ours. There are others who think that we have caught up on the roasts. Our beef is very good, our mutton does not equal always the English Southdowns; but we are even improving in the blacknosed woolly brethren who conceal such delicious juices under their warm coats.

A roast saddle of mutton with currant jelly—but let us not linger over this thrilling theme. Our venison is the best in the world.

As for turkeys,—*we discovered them*, and it is fair to say that, after looking the world over, there is no better bird than a Rhode Island Turkey, particularly if it is sent to you as a present from a friend. Hang him a week, with a truffle in him, and stuff him with chestnuts.

As for chickens—there France has us at a disadvantage. There seems to be a secret of fowl-feeding, or rearing, in France which we have not mastered. Still we can get good chickens in America, and noble capons, but they are very expensive.

The *entrées*—here we must go again to those early missionaries to a savage shore, the Delmonicos. They were the high priests of the *entrée*.

The salads—those daughters of luxury, those delicate expressions, in food, of the art of dress—deserve a separate chapter.

And now the *sorbet* cools our throats and leads us up to the game.

The American desserts are particularly rich and profuse. Our pies have been laughed at, but they also are fit to eat, especially mince-pie, which is first cousin to an English plum-pudding.

Our puddings are like our Western scenery, heavy but magnificent. Our ices have reached, under our foreign imported artists, the greatest perfection. Our fruit is abundant and highly flavoured. We have not yet perhaps known how to draw the line as to desserts. The great *too much* prevails.

Do we not make our dinners too long and too heavy? How great an artist would he be who should so graduate a dinner that there would be no to-morrow in it! We eat more like Heliogabalus than like that *gourmet* who took the *beccafico* out of the olive which had been hidden in the pigeon, which had in its turn been warmed in the chicken, which was cooked in the ox, which was roasted whole for the birthday of a king. The *gourmet* discarded the rest, but ate the *beccafico*.

The first duty of a guest who is asked to one of these dinners is to be punctual. Who wishes to sit next to Mr. Many-Courses, when he has been kept waiting for his dinner? Imagine the feelings of an amiable host and hostess who, after taking the trouble to get up an excellent dinner, feel that it is being spoiled by the tardiness of one guest! They are nervously watching Mr. Many-Courses, for hungry animals are frequently snappish, and sometimes dangerous.

The hostess who knows how to invite her guests and to seat them afterwards is a power in the State. She helps to refine, elevate, and purify our great American conglomerate. She has not the Englishman's Bible, "The Peerage," to help her seat her guests; she must trust to her own intelligence to do that. Our great American conglomerate repels all idea of rank, or the precedence idea, which is so well understood in England.

Hereditary distinction we have not, for although there are some families which can claim a grandfather, they are few. A grandfather is of little importance to the men who make themselves. Aristocracy in America is one of talent or money.

Even those more choice intelligences, which in older countries are put on glass pedestals, are not so elevated here as to excite jealousy. We all adore the good diner-out, but somebody would be jealous if he had always the best seat. Therefore the hostess has to contend with much that is puzzling in the seating of her guests; but if she says to herself, "I will place those people near each other who are sympathetic," she will govern her festive board with the intelligence of Elizabeth, and the generosity of Queen Margharita.

She must avoid too many highly scented flowers. People are sometimes weary of the "rapture of roses." Horace says: "Avoid, at an agreeable entertainment, discordant music, and muddy perfume, and poppies mixed with Sardinian honey; they give offence." Which is only another way of saying that some music may be too heavy, and the perfume of flowers too strong.

Remember, young hostess, or old hostess, that your dinner is to be made up of people who have to sit two hours chatting with each other, and that this is of itself a severe ordeal of patience.

Good breeding is said to be the apotheosis of self-restraint, and so is good feeding. Good breeding puts nature under restraint, controls the temper, and refines the speech. Good feeding, unless it is as well governed as it should be, inflames the nose and the temper, and enlarges the girth most unbecomingly. Good breeding is the guardian angel of a woman. Good feeding, that is, conscientious dining, must be the patron saint of a man! A truly well bred and well fed man is quiet in dress, does not talk slang, is not prosy, is never unbecomingly silent, nor is he too garrulous. He is always respectful to everybody, kind to the weak, helpful to the feeble. He may not be an especially lofty character, but good feeding inducts him into the character and duties of a gentleman. He simulates a virtue if he has it not, especially after dinner. *Noblesse oblige* is his motto, and he feels what is due to himself.

Can we be a thorough-bred, or a thorough-fed, all by ourselves? It is easy enough to learn when and where to leave a card, how to behave at a dinner, how to use a fork, how to receive and how to drop an acquaintance; but what a varied education is that which leads up to good feeding, to becoming a conscientious diner. It is not given to every one, this lofty grace.

A dinner should be a good basis for a mutual understanding. They say that few great enterprises have been conducted without it. People are sure to like each other much better after dining together. It is better to go home from a dinner remembering how clever everybody was, than to go home merely to wonder at the opulence that could compass such a pageant.

A dinner should put every one into his best talking condition. The quips and quirks of excited fancy should come gracefully, for society well arranged brings about the attrition of wits. If one is comfortable and well-fed—not gorged—he is in his best condition.

The more civilized the world gets, the more difficult it is to amuse it. It is the common complaint of the children of luxury that dinners are dull and society stupid. How can the reformer make society more amusing and less dangerous? Eliminate scandal and back-biting.

The danger and trials and difficulties of dinner-giving are manifold. First, whom shall we ask? Will they come? It is often the fate of the hostess, in the busy season, to invite forty people before she gets twelve. Having got the twelve, she then has perhaps a few days before the dinner to receive the unwelcome news that Jones has a cold, Mrs. Brown has lost a relative, and Miss Malcontent has gone to Washington. The dinner has to be reconstructed; deprived of its original intention it becomes a balloon which has lost ballast. It goes drifting about, and there is no health in it and no purpose. This is especially true also of those dinners which are conducted on debt-paying principles.

How many hard-worked, rich men in America are bored to death by the gilded and over-burdened splendour of their wives' dinners and those to which they are to go. They sit looking at their hands during two or three courses, poor dyspeptics who cannot eat. To relieve them, to bring them into communion with their next neighbour, with whom they have nothing in common, what shall one do? Oh, that depressing cloud which settles over the jaded senses of even the conscientious diner, as he fails to make his neighbour on either side say anything but yes or no!

We must, perhaps, before we give the perfect dinner, renounce the idea that dinner should be on a commercial basis. Of course our social debts must be paid. It is a large subject, like the lighting of a city, the cleaning of the streets, and must be approached carefully, so that the lesser evil may not swamp the greater good. Do not invite twelve people to bore them.

The dinner hour differs in different cities,—from seven to half-past seven, to eight, and eight and a half; all these have their adherents. In London, many a party does not sit down until nine. Hence the necessity of a hearty meal at five o'clock tea. The royalties, all blessed with good appetites, eat eggs on toast, hot scones and other good things at five o'clock tea, and take often an *avant goût* also at seven.

In our country half-past seven is generally the most convenient hour, unless one is going to the play afterward, when seven is better. A dinner should not last more than an hour and a half. But it does last sometimes three hours.

Ladies dress for a large dinner often in low neck and short sleeves, wear their jewels, and altogether their finest things. But now Pompadour waists are allowed. For a small dinner, the Pompadour dress, half-open at the throat, with a few jewels, is in better taste.

Men should be always in full dress,—black coat, waistcoat, and trousers, and white cravat. There is no variation from this dress at a dinner, large or small.

For ladies in delicate health who cannot expose throat or arms, there is always the largest liberty allowed; but the dinner dress must be handsome.

In leaving the house and ordering the carriage, name the earliest hour rather than the latest; it is better to keep one's coachman waiting than to weary one's hostess. It is quite impossible to say when one will leave, as there may be music, recitations, and so on, after the dinner. It is now quite the fashion, as in London, to ask people in after the dinner.

Everybody should go to a dinner intending to be agreeable.

"E'en at a dinner some will be unblessed,
However good the viands, and well dressed;
They always come to table with a scowl,
Squint with a face of verjuice o'er each dish,
Fault the poor flesh, and quarrel with the fish,
Curse cook, and wife, and loathing, eat and growl."

Such men should never be asked twice; yet such were Dr. Johnson, and later on, Abraham Hayward, the English critic, who were invited out every night of their lives. It is a poor requital for hospitality, to allow any personal ill-temper to interfere with the pleasure of the feast. Some hostesses send around the champagne early to unloose the tongues; and this has generally a good effect if the party be dull. Excessive heat in a room is the most benumbing of all overweights. Let the hostess have plenty of oxygen to begin with.

For a little dinner of eight we might suggest that the hostess write:—

DEAR MRS. SULLIVAN,—Will you and Mr. Sullivan dine with us on Thursday at half-past seven to meet Mr. and Mrs. Evarts, quite informally?

Ever yours truly,
MARY MONTGOMERY.

This accepted, which it should be in the first person, cordially, as it is written, let us see what we would have for dinner—

Sherry.   Soup.   Sorrel, *à l'essence de veau.*

Lobsters, *sauté à la Bonnefoy.*   Chablis.

Veal Cutlets, *à la Zingara.*

Fried sweet potatoes.   Champagne.

Roast Red-Head Ducks.   Currant jelly.

Claret.   Curled Celery in glasses.   Olives.

Cheese.   Salad.

Frozen Pudding.

Grapes.

Coffee.   Liqueurs.

Or, if you please, a brown soup, a white fish or bass, boiled, a saddle of mutton, a pair of prairie chickens and salad, a plate of broiled mushrooms, a *sorbet* of Maraschino, cheese, ice-cream, fruit. It is not a bad "look-out," is it?

How well the Italians understand the little dinner! They are frugal but conscientious diners until they get to the dessert.

Their dishes have a relish of the forest and the field. First comes wild boar, stewed in a delicious condiment called sour-sweet sauce, composed of almonds, pistachio nuts, and plums. Quails, with a twang of aromatic herbs, are followed by macaroni flavoured with spiced livers, cocks' combs, and eggs called *risotto*, then golden *fritto*, cooked in the purest *cru* of olive oil, and *quocchi* cakes, of newly ground Indian corn, which is all that our roasted green corn is, without the trouble of gnawing it off the cob,—a process abhorrent to the conscientious diner unless he is alone. One should first take monastic vows of extreme austerity before he eats the forbidden fruit, onion, or the delicious corn. But when we can conquer Italian cooking, we can eat these two delicious things, nor fear to whisper to our best friend, nor fear to be seen eating.

The triumphs of the *dolce* belong also to the Italians. Their sugared fruits, ices, and pastry are all matchless; and their wines, Chianti, Broglio, and Vino Santo, a kind of Malaga, as "frankly luscious as the first grape can make it," are all delicious.

VARIOUS MODES OF GASTRONOMIC GRAT-IFICATION.

Phyllis, I have a cask full of Albanian wine upwards of nine years old; I have parsley in the garden for the weaving of chaplets. The house shines cheerfully with plate; all hands are busy.

HORACE, *Ode XI.*

Some old French wit spoke of an "idea which could be canonized." Perhaps yet we may have a Saint Table-Cloth. There have been worse saints than Saint Table-Cloth and clean linen, since the days of Louis XIII!

We notice in the old pictures of feasting that the table-cloth was of itself a picture,—lace, in squares, blocks, and stripes, sometimes only lace over a colour, but generally mixed with linen.

It was the highest ambition of the Dutch housewife to have much double damask of snowy whiteness in her table-linen chest. That is still the grand reliable table-linen. No one can go astray who uses it.

Table-linen is now embroidered in coloured cottons, or half of its threads are drawn out and it is then sewed over into lace-work. It is then thrown over a colour, generally bright red. But pale lilac is more refined, and very becoming to the lace-work.

Not a particle of coarse food must go on that table-cloth. Everything must be brought to each guest from the broad, magnificent buffet; all must be served *à la Russe* from behind a grand, impenetrable screen, which should fence off every dining-room from the butler's pantry and the kitchen. All that goes on behind that screen is the butler's business, and not ours. The butler is a portly man, presumably, with a clean-shaven face, of English parentage. He has the key of the wine-cellar and of the silver-chest, two heavy responsibilities; for nowadays, not to go into the question of the wines, the silver-chest is getting weighty. Silver and silver-gilt dishes, banished for some years, are now reasserting their pre-eminent fitness for the dinner-table: The plates may be of solid silver; so are the high candlesticks and the salt-cellars, of various and beautiful designs after Benvenuto Cellini.

Old silver is reappearing, and happy the hostess who has a real Queen Anne teapot. The soup-tureen of silver is again used, and so are the old beer-mugs. Our Dutch ancestors were much alive to good silver; he may rejoice who, joking apart, had a Dutch uncle. I, for one, do not like to eat off a metallic plate, be it of silver or gold. It is disagreeable to hear the knife scrape on it, even with the delicate business of cutting a morsel of red canvas-back. Gastronomic gratification should be so highly refined that it trembles at a crumpled rose-leaf. Porcelain plates seem to be perfect, if they have not on them the beautiful head of Lamballe. Nobody at a dinner desires to cut her head off again, or to be reminded of the French Revolution. Nor should we hurry. A master says, "I have arrived at such a point that if the calls of business or pleasure did not interpose, there would be no fixed date for finding what time might elapse between the first glass of sherry and the final Maraschino."

However, the pleasures of a dinner may be too prolonged. Men like to sit longer eating and drinking than women; so when a dinner is of both sexes it should not continue more than one hour and a half. Horace, that prince of diners, objected to the long-drawn-out meal. "Then we drank, each as much as he felt the need," meant no orgy amongst the Greeks.

But if the talk lingers after the biscuit and cheese the hostess need not interrupt it.

Talleyrand is said to have introduced into France the custom of taking Parmesan with the soup, and the Madeira after it.

There are many conflicting opinions about the proper place for the cheese in order of serving. The old fashion was to serve it last. It is now served with, or after, the salad. "A dessert without cheese is like a beautiful woman with one eye," says an old gourmet.

"Eat cheese after fruit, to prepare the palate for fresh wine," says another.

"After melon, wine is a felon."

If it is true that "an American devours, an Englishman eats, and a Frenchman dines," then we must take the French fashion and give the cheese after the salad.

Toasted cheese savouries are very nice. The Roman punch should be served just before the game. It is a very refreshing interlude. Some wit called it at Mrs. Hayes' dinners "the life-saving station."

When the ices are removed a dessert-plate of glass, with a finger-bowl, is placed before each person, with two glasses, one for sherry, one for claret, or Burgundy; and the grapes, peaches, pears, and other fruits are then passed.

The hostess makes the sign for retiring to a *salon* perhaps rich with magnificent hangings of old gold, with pictures, with vases of Dresden, of Sèvres, of Kiota, with statuary, and specimens of Capo di Monti. There coffee may be brought and served by the footmen in cups which Catherine of Russia might have given to Potemkin. The gentlemen, in England and America, remain behind to smoke.

There is much exquisite porcelain in use in the opulent houses of America. It is getting to be a famous fad with us, and nothing adds more to one's pleasure in a good dinner than to have it served on pretty plates. And let us learn to say "footman," and not "waiter;" the latter personage belongs to a club or a hotel. It would prevent disagreeable mistakes if we would make this correction in our ordinary conversation.

In the arrangement of a splendid dinner let us see what should be the bill of fare.

This is hard to answer, as the delicacies vary with the season. But we will venture on one:—

Oysters on the half-shell.

Sherry.	Soups:	
Crème d'Asperges,		Julienne.
	Fish:	Chablis.

Fried Smelts, or Salmon.

Fresh Cucumbers.

| Champagne. | *Filet de Bœuf,* with Truffles and Mushrooms. | Claret. |

Fried Potatoes.

Entrées:

| *Poulet à la Maréchale.* | | Petits Pois. |

Timbale de Macaroni.

Sweetbreads.

Vegetables.		Artichokes.
Sorbet.		Roman Punch.
Steinberger.	Game:	

Canvas-back or Wild Duck with Currant Jelly.

Quail with Water-Cresses.

| Salad of Lettuce. | | Salad of Tomato. |
| Rudesheimer. | | *Pâté de foie gras.* |

Hot dessert:

Cabinet Pudding.

Cold dessert:

Crème glacée aux tutti frutti.

Marron glacés.	Cakes.	Preserved ginger.
Madeira.	Cheese.	Port.
Café.		Cordials.

I apologize to my reader for mixing thus French and English. It is a vulgar habit, and should be avoided. But it is almost impossible to avoid it when speaking of a dinner; the cooks being French, the *menus* are written in French, and the names of certain dishes are usually written in French. Now all people understand French, or should do so. If they do not, it is very easy to learn that the *"vol au vent de volaille"* is simply chicken pie, that potatoes are still potatoes under whatever alias they are served, and so on.

No such dinner as this can be well served in a private house unless the cook is a *chef*, a *cordon bleu*,—here we must use French again,—and unless the service is perfect this dinner will be a failure. It is better to order such a dinner from Delmonico's or Sherry's or from the best man you can command. Do not attempt and fail.

But the little dinners given by housekeepers whose service is perfect are apt to be more eatable and palatable than the best dinner from a restaurant, where all the food is cooked by gas, and tastes alike.

The number of guests is determined by the size of the room. The etiquette of entering the dining-room is this: the host goes first, with the most distinguished lady. The hostess follows last, with the most distinguished gentleman.

Great care and attention must be observed in seating the guests. This is the province of the hostess, who must consider the subject carefully. All this must be written out, and a diagram made of the table. The name of each lady is written on a card and enclosed in an envelope, on the outside of which is inscribed the name of the gentleman who has the honour to take her in. This envelope must be given each man by the servant in the dressing-room, or he must find it on the hall table. Then, with the dinner-card at each place, the guests find their own places.

The lady of the house should be dressed and in the drawing-room at least five minutes before the guests are to arrive, which should be punctually. How long must a hostess wait for a tardy guest? Only fifteen minutes.

It is well to say to the butler, "Dinner must be served at half-past seven," and the guests may be asked at seven. That generally ensures the arrival of all before the fish is spoiled. Let the company then go in to dinner, allowing the late-comer to follow. He must come in alone, blushing for his sins. These facts may help a hostess: No great dinner in Europe waits for any one; royalty is always punctual. In seating your guests do not put husband and wife, sisters or relatives together.

An old courtesy book of 1290 says:—

> "Consider about placing
> Each person in the post that befits him.
> Between relations it behooves
> To place others midway sometimes."

We should respect the *superstitions* of the dinner-table. No one should be helped twice to soup; it means an early death. Few are free from the feeling that thirteen is an unlucky number; so avoid that, as no one wishes to make a guest uncomfortable. As we have said, Gasthea is an irritable muse; she must be flattered and pampered. No one must put salt on another's plate. There is a strong prejudice against spilling the salt; but evil consequences can be avoided by throwing a pinch of salt over the left shoulder.

These remarks may seem frivolous to those unhappy persons who have not the privilege of being superstitious. It gives great zest to life to have a few harmless superstitions. It is the cheese *fondu* of the mental faculties; and we may add that a consideration of these maxims, handed down from a glorious past of gastronomes, contributes to the various modes of gastronomic gratification. We must remember that the tongue of man, by the delicacy of its structure, gives ample evidences of the high functions to which it is destined. The Roman epicures cultivated their taste so perfectly that they could tell if a fish were caught above or below a bridge. Organic perfection, epicureanism, or the art of good living, belongs to man alone. The pleasure of eating is the only one, taken in moderation, which is common to every time, age, and condition, which is enjoyed without fatigue or danger, which must be repeated two or three times a day. It can combine with our other pleasures, or console us for their loss.

"*Un bon diner, c'est un consolation pour les illusions perdus.*" And we have an especial satisfaction, when in the act of eating, that we are prolonging our existence, and enabling ourselves to become good citizens whilst enjoying ourselves.

Thus the pleasures of the table, the act of dining, the various modes of gastronomic gratification should receive our most respectful consideration. "Let the soup be hot, and the wines cool. Let the coffee be perfect, and the liqueurs chosen with peculiar care. Let the guests be detained by the social enjoyment, and animated with the hope that before the evening is over there is still some pleasure in store."

Our modern hostesses who understand the art of entertaining often have music, or some recitations, in the drawing-room after the dinner; and in England it is often made the occasion of an evening party.

Thus gourmandize is that social love of good dinners which combines in one Athenian elegance, Roman luxury, and Parisian refinement. It implies discretion to arrange, skill to prepare, and taste to direct. It cannot be done superficially, and if done well it takes time, experience, and care. "To be a success, a dinner must be thought out."

"By right divine, man is the king of nature, and all that the earth produces is for him. It is for him that the quail is fattened, the grape ripened. For him alone the Mocha possesses so agreeable an aroma, for him the sugar has such wholesome properties."

He, and he alone, banquets in company, and so far from good living being hurtful to health, Brillat Savarin declares that the *gourmets* have a larger dose of vitality than other men. But they have their sorrows, and the worst of them is a bad dinner, — an ill-considered, wretchedly composed, over-burdened repast, in which there is little enjoyment for the brain, and a constant disappointment to the palate.

"Let the dishes be exceedingly choice and but few in number, and the wines of the best quality. Let the order of serving be from the more substantial to the lighter." Let the eating proceed without hurry or bustle, since the dinner is the last business of the day; and let the guests look upon themselves as travellers about to reach the same destination together.

A dinner is not, as we see, a matter of butler or *chef* alone. "It is the personal trouble which a host and hostess are willing to take; it is the intimate association of a cultivated nature with the practical business of entertaining, which makes the perfect dinner.

"Conviviality concerns everything, hence it produces fruits of all flavours. All the ingenuity of man has been for centuries concentrated upon increasing and intensifying the pleasures of the table."

The Greeks used flowers to adorn vases and to crown the guests. They ate under the vault of heaven, in gardens, in groves, in the presence of all the marvels of nature. To the pleasures of the table were joined the charms of music and the sound of instruments. Whilst the court of the king of the Phoenicians were feasting, Phenius, a minstrel, celebrated the deeds of the warriors of bygone times. Often, too, dancers and jugglers and comic actors, of both sexes and in every costume, came to engage the eye, without lessening the pleasures of the table.

We eat in heated rooms, too much heated perhaps, and brilliantly lighted, as they should be. The present fancy for shaded lamps, and easily ignitible shades, leads to impromptu conflagrations which are apt to injure Saint Table-Cloth. That poor martyr is burned at the steak quite too often. Our dancers and jugglers are introduced after dinner, not during dinner; and we have our warriors at the table amongst the guests. Nor do we hire Phenius, a minstrel, to discourse of their great deeds.

I copy from a recent paper the following remarks. Mr. Elbridge T. Gerry, says: "There are in society some newly admitted members who, with the best intentions imaginable, are never able to do things in just the proper style. They are persons of wealth, fairly good breeding and possessed of a desire to entertain. With all the good-humoured witticisms that the newspapers indulge in on this subject, it is nevertheless a fact that the art of entertaining requires deep and careful study, as well as natural aptitude."

Some of the greatest authors have stated this in poetry and prose.

"A typical member of this new class recently gave a dinner to a number of persons in society. It was a very dull affair. There was prodigality in everything, but no taste, and no refinement. The fellow amused me by telling us he had no trouble in getting up a fine dinner; he had only to tell his butler and *chef* to get up a meal for so many persons, and the whole thing was done. There are few persons fortunate enough to possess *chefs* and butlers of that kind; he certainly was not. Of the persons who attended his dinner, nine out of ten were displeased and will never attend another. It does not take long for the experienced member of society to know whether a host or hostess is qualified to entertain, and the climbers soon find it a hard piece of business to secure guests."

But on the other hand, we can reason that so fond of the various modes of gastronomic gratification is the human race, that the dinner giver is a very popular variety of the *genus homo*; nor does the host or hostess generally find it a hard matter to secure guests. Indeed there is a vulgar proverb to the effect that if the Devil gives a ball, all the angels will go to it.

"If you want an animal to love you, feed it." So that the host can stand a great deal of criticism. We should, however, take a hint from the Arabs, nor abuse the salt; it is almost worse than spilling it.

Lady Morgan described the cookery of France as being "the standard and gauge of modern civilization;" and when, during the peace which followed Waterloo, Brillat Savarin turned his thoughts to the æsthetics of the dinner-table, he probably added more largely to the health and happiness of the human race than any other known philanthropist. We must not forget what had gone before in the developments and refinements of the reigns of Louis XIV., XV., and the Regent; we must not forget the honour done to gastronomy by such statesmen as Colbert, such soldiers as Condé, nor by such a wit and beauty as Madame de Sevigné.

OF SOUPS.

"Oh, a splendid soup is the true pea-green,
I for it often call,
And up it comes, in a smart tureen,
When I dine in my banquet hall.
When a leg of mutton at home is boiled,
The liquor I always keep,
And in that liquor, before 't is spoiled,
A peck of peas I steep;
When boiled till tender they have been
I rub through a sieve the peas so green.
"Though the trouble the indolent may shock,

I rub with all my power,
And having returned them to the stock,
I stew them for an hour;
Of younger peas I take some more,
The mixture to improve,
Thrown in a little time before
The soup from the fire I move.
Then seldom a better soup is seen
Than the old familiar soup pea-green."

The best of this poetical recipe is that it is not only funny, but a capital formula.

"The giblet may tire, the gravy pall,
And the truth may lose its charm;
But the green pea triumphs over them all
And does not the slightest harm."

Some of us, however, prefer turtle. It would seem sometimes as if turtle soup were the synonym for a good dinner, and as if it dated back to the days of good Queen Bess. But fashion did not set its seal on turtle soup until about seventy years ago; as an entry in the "Gentleman's Magazine" mentions calipash and calipee as rarities. It is now inseparable from the Lord Mayor's dinner. When we notice ninety-nine recipes for soup in the latest French cookery book, and when we see the fate of a dinner made or marred by the first dish, we must concede that it will be a stumbling-block to the young housekeeper.

Add to that the curious fact that no Irishwoman can make a good soup until she has been taught by years of experience, and we have the first problem in the dangerous process of dinner-giving staring us in the face. A greasy, watery, ill-considered soup will take away the appetite of even a hungry man; while a delicate white or brown soup, or the *purées* of peas and asparagus, may well whet the appetite of the most pampered *gourmet*.

The subject of soup-making may well be studied. A good soup is at once economical and healthful, and of the first importance in the construction of a dinner. Soup should be made the day before it is to be eaten, by boiling either a knuckle of veal for a white soup, three or four pounds of beef, with the bone well cracked, for a clear *consommé*, or by putting the bones of fish, chickens, and meat into water with salt and pepper, and thus making an economical soup, which may, however, be very good. The French put everything into the soup pot,—bones, scraps, pot liquor, the water in which onions have been boiled, in fact in which all vegetables including beans and potatoes have been boiled; even as a French writer says "rejected MSS. may be thrown into the soup pot;" and the result in France is always good. It is to be observed that every soup should be allowed to cool, and all the fat should be skimmed off, so that the residuum may be as clear as wine.

Delicate soups, clear *consommé*, and white soups *à la Reine*, are great favourites in America, but in England they make a strong, savoury article, which they call gravy soup. It is well to know how to prepare this, as it makes a variety.

> Cut two pounds of beef from the neck into dice, and fry until brown. Break small two or three pounds of bones, and fry lightly. Bones from which streaked bacon has been cut make an excellent addition, but too many must not be used, lest the soup be salt. Slice and fry brown a pound of onions, put them with the meat and bones and three quarts of cold water into the soup pot; let it boil up, and having skimmed add two large turnips, a carrot cut in slices, a small bundle of sweet herbs, and a half a dozen pepper-corns. Let the soup boil gently for four or five hours, and about one hour before it is finished add a little piece of celery, or celery-seed tied in muslin. This is a most delicious flavour. When done, strain the soup and set it away for a night to get cold. Remove the fat and next day let it boil up, stirring in two spoonfuls of corn starch, moistened with cold water. Season with salt and pepper to taste, not too salt; add forcemeat balls to the soup, and you have a whole dinner in your soup.

An oxtail soup is made like the above, only adding the tail, which is divided into joints, which are fried brown. Then these joints should be boiled until the meat comes easily off the bones. When the soup is ready put in two lumps of sugar, a glass of port wine, and pour all into the tureen.

The Julienne soup, so delicious in summer, should be a nice clear stock, with the addition of prepared vegetables. Unless the cook can buy the excellent compressed vegetables which are to be had at the Italian warehouses, it is well to follow this order:—

> Wash and scrape a large carrot, cut away all the yellow parts from the middle, and slice the red outside. Take an equal quantity

of turnips and three small onions, cut in a similar manner. Put them in a stewpan with two ounces of butter and a pinch of powdered sugar, stir over the fire until a nice brown colour, then add a quart of clear, well-flavoured stock, and let all simmer together gently for three hours. When done, skim the fat off very carefully, and ten minutes before serving add a lettuce cut in shreds and blanched for a minute in boiling water. Simmer for five minutes and the soup will be ready. This is a most excellent soup if well made.

Mock-turtle soup is easily made:—

Boil the bones of the head three hours, add a piece of gravy meat cut in dice and fried brown, three onions sliced and fried brown, a carrot, a turnip, celery, and a small bundle of sweet herbs; boil gently for three hours and take off the fat. When it is ready to be served add a glass of sherry and slices of lemon. The various parts of a calf's-head can be cooked and used as force-meat balls, and made to look exactly like turtle. This soup is found canned and is almost as good as the real article.

Dried-pea soup, *crème d'asperge*, and bean soup, in fact all the *purées*, are very healthful and elegant soups. The *purée* is the mashed mass of pea or bean, which is added to the stock.

Boil a pint of large peas in a quart of water with a sprig of parsley or mint, and a dozen or so of green onions. When the peas are done strain and rub them through a sieve, put the *purée* back into the liquor the peas were boiled in, add a pint of good veal or beef broth, a lump of sugar, and pepper and salt to taste. Let the soup get thoroughly hot without boiling, stir in an ounce of good butter, and the soup is ready.

A plain but quick and delicious soup may be made by using a can of corn, with a small piece of pork. This warmed up quickly, with a little milk added, is very good.

As for a *crème d'asperge*, it is better to employ a *chef* to teach the new cook.

Mulligatawny soup is a visitor from India. It should not be too strong of curry powder for the average taste. The stock should be made of chicken or veal, or the liquor in which chickens have been boiled.

Slice and fry in butter six large onions, add four sharp, sour apples, cored and quartered, but not peeled. Let them boil in a little of the stock until quite tender, then mix with them a quarter of a pound of flour, and a small teaspoonful of curry powder. Take a quart of the stock and when the soup has boiled skim it; let it simmer for half an hour, then carefully take off all the fat, strain the soup, and rub the onions through a sieve. When ready to heat the soup for the dinner-table add any pieces of meat or chicken

cut into small, delicate shapes. When these have been boiled together for ten minutes the soup will be ready; salt to taste. Boiled
rice should be sent in on a separate dish.

Sorrel soup is a great favourite with the French people. We do not make
enough of sorrel in this country; it adds an excellent flavour.

Carefully wash a pound of sorrel, and having picked, cut it in
shreds, put it into a stewpan with two ounces of fresh butter and
stir it over the fire for ten minutes. Stir in an ounce of flour, mix
well together and add a pint and a half of good white stock made
as for veal broth. Let it simmer for half an hour. Having skimmed
the soup, stir in the yolks of three eggs beaten up in half a pint
of milk or cream. Stir in a little pat of butter, and when dissolved
pour the whole over thin pieces of toasted bread into the tureen.

With the large family of the broths every housewife should become acquainted. They are invaluable for the sick, especially broths of chicken and mutton. For
veal broth the following is an elaborate, but excellent recipe:

Get three or four pounds of scrag, or a knuckle of veal,
chopped into small pieces, also a ham bone, or slice of ham, and
cover with water; let it boil up, skim it until no more rises. Put in
four or five onions, a turnip, and later a bit of celery or celery seed
tied in muslin, a little salt, and white pepper. Let it boil gently for
four hours; strain the gravy and having taken off all the fat return
the residue to the pot and let it boil; then slightly thicken with
corn flour, about one teaspoonful to a quart of soup; let it simmer
before serving. Three pounds of veal should make two quarts of
good soup.

A sheep's-head soup is famous all over Scotland and is made as follows:—

Get the head of a sheep with the skin on, soak it in tepid water,
take out the tongue and brains, break all the thin bones inside the
cheek, and carefully wash it in several waters; put it on in a quart
of water with a teaspoonful of salt and let it boil ten minutes. Pour
away this water and put two quarts more with one pound of a
scrag of mutton; add, cut up, six onions, two turnips, two carrots,
a sprig of parsley, and season with pepper and salt. Let it boil
gently for four or five hours, when the head and neck will not be
too much cooked for the family dinner, and may be served either
with parsley or onion sauce. It is a most savoury morsel. Strain the
soup, and let it cool so as to remove every particle of fat. Rub the
vegetables through a sieve to a fine *purée*. Mix a tablespoonful of
flour in a quarter of a pint of milk; make the soup boil up and stir
it in with the vegetables.

Have the tongue boiled until it is very tender, skin and trim
it, have the brains also well cooked, and chop and pound them
very fine with the tongue, mix them with an equal weight of sifted

bread-crumbs, a tablespoonful of chopped green parsley, pepper, salt, and egg, and if necessary a small quantity of flour to enable you to roll the mixture into little balls. Put an ounce of butter into a small frying-pan and fry the balls until a nice brown, lay them on paper before the fire to drain away all the fat, and put them into the soup after it is poured into the tureen. Scald and chop some green parsley and serve separately on a plate.

Thackeray thought so much of a boiled sheep's head that he made it the point of one of his humorous poems.

"By that grand vow that bound thee
Forever to my side,
And by the ring that made thee
My darling and my bride!
Thou wilt not fail or falter
But bend thee to the task—
A boiled sheep's head on Sunday
Is all the boon I ask!"

In France, cabbage is much used in soup.

"Ha, what is this that rises to my touch
So like a cushion—can it be a cabbage?
It is, it is, that deeply inspired flower
Which boys do flout us with, but yet—I love thee,
Thou giant rose, wrapped in a green surtout.
Doubtless in Eden thou didst blush as bright
As these thy puny brethren, and thy breath
Sweetened the fragrance of her spicy air;
And now thou seemst like a bankrupt beau
Stripped of his gaudy hues and essences,
And growing portly in his sober garments."

The cabbage is without honour in America; and yet if boiled in water which is thrown away, having absorbed all its grosser essences, and then boiled again and chopped and dressed with butter and cream, it is an excellent vegetable. Its disagreeable odour has led to its expulsion from many a house, but corn-beef and cabbage are not to be despised.

Cauliflower, which Thackeray calls the "apotheosis of cabbage," is the most delicate of vegetables; and a *purée* of cauliflower shall close our chapter on soups.

Boil in salted water, using a small piece of butter, two heads of cauliflower, drain and pass them through a colander, dilute with two quarts of sauce and a quart of chicken broth, season with salt, white pepper, and grated nutmeg. Add a teaspoonful of fine white sugar, then pass the whole forcibly with a wooden presser through a fine sieve,—the finer the sieve the better the *purée*. Put the residue in a stewpan, set it on the fire, stir all the while till it boils, let it boil for ten minutes, strain well, add a mixture made with the yolks of six eggs and half a pint of cream, finish with four ounces of table butter, and serve with small, fried, square *croûtons*.

A *purée* of celery is equally excellent; but all these soups require an intelligent cook. It is better to have one's cook taught to make soups by an expert, for it is the most difficult of all the dishes, if thoroughly good. The plain soup, free from grease and well flavoured, is easy enough after a little training, "but the chief ingredient of soup is brains," according to a London *chef*. It is, however, a good practice for an amateur cook to experiment and to try these various recipes, all of which are practicable.

FISH.

What is thy diet? Canst thou gulf a shoal
Of herrings? Or hast thou gorge and room
To bolt fat porpoises and dolphins whole
By dozens, e'en as oysters we consume?

PUNCH.

The world's mine oyster, which I with sword will open.

HOTSPUR.

The Egyptians, strange to say, did not deify fish, that important article of their food. We read of the enormous yield of Lake Mœris, which was dammed up by the great Rameses, and whose draught of fishes brought him so enormous a revenue.

One of the most fascinating of all the Egyptian Queens, Sonivaphra, received the revenues of one of these fisheries to keep her in shoe-strings, — probably another name for pin money.

And yet the Egyptians, while mummying the cats and dogs and beetles, and such small deer, made no gods of the good carp or other fish which must have stocked the river Nile. They emblazoned the crocodile on their monuments, but never a fish. It is a singular foreshadowing of that great vice of the human race, ingratitude.

The Romans were fond of fish, and the records of their gastronomy abound in fish stories. We read of Licinius Crassus, the orator, that he lived in a house of great elegance and beauty. This house was called the "Venus of the Palatine," and was remarkable for its size, the taste of the furniture, and the beauty of the grounds. It was adorned with pillars of Hymettian marbles, with expensive vases and *triclinia* inlaid with brass; his gardens were provided with fish-ponds, and noble lotus-trees shaded his walks. Abenobarbus, his colleague in the censorship, found fault with such luxury, such "corruption of manners," and complained of his crying for the loss of a lamprey as if it had been a favourite daughter!

This, however, was a tame lamprey, which used to come to the call of Crassus and feed out of his hand. Crassus retorted by a public speech against his colleague, and by his great power of ridicule turned him into derision, jested upon his name, and to the accusation of weeping for a lamprey, replied that it was more than Abenobarbus had done for the loss of any of his three wives!

In the sixteenth century, that golden age of the Vatican, the splendid court of Leo X. was the centre of artistic and literary life, and the witty and pleasure-loving

Pope made its gardens the scene of his banquets and concerts, where he listened to the recitations of the poets who sprung up under his protection. There beneath the shadow of the ilex and the lauristines, in a circle so refined that ladies were admitted, Leo himself leaned on the shoulder of the handsome Raphael, who was allowed to caress and admire the Medicean white hand of his noble patron. We read that this famous Pope was so fastidious as to the fish dinners of Lent, that he invented twenty different recipes for the chowder of that day! Walking in disguise with Raphael through the fish-market, he espied a boy who, on his knees, was presenting a fish to a pretty *contadina*. The scene took form and immortality in the famous *Vierge au Poisson*, in which, conducted by the Angel Gabriel, the youthful Saint John presents the fish to the Virgin and child,—a beautiful picture for the church whose patron saint was a fisherman.

Indeed, that picture of the sea of Galilee, and the sacred meaning attached to the etymology of the word "fish," has given the finny wanderer of the seas a peculiar and valuable personality. All this, with the selection by our Lord of so many of his disciples from amongst the fishermen, the many poetical associations which form around this, the cheapest and most delicate form of food with which the Creator has stocked this world of ours, would, if followed out, afford a volume of suggestion, quotation, poetry, and romance with which to embellish the art of entertaining.

Fish is now believed to produce aliment for the brain, and as such is recommended to all authors and editors, statesmen, poets and lawyers, clergymen and mathematicians,—all who draw on that finer fibre of the brain which is used for the production of poetry or prose.

England is famed for its good fish, as why should it not be, with the ocean around it? The turbot is, *par excellence*, the fish for a Lord Mayor's dinner, and it is admirable *à la crème* for anybody's dinner. Excellent is the whitebait of Richmond, that mysterious little dwarf. Eaten with slices of brown bread and butter it is a very delicious morsel, and the whiting, which always comes to the table with his tail in his mouth, beautifully browned outside, white as snow within, what so excellent as a whiting, except a *sole au gratin* with sauce Tartare?

Fresh herrings in Scotland are delicious, almost equal to the red mullets which Cæsar once ate at Marseilles. The fresh sardines at Nice, and all along the Mediterranean, are very delicate, as are the thousand shell-fish. The langoose, or large lobster of France and the Mediterranean, is a surprise to the American traveller. Not so delicate as our American lobster, it still is admirable for a salad. It is so large that the flesh—if a fish has flesh—can be sliced up and served like cold roast turkey.

The salmon, king of fish, inspires in his capture, in Scotland rivers, in Labrador, in Canada, some of the best writing of the day. William Black, in Scotland, and Dr. Wier Mitchell, of Philadelphia, can tell stories of salmon-fishing which are as brilliant as Victor Hugo's description of Waterloo, or of that mysterious jelly-fish in his novel, "The Toilers of the Sea."

The New York market boasts the red snapper, the sheepshead, the salmon, the salmon-trout, the Spanish mackerel, most toothsome of viands, the sea bass, cod, halibut, the shad, the greatest profusion of excellent oysters and clams, the cheap pan-fish, and endless eels. The French make many fine dishes of eels, as the Romans did.

To be good, fish must be fresh. It is absolutely indispensable, to retain certain flavours, that the fish should go from one element to another, out of the water into the fire, and onto the gridiron or into the frying pan as soon as possible. Therefore, if the housewife has a fish seasonable and fresh, and a gridiron, she can make a good dish for a hungry man.

We shall begin with the cheapest of the products of the water, and although they may squirm out of our hands, try to bring to the table the despised eels.

An old proverb said that matrimony was a bag in which there were ninety-nine snakes and one eel, and the young lady who put her hand into this agreeable company had small chance at the eel. It would seem at first blush as if no one would care particularly for the eel. In old England, eels were exceedingly popular, and the monks dearly loved to feed upon them. The cellarist of Barking Abbey, Essex, in the ancient times of monastic foundations, was, amongst other eatables, to provide stewed eels in Lent and to bake eels on Shrove Tuesday. There were artificial receptacles made for eels. The cruel custom of salting eels alive is mentioned by some old writers.

"When the old serpent appeared in the guise of a stewed eel it was impossible to resist him."

Eels *en matelote* should be cut in three-inch pieces, and salted; fry an onion brown in a little dripping, add half a pint of broth to the brown onion, part of a bay leaf, six broken pepper-corns, four whole cloves, and a gill of claret. Add the eels to this and simmer until thoroughly cooked. Remove the eels, put them on a hot dish, add a teaspoonful of brown flour to the sauce, strain and pour over the eels. Spatch-cooked eels are good.

Fricasseed eels: Cut three pounds of eels into pieces of three inches in length, put them into a stewpan, and cover them with Rhine wine, or two thirds water and one third vinegar; add fifteen oysters, two pieces of lemon, a bouquet of herbs, one onion quartered, six cloves, three stalks of celery, a pinch of cayenne pepper, and salt to taste. Stew the eels one hour, remove them from the dish, strain the liquor. Put it back into the saucepan with a gill of cream and an ounce of butter rolled in flour, simmer gently a few minutes, pour over the fish, and you have a dish for a king.

Stewed eels are great favourites with *gourmets*, cooked as follows:—

Cut into three-inch pieces two pounds of medium-sized cleaned eels. Rub the inside of each piece with salt. Let them stand half an hour, then parboil them. Boil an onion in a quart of milk and remove the onion. Drain the eels from the water and add them to the milk. Season with half a teaspoonful of chopped parsley, salt and pepper, and the smallest bit of mace. Simmer until the flesh falls from the bones.

Fried eels should be slightly salted before cooking. Do not cover them with batter, but dredge them with just flour enough to absorb all moisture, then cover them with boiling lard.

As for the thousand and one recipes for cooking an oyster, no one need tell an American hostess much on that subject. Raw, roasted, boiled, stewed, scalloped and baked in patties, what so savoury as the oyster? They should be bought alive, and opened with care by an expert, for the bits of shell are dangerous. If eaten raw, pieces of lemon should be served with them. Plates of majolica to hold five or seven oysters are now to be bought at all the best crockery stores.

To stew oysters well, cream and butter should be added, and the whole mixture done in a silver dish over an alcohol lamp. Broiled oysters should be dipped first in melted butter, then in bread crumbs, then put in a very fine wire gridiron, and broiled over a bright bed of coals. Scalloped oysters should be carefully dried with a clean napkin, then laid in a deep dish on a bed of crumbs and fresh butter, all softened by the liquor of the oyster; a layer of oysters and a layer of crumbs should follow each other, with little walnuts of butter put between. The mixture should be put in a very hot oven and baked a delicate brown, but not dried.

The plain fried oyster is very popular, but it should not be cooked in small houses just before an entertainment, as the odour is not appetizing. To dip them in egg batter, then in bread-crumbs, and fry them in drippings is a common and good fashion. A more elaborate fashion is to beat up the yolks of four eggs with three tablespoonfuls of sweet oil, and season them with a teaspoonful of salt, and a saltspoonful of cayenne pepper. Beat up thoroughly, dip each oyster in this mixture and then in bread crumbs, and fry in hot oil. The best and most elegant way of cooking an oyster is, however, "*à la poulette.*"

> Scald the oysters in their own liquor, drain them, and add to the liquor, salt, half an ounce of butter, the juice of half a lemon, a gill of cream, and a teaspoonful of dissolved flour. Beat the yolk of one egg, and add to the sauce, stir until the sauce thickens; place the oysters on a hot dish, pour the sauce over them, add a little chopped parsley and serve.

A simpler and more primitive but excellent way of cooking oysters is to clean the shells thoroughly, and place them in the coals in an open fireplace, or to roast them in hot ashes until the shells snap open.

When the oyster departs then the clam takes his place, and is delicious as an *avant goût* or an appetizer at a dinner. If clams are broiled they must be done quickly, else they become hard and indigestible.

The soft-shell clam, scalloped, makes a good dish. Clean the shells well, then put two clams to each shell, with half a teaspoonful of minced celery. Cut a slice of fat bacon small, add a little to each shell, put bread crumbs on top and a little pat of butter, bake in the oven until brown. A clam broth is a delicious and healthful beverage for sick or well; add cream and a spoonful of sherry to it, and it becomes a fabulously fine thing. In this mixture the clams must be strained out before the cream and wine are added.

But if the clam is good what shall we say of crabs. Hard-shell crabs must be boiled about twelve minutes, drained, and set away to cool. Eaten with sandwiches and a dressing they are considered a delicacy for supper. They can be more cooked with chopped eggs, or treated like a chicken pasty, and cooked in a paste shell they are very good.

Take half an ounce of butter, half an onion minced, half a pound of minced raw veal, and a small carrot shredded, a chopped crab, a pint of boiling cream; simmer an hour, then strain into a saucepan, and what a sauce you have!

The soft-shell crab is an invalid. He is caught when he is helpless, feverish, and not at all, one would say, healthy. He is killed by the jarring of the train, by thunder, by some passing noisy cart, and some say by a fall in stocks, or a sudden change in political circles.

Such sensitive creatures must be cooked as soon as possible. It is only necessary to remove the feathery substance under the pointed sides of the shells, rinse them in cold water, drain, season with salt and pepper, dredge them in flour and fry in hot fat. Crab patties and crabs cooked in any other way than this fail to please the epicure. Nothing with so pronounced an individuality as a soft-shelled crab should be disguised.

A devilled crab is considered good, but it should be cooked by a negro expert from Maryland.

Scallops are essentially good in stews, or fried, and when, cut in small pieces, with a pint of milk, a little butter, and a little salt, they again return to their beautiful shells and are baked as a scallop, they are delicious. Put in pork fat, and fried, they are also very fine.

The lobster is now considered very healthful, and as conveying more phosphorus into the human system than any other fish. Broiled, devilled, stewed, cooked in a fashion called *Bourdelaise*, it is the most delicious of dishes, and as a salad what can equal it?

A baked whitefish with Bordeaux sauce is very fine.

> Clean and stuff the fish with bread-crumbs, onions, butter, and sweet marjoram. Put it in a baking pan, add a liberal quantity of butter previously rolled in flour, put in the pan a pint of claret, and bake for an hour. Remove the fish and strain the gravy, put in a teaspoonful of brown flour and a pinch of cayenne pepper.

Halibut with an egg sauce and a border of parsley is a dish for a banquet, only the cook must know how to make egg sauce. Supposing we tell her?

> Put two ounces of butter in a stew-pan; when it melts, add one ounce of flour. Stir for one minute or more, but do not brown. Then add by degrees two gills of boiling water, stirring until

smooth, and boiling about two minutes. If not perfectly smooth, pass it through a sieve; then add another ounce of butter cut in pieces. When the butter is melted, add three hard-boiled eggs, chopped not too fine, season with pepper and salt, and serve immediately.

This sauce is admirable for cod, and for all boiled fish.

But the "perfectest thing on earth" is a broiled fish, a shad for instance; and one of the best preventives against burning is to rub olive oil on the fish before putting it on the gridiron. Charcoal affords the best fire, and it must be free from all smoke and flame.

A little sweet butter, half a teaspoonful of chopped parsley and the juice of a lemon should be melted together, and stand ready to be poured over the broiled fish.

Mr. Lowell, in one of his delightful, witty papers in the Atlantic Monthly years ago, regretted that he could not find a gridiron near the St. Lawrence, although its patron saint suffered martyrdom on that excellent kitchen utensil. It is a lamentable fact that wood fires and gridirons are giving out. They contain within themselves the merits of all the kitchen ranges, all the lost juices of that early American cookery, which one who has tasted it can never forget. Where are the broils of our childhood?

Codfish is a family stand-by, but a tasteless fish unless covered with oysters or something very good; but salt-codfish balls are a great luxury.

Brook trout, boiled, baked, and broiled, are all inferior to the fry. The frying-pan has to answer for a multitude of sins, but nothing so base can be found as to deprive it of its great glory in sending us a fried brook-trout. "Clean and rinse a quarter-of-a-pound trout in cold water," says one recipe.

Why not a pound-and-a-quarter trout? The recipe begins later on: after some pork has been fried in the pan, throw in your carefully cleaned fish, no matter what their weight may be, turn them three times most carefully. Send to table without adding or detracting from their flavour.

This is for the sportsman who cooks his trout himself by a wood fire in the woods; and no other man ever arrives at just that perfect way of cooking a trout. When the trout has come down from cooling springs to the hot city, it requires a seasoning of salt, pepper, and lemon-juice.

Frogs—frogs as cooked in France, *grenouilles à la poulette*—are a most luxurious delicacy. They are very expensive and are to be bought at the *marché St. Honoré*. As only the hind legs are eaten, and the price is fifteen francs a dozen, they are not often seen. We might have them in this country for the catching. Of their tenderness, succulence, and delicacy of flavour there can be no question. They are clean feeders, and undoubtedly wholesome.

Sala, writing in "Breakfasts in Bed" does not praise *bouillabaisse*. He declares that the cooks plunge a rolling-pin in tallow and then with it stir that *pot pourri* of red mullet, tomatoes, red pepper, red Burgundy, oil, and garlic to which Thackeray has written so delightful a lyric. "Against fish soups, turtle, terrapin, oyster, and bisque," he says, "I can offer no objection." The Italians again have their good *zuppa marinara*, which is not all like the *bouillabaisse*, and the Russians make a very appetizing fish pottage which is called *batwina*, the stock of which is composed of *kraus*, or half-brewed barley beer, and oil. Into this is put the fish known as the sterlet of the Volga, or the sassina of the Gulf of Finland, together with bay leaves, pepper, and lumps of ice. *Batwina* is better than *bouillabaisse*.

THE SALAD.

"Epicurean cooks shall sharpen with cloyless sauce the appetite."

Of all the vegetables of which a salad can be made, lettuce is the greatest favourite. That lettuce which is *panachée*, says the *Almanach des Gourmands*, that is, when it has streaked or variegated leaves, is truly *une salade de distinction*. We prefer in this country the fine, crisp, solid little heads, of which the leaves are bright green. The milky juices of the lettuce are soporific, like opium seeds, and predispose the eater to sleep, or to repose of temper and to philosophic thought.

After, or before, lettuce comes the fragrant celery, always an appetizer. Then the tomato, a noble fruit as sweet in smell as Araby the blest, which makes an illustrious salad. Its medicinal virtue is as great as its gastronomical goodness. It is the friend of the well, for it keeps them well, and the friend of the sick, for it brings them back to the lost sheep-folds of hygeia.

There are water-cress and dandelion, common mustard, boiled asparagus, and beet root, potato salad, beloved of the Germans, the cucumber, most fragrant and delicate of salads, a salad of eggs, of lobsters, of chickens, sausages, herrings, and sardines. Anything that is edible can be made into a salad, and a vegetable mixture of cold French beans, boiled peas, carrots and potato, onion, green peppers, and cucumber, covered with fresh mayonnaise dressing, is served ice cold in France, to admiration.

To learn to make a salad is the most important of qualifications for one who would master the art of entertaining.

Here is a good recipe for the dressing:—

Two yolks of eggs, a teaspoonful of salt, and three of mustard,—it should have been mixed with hot water before using,—a little cayenne pepper, a spoonful of vinegar; pound the eggs and mix well. Common vinegar is preferred by many, but some like tarragon vinegar better. Stir this gently for a minute, then add two full spoonfuls of best oil of Lucca.

"A sage for the mustard, a miser for the vinegar, a spendthrift for the oil, and a madman to stir" is the old saw. Add a teaspoonful of brown sugar, half a dozen little spring onions cut fine, three or four slices of beet root, the white of the egg, not cut too small, and then the lettuce itself, which should be torn from the head stock by the fingers.

Some French salad dressers say *fatiguez la salade*, which means, shake it, mix it, and bruise it; but the modern arrangement is to delicately cover the leaves with the dressing, and not to bruise them. This is an old-fashioned salad.

An excellent salad of cold boiled potatoes cut into slices about an inch thick, may be made with thin slices of fresh beet root, and onions cut very thin, and very little of them, with the same dressing, minus the sugar.

Francatelli speaks of a Russian salad with lobster, a German salad with herrings, and an Italian salad with potatoes; but these come more under the head of the mayonnaises than of the simpler salads.

The cucumber comes next to lettuce, as a purely vegetable salad, and is most desirable with fish. Dr. Johnson declared that the best thing you could do with a cucumber, after you had prepared it with much care and thought, was to throw it out of the window; but Dr. Johnson, although he could write Rasselas and a dictionary, knew nothing about the art of entertaining. He was an eater, a glutton, a *gourmand*, not a *gourmet*. How should he dare to speak against a cucumber salad?

Endive and chiccory should be added to the list of vegetable salads. Neither of them is good, however.

An old-fashioned French salad is made thus: "Chop three anchovies, an onion, and some parsley small; put them in a bowl with two tablespoonfuls of vinegar, one of oil, a little mustard and salt. When well mixed, add some slices of cold roast beef not exceeding two or three inches long. Make three hours before eating. Garnish with parsley." This is by no means a bad way of serving up yesterday's roast beef.

The etymology of salad is said to be "sal," or something salted. Shakspeare mentions the salad five or six times. In Henry VI., Jack Cade, in his extremity of peril when hiding from his pursuers in Ida's garden, says he has climbed over the wall to see if he could eat grass, or pick a salad, which he says "will not come amiss to cool a man's stomach in the hot weather." In Antony and Cleopatra, the passionate queen speaks of her "salad days" when she was "green in judgment, cool in blood." This means, however, something raw or unripe. Hamlet uses the word with the more ancient orthography of "sallet," and says in his speech to the players, "I remember when there were no sallets in these times to make them savoury." By this he meant there was nothing piquant in them, no Attic salt. One author, not so illustrious, claims that the noblest prerogative of man is that he is a cooking animal, and a salad eater.

"The lion is generous as a hero, the rat artful as a lawyer, the dove gentle as a lover, the beaver is a good engineer, the monkey is a clever actor, but none of them can make a salad. The wisest sheep never thought of culling and testing his grasses, seasoning them with thyme or tarragon, softening them with oil, exasperating them with mustard, sharpening them with vinegar, spiritualizing them with a suspicion of onions, in that no sheep has made a salad. Their only sauce is hunger.

"Salads," says this pleasant writer, "were invented by Adam and Eve, — probably made of pomegranates as to-day in Spain."

Of all salads, lobster is the most picturesque and beautiful. Its very scarlet is a trumpet tone to appetite. It lies embedded in green leaves like a magnificent tropical cactus. A good dressing for lobster is essence of anchovy, mushroom ketchup, hard-boiled eggs, and a little cream.

Mashed potatoes, rubbed down with cream, or simply mixed with vinegar, are no bad substitute for eggs, and impart to the salad a new and not unpleasing flavour. French beans, the most delicate of vegetables, give the salad eater a new sensation. A dressing can be mixed in the following proportions: "Four mustard ladles of mustard, four salt ladles of salt. Three spoonfuls of best Italian oil, twelve of vinegar, three unboiled eggs. All are to be carefully rubbed together." This is for those who like sours and not sweets. An old French *émigré*, who had to make his living in England during the time of the Regency, a man of taste and refinement, an epicurean Marquis, carried to noblemen's houses his mahogany box full of essences, spices, and condiments, and made his salad in this way: he chopped up three anchovies with a little shallot and some parsley; these he threw into a bowl with a little mustard and salt, two tablespoonfuls of oil, and one brimming over with vinegar. When thoroughly merged he added his lettuce, or celery, or potato, extremely thin, short slices of best Westphalia ham, or the finest roast beef, which he had steeped in the vinegar. He garnished with parsley and a few layers of bacon. This man was called *Le Roi de la salade*.

A cod mayonnaise is a good dish:—

> Boil a large cod in the morning. Let it cool; then remove the skin and bones. For sauce put some thick cream in a porcelain sauce-pan and thicken it with corn-flour which has been mixed with cold water. When it begins to boil stir in the beaten yolks of two eggs. As it cools beat it well to prevent it from being lumpy, and when nearly cold stir in the juice of two lemons, a little tarragon vinegar, a pinch of salt, and a *soupçon* of cayenne pepper. Peel and slice some very ripe tomatoes or cold potatoes, steep them in vinegar with cayenne, pounded ginger, and plenty of salt. Lay these around the fish and cover with cream sauce. The tomatoes and potatoes should be carefully drained before they are placed around the fish.

A salmon covered with a green sauce is a famous dish for a ball supper; indeed, there are thirty or forty salads with a cold fish foundation.

This art of dressing cold vegetables with pepper, salt, oil, and vinegar, should be studied. In France they give you these salads to perfection at the *déjeuner à la fourchette*. Fillippini, of Delmonico's, in his admirable work, "The Table," adds Swedish salad, String Bean Salad, Russian Salad, Salad Macédoine, *Escarolle, Doucette, Dandelion à la coutoise, Baib de Capucine*, Cauliflower salad, and *Salad a l'Italian*. I advise any young housekeeper to buy this book of his, as suggestive. It is too elaborate and learned, however, for practical application to any household except one in which a French cook is kept.

A mayonnaise dressing is a triumph of art when well made:—

A tablespoonful of mustard, one teaspoonful of salt, the yolk of three uncooked eggs, the juice of half a lemon, a quarter of a cupful of butter, a pint of oil, and a cupful of whipped cream. Beat the yolks and dry ingredients until they are very light, with a wooden spoon or with a wire beater. The bowl in which the dressing is being made should be set in a pan of ice water. Add oil, a few drops at a time, until the dressing becomes thick and rather hard. After it has reached this stage the oil can be added more rapidly. When it gets so thick as to be difficult to beat add a little vinegar, then add the juice of the lemon and the whipped cream, and place on ice until desired to be used.

Another dressing can be made more quickly:—

The yolk of a raw egg, a tablespoonful of mixed mustard, one fourth of a teaspoonful of salt, six tablespoonfuls of oil. Stir the yolk, mustard, and salt together with a fork until they begin to thicken; add the oil gradually, stirring all the time.

An excellent salad dressing is also made by using the yolk of hard-boiled eggs, some cold mashed potatoes well pressed together with a fork, oil, vinegar, mustard, and salt rubbed in, in the proportions of two of oil to one of vinegar.

A salad must be fresh and freshly made, to be good. Never serve a salad the second day; and it is not well to cover a delicate salad with too much mayonnaise. The very heart of the celery or the delicate inner leaves of the lettuce are the best for dinners. The heavy chicken and lobster, cabbage and potato salads, are dishes for lunches and suppers.

The chief employment of a kitchen maid, in France, where a man cook is kept, is to wash the vegetables; and you see her swinging the salad in a wire safe after washing it delicately in fresh water. The care bestowed on these minor morals of cookery, so often wholly neglected, adds the finishing touch to the excellence of a French dinner.

For a green mayonnaise dressing, so much admired on salmon, use a little chopped spinach and finely chopped parsley. The juice from boiled beets can be used to make a fine red dressing. Two of these dishes will make a plain, country lunch-table very nice, and will have an appetizing effect, as has anything that betokens care, forethought, neatness, and taste.

Some people cannot eat oil. Often the best oil cannot be bought in a retired and rural neighbourhood. But an excellent substitute is fresh butter or clarified chicken-fat, very carefully prepared, and icy cold. The yolks of four raw eggs, one tablespoonful of salt, one of mustard, the juice of a lemon, and a speck of cayenne pepper should be used.

Two drops of onion juice, or a bit of onion sliced, will add great piquancy to salad dressing, if every one likes onion.

I have never tried the following recipe,—I have tried all the others,—but I have heard that it was very good:

Four tablespoonfuls of butter, one of flour, one tablespoonful of salt, one of sugar, one heaping teaspoonful of mustard, a speck of cayenne, one cupful of milk, half a cupful of vinegar, three eggs. Let the butter get hot in a saucepan. Add the flour and stir until smooth, being careful not to brown. Add the milk and boil up. Place the saucepan in another of hot water. Beat the eggs, salt, pepper, sugar, and mustard together, and add the vinegar. Stir this into the boiling mixture and stir until it thickens like soft custard, which will be about five minutes. Set away to cool, and when cold, bottle and place in the ice-chest. This will keep two weeks.

If one wishes to use prepared mayonnaise it is better to buy that which is sold at the grocers. It has not the charm of a fresh dressing, however, but is rather like those elaborated impromptus which some studied talkers get off.

A very pretty salad can be made of nasturtium-blossoms, buttercups, a head of lettuce, and a pint of water-cresses. It is to be covered with the French dressing and eaten immediately.

Asparagus is so good in itself that it seems a shame to dress it as a salad; yet it is very good eaten with oil, vinegar, and salt. Cauliflower, cold, is delicious as a salad, and can be made very ornamental with a garniture of beet root, which is a good ingredient for a salad of salt codfish, boiled.

Sardine salads are very appetizing for lunch. Arrange a cold salmon or codfish on a bed of lettuce. Split six sardines, remove the bones, and mix them into the dressing. Garnish the whole dish with sardines, and cover with the dressing.

All kinds of cooked fish can be served with salads. Lettuce is the best green salad to serve with them; but all cooked and cold vegetables go well with fish. Add capers to the mayonnaise.

A housekeeper who has conquered the salad question can always add to the plainest dinner a desirable dish. She can feed the hungry, and she can stimulate the most jaded fancy of the over-fastidious *gourmet* by these delicate and consummate luxuries.

Here is Sydney Smith's recipe for a salad: —

"To make this condiment your poet begs
The pounded yellow of two hard-boiled eggs;
Two boiled potatoes, passed through kitchen sieve,
Smoothness and softness to the salad give.
Let onion atoms wink within the bowl,
And half suspected, animate the whole;
Of mordant mustard, add a single spoon,
(Distrust the condiment that bites too soon),
But deem it not, thou man of herbs, a fault,
To add a double quantity of salt.
Four times the spoon with oil of Lucca crown,
And twice with vinegar, procured from town;

And lastly, o'er the favoured compound toss
A magic *soupçon* of anchovy sauce.
Oh, green and glorious! Oh, herbaceous treat!
'T would tempt the dying anchorite to eat!
Back to the world would turn his fleeting soul,
To plunge his fingers in a salad bowl!
Serenely full, the epicure would say,
'Fate cannot harm me,—I have dined to-day.'"

LOBSTER SALAD.

"Take, take lobsters and lettuces,
Mind that they send you the fish that you order;
Take, take a decent sized salad bowl,
One that's sufficiently deep in the border;
Cut into many a slice,
All of the fish that's nice;
Place in the bowl with due neatness and order;
Then hard-boiled eggs you may
Add in a neat array,
All toward the bowl, just by way of a border.
"Take from the cellar of salt a proportion,
Take from the castors both pepper and oil,
With vinegar too, but a moderate portion,—
Too much of acid your salad will spoil;
Mix them together,
You need not mind whether
You blend them exactly in apple-pie order,
But when you've stirred away,
Mix up the whole you may,
All but the eggs which are used as a border.
"Take, take plenty of seasoning;
A teaspoonful of parsley that's chopped in small pieces
Though, though, the point will bear reasoning,
A small taste of onion the flavour increases
As the sauce curdle may,
Should it, the process stay.
Patiently do it again in good order;
For if you chance to spoil
Vinegar, eggs, and oil,
Still to proceed would on lunacy border."

A Spanish salad, *gaspacho*, is a favourite food of the Andalusian peasant. It is but bread soaked in oil and water, with a large Spanish onion peeled, and a fresh cucumber.

Slice three tomatoes, take out the grain and cut up the fruit.
Arrange carefully all these materials in a shallow earthen pan, tier

upon tier, salting and peppering each to taste, pouring in oil plentifully, and vinegar. Last of all, let the salad lie in some cool spot for an hour or two, then sprinkle over it two handfuls of breadcrumbs.

In Spanish peasant houses, the big wooden bowl hanging below the eaves to keep it cool is always ready for attack. The oil in Spain is not to our taste; but the salad made as above, with good oil, is delicious. It should have a sprinkling of red pepper.

DESSERTS.

There is not in the wide world so tempting a sweet
As that trifle where custard and macaroons meet.
Oh! the latest sweet tooth from my head must depart
Ere the taste of that trifle shall not win my heart.

Yet it is not the sugar that's thrown in between,
Nor the peel of the lemon so candied and green,
'T is not the rich cream that's whipped up by a mill,
Oh, no; it is something more exquisite still!

The great meaning of dessert is to offer "something more exquisite still." And it is the province of the housekeeper, be she young or old, to study how this can be done.

Nothing in European dinners can compare with the American custards, puddings, and pies. We are accused as a nation of having eaten too many sweets, and of having ruined our teeth thereby; but who that has languished in England over the insipid desserts at hotels, and the tooth-sharpeners called "sweets," meaning tarts as sour as an east wind, has not sighed for an American pie? In Paris the cakes are pretty to look at, but oh, how they break their promise when you eat them! Nothing but sweetened white of egg. One thing they surpass us in, — *omelette soufflé*; and a *gâteau St. Honoré* is good, but with that word of praise we dismiss the great French nation.

Just look at our grand list of fruit desserts: apple charlotte, apricots with rice, banana charlotte, banana fritters, blackberry short-cake, strawberry short-cake, velvet cream with strawberries, fresh pine-apples in jelly, frozen bananas, frozen peaches in cream, orange cocoanut salad, orange salad, peach fritters, peach meringue, peach short-cake, plum salad, salad of mixed fruits, sliced pears with whipped cream, stewed pears, plain, and pumpkin pie! But oh! there is "something more exquisite still," and that is an apple pie.

"All new dishes fade, the newest oft the fleetest;
Of all the pies ever made, the apple's still the sweetest.
Cut and come again, the syrup upward springing,
While life and taste remain, to thee my heart is clinging.
Who a pie would make, first his apple slices,
Then he ought to take some cloves and the best of spices,
Grate some lemon rind, butter add discreetly,
Then some sugar mix, but mind, — the pie not made too sweetly.
If a cook of taste be competent to make it,

In the finest paste will enclose and bake it."

During years of foreign travel I have never met a dish so perfect as the American apple pie can be, with cream.

Then look at our puddings; they are richer, sweeter, more varied than any in the world, the English plum-pudding excepted. That is a ponderous dainty, which few can eat. It looks well when dressed with holly and lighted up, but it is not to be eaten every day. Baked bread pudding, carrot pudding, exceedingly delicate, chocolate pudding, cold cabinet-pudding, boiled rice-pudding with custard sauce, poor man's rice-pudding, green-apple pudding, Indian pudding, minute pudding, tapioca pudding, and all the custards boiled and baked with infinite variety of flavour,—these are the every-day luxuries, and they are very great ones, of the American table.

One charming thing about dessert and American dishes is that ladies can make them. They do not flush the face or derange the white apron. They are pleasant things to dally with,—milk and eggs, and spice and sugar. A model kitchen is every lady's delight. In these days of tiles, and marble pastry-boards, and modern improvements, what pretty things kitchens are.

The model dairy, too, is a delight, with its upright milk-pans, in which the cream is marked off by a neat little thermometer, and its fire-brick floor. How cool and neat it is! Sometimes a stream of fresh water flows under the floor, as the river runs under the Château of Chenonceaux, where Diane de Poitiers dressed her golden hair.

In the model kitchen is the exquisite range, with its polished *batterie de cuisine*. Every brilliant saucepan seems to say, "Come and cook in me;" every porcelain-lined pan urges upon one the necessity of stewing nectarines in white sugar; every bright can suggests the word "conserve," which always makes the mouth water; every clatter of the skewers says, "Dainty dishes, come and make me." All this is quite fascinating to an amateur.

No pretty woman, if she did but know it, is ever so pretty as when she is playing cook, and doing it well. The clean white apron, the short, clean, cambric gown, the little cap, the white, bare arms,—the glorified creams and jellies, pies and Charlotte Russe, cakes and puddings, which fall from such fingers are ambrosial food.

There is a great passion, in the properly regulated woman's heart, for the cleanly part of the household work. The love of a dairy is, with many a duchess, part of the business of her rank. In our country, where ladies are compelled to put a hand, once perhaps too often, owing to the insufficiency of servants, to the cooking, it is less a pastime, but a knowledge of it is indispensable. To cook a heavy dinner in hot weather, to wash the dishes afterward, this is sober prose, and by a very dull author; but to make the dessert, this is poetry. In the early morning the hostess should go into her neat dairy to skim the cream; it will be much thicker if she does. She will prepare all things for the desserts of the day. She will make her well-flavoured custard and set it in the ice-chest. She will place her compote of pears securely on a high shelf, away from that ubiquitous cat who has, in most families, so remarkable and so irrepressible an appetite.

Then she should make a visit to the kitchen before dinner, to see to it that the roast birds are garnished with water-cress, that the vegetables are properly prepared, that the dishes are without a smear on their lower surface. All this attention makes good servants and very good dinners.

In the matter of flavouring, the coloured race has us at a great disadvantage. Any old coloured cook can distance her white "Missus" there. This highly gifted race seem to have a sixth sense on the subject of flavours. The rich tropical nature breaks out in reminiscences of orange-blossoms, pineapple, guava, cocoanut, and mandarin orange. Never can the descendants of the poor, half-starved, frozen exiles of Plymouth Rock hope to achieve such custards and puddings as these Ethiops pour out. It is as if some luxurious and beneficent gift had left us when we were made poets, orators, philosophers, preachers, and authors, when we were given what we proudly term a higher intelligence. Who would not exchange all the cold, mathematical, intellectual supremacy of which we boast for that luscious gift of making pies and puddings *à ravir*?

The making of pastry is so delicate and so varied a task that we can only say, approach it with cold hands, cold ice-water, roll it on a marble slab, then bake it in a very hot oven.

Learn to stew well. Stew your fruit in a porcelain stewpan before putting it in your tarts. It is one of the most wholesome forms of cookery; a French novelist calls the stewpan the "favourite arm, the talisman of the cook." A celebrated physician said that the action of the stewpan was like that of the stomach, and it is a great gain if we can help that along. Stewing gooseberries, cherries, and even apples with sugar and lemon-peel before putting them in the tart, ensures a good pie.

Whipped white of egg is an elegant addition to most dessert dishes, and every lady should provide herself with wire whisks.

Whipped to a strong froth with sugar, and lemon or vanilla flavouring, this garnish makes an ordinary into a superior pudding. New-laid eggs are exceedingly difficult to beat up well. Take those which have been laid several days. Have a deep bowl with a circular bottom, and in beating the eggs keep the whisk as much as possible in an upright position, moving it very rapidly; a little boiling water, a tablespoonful to two eggs, and a teaspoonful of sifted sugar put to them before beating is commenced, facilitates the operation.

For *omelette soufflé* the white of eggs, beaten, should be firm enough to cut.

An orange-custard pudding is so very good that we must give a time-honoured recipe:—

> Boil a pint of new milk, pour it upon three eggs lightly beaten, mix in the grated peel of an orange, and two ounces of loaf sugar; beat all together for ten minutes, then pour the custard into a pie dish, set it into another containing a little water, and put it in a moderate oven. When the custard is set, which generally takes about half an hour, take it out and let it get cold. Then sprinkle

over rather thickly some very fine sugar, and brown with a sala-
mander. This should be eaten cold.

Of rice and tapioca puddings the variety is endless, and they are most healthful. A wife who will give her dyspeptic husband a good pudding every day may
perhaps save his life, his fortunes, and if he is an author, his literary reputation.

An antiquary of the last century wrote, "Cookery was ever reckoned a branch
of the art medical; the verb *curare* signifies equally to dress vegetables and to cure
a distemper, and everybody has heard of Dr. Diet, and kitchen physic."

Indeed that most sacred part of a woman's duty, learning to cook for the sick,
can be studied through desserts. A lady, very ill in Paris through a long winter, declared that she would have been cured had she once tasted cream-toast, or tapioca
pudding; both were luxuries which she never encountered.

Then come all the jellies; and it is better to make your own gelatine from the
real calves'-feet than to use patent gelatine. The latter, however, is very good, and
saves time. It also makes excellent foundation for all the so-called creams.

Some ardent housekeepers put up all their jams, preserves, and currant jelly;
some even make the cordials curaçoa, noyau, peach brandy, ginger cordial, and
cherry brandy, but this is unnecessary. They can be bought cheaper and better
than they can be made.

The history of liqueurs is a curious one. Does any one ever think, as he tastes
Chartreuse, of the gloomy monks who dig their own graves, and never speak save
to say, "Mes frères, il faut mourir," who alone can make this sparkling and delicate
liqueur which figures at every grand feast?

I have made an expedition to their splendid mountain-bound convent. It is
one of the most glorious drives in Europe, and rises into Alpine grandeur and
solemnity. There, amid winter's cold and summer's heat, the Chartreuse lives in
severe penance, making his hospitable liqueur which enchants the world, out of
the chamomile and other herbs which grow around his convent.

The best French liqueurs were made formerly at La Côte by the Visetandine
nuns. Kirschwasser is made from the cherries which grow in the Alpine Tyrol, in
one small province which produces nothing else.

Liqueurs were invented for Louis XIV. in his old age. A cordial was made by
mixing brandy with sugar and scents.

In making a mince pie, do not forget the excellent brandy, and the dash of
orange curaçoa, which should be put in by the lady herself. Else why is it that
otherwise the mince pie seems to lack the inspiriting and hidden fire. We read that
there is "many a slip 'twixt the cup and the lip." Perhaps the cook could tell, but
one may be very sure she will not.

The modern, elegant devices by which strawberries, violets, and roseleaves,
orange blossoms, and indeed all berries can be candied fresh in sugar, afford a
pretty pastime for amateur cooks. But if near a confectioner in the city these can
be bought cheaper than they can be made. It may amuse an invalid to make them,

and the art is easily learned.

The cheese *fondu* is a great favourite at foreign desserts. It is of Swiss origin. It is a healthful, savoury, and appetizing dish, quickly dressed and good to put at the end of a dinner for unexpected guests.

> Take as many eggs as there are guests, and then about a third as much by weight of the best Gruyères cheese, and the half of that of butter. Break and beat up well the eggs in a saucepan, then add the butter and the cheese, grated or cut in small pieces; place the saucepan on the fire, and stir with a wooden spoon till it is of a thick and soft consistence; put in salt according to the age of the cheese,—fresh cheese requires the most,—and a strong dose of pepper, then bake it like macaroni and send to table hot.

One pie we have which is national; it is that made of the pumpkin, and it is notoriously good. Also we may claim the squash pie and the sweet-potato pie, both of which merit the highest encomiums.

Our fruits are so plentiful and so good that few housekeepers can fail of having a good dessert of fruits alone. But do not force the seasons. Take them as they come. When fruits are cheapest then they are best. Our peaches have more flavour than those of Europe, and our grapes are unrivalled. Of plums and pears, France has better than we can boast, but our strawberries are as good and as plentiful as in England.

In fact, all the wild berries which are now getting to be cultivated berries, like blackberries, blueberries, huckleberries, and raspberries, are better than similar fruits abroad. The wild strawberry of the Alps is, however, delicious in flavour and sweetness.

A very grand dessert is furnished with ices of every flavour, jellies holding fruit and flavoured with maraschino, all sorts of bonbons, nuts in sugar, candied grapes and oranges, fresh fruits in season, and ending with liqueurs and black coffee.

A simple pudding, or pie followed by grapes and peaches, with the cup of black coffee afterward, is the national dessert of our United States. In winter it may be enriched by a Newtown pippin or a King of Tompkins County apple, some boiled chestnuts and a few other nuts, some Florida oranges, or those delicious little mandarins, perhaps raised by the immortal Rip Van Winkle, our own Joe Jefferson, on his Louisiana estate. He seems to have infused them with the flavour of his own rare and cheerful genius. He has raised a laugh before this, as well as the best mandarin oranges. Some dyspeptics declare that to chew seven roasted almonds after dinner does them good. And the roasted almonds fitly close the chapter on desserts.

GERMAN EATING AND DRINKING.

"I wonder if Charlemagne ever drank
A tankard of Assmanschausen. Nay!
If he had, his empire never would rank
As it does with the royalist realms to-day;
For the goddess that laughs within the cup
Had wiled and won him from blood and war,
And shown, as he drained her long draughts up,
There was something better worth living for
Than kingcraft keeping his gruff brow sad.
I wish from my very soul she had."

The deep, dark, swiftly flowing Rhine, its legends, its forests of silver firs and pines, its mountains crowned with castles, and its hillsides blushing with the bending vine, the convent's ancient walls, the glistening spire, the maidens with their plaited hair, and "hands that offer early flowers," all the bright, beautiful, romantic landscape, the dancing waves which wash its historic shores, its donjon keeps and haunted Tenter Rock, its

"Beetling walls with ivy grown,
Frowning heights of mossy stone," —

all this beauty is placed in the land of the sauer-kraut, the herring salad, the sweet stewed fruit with pork, pig and prune sauce, carp stewed in beer, raw goose-flesh or Göttingen sausages, potato sweetened, and cabbage soured, — in a land, in short, whose kitchen is an abomination to all other nations.

Not that one does not get an excellent dinner at a German hotel in a great city. But all the cooks are French. The powerful young emperor has, however, given his orders that all *menus* shall hereafter be written in German; the language of Ude, Soyer, Valet, and Francatelli, Brillat, Savarin, and Béchamel, is to be replaced by German.

But if the viands are not good, the wines are highly praised by the *gourmet*; and as these wines are often exported, it is said that one gets a better German wine in New York than at a second-class hotel at Bonn or Cologne or Düsseldorf, — on the same principle that fish at Newport is less fresh than at New York, for it is all bought, sent to New York, and then sent back to Newport. In other words, the exporters are careful to keep up the reputation of their exported wines.

Assmanschausen is a red Rhine wine of high degree; some *gourmets* call it the Burgundy of the Rhine. This poetic beverage is found within the gorge of the

Rhine.

The bend which the noble river assumes at the Rheingau is said to have the effect of concentrating the sun's rays, reflected from the surface of the water as from a mirror, upon the vine-clad slopes; and it is to this circumstance, combined with the favourable nature of the soil, and to the vineyards being completely sheltered from the north winds by the Taunus range, that the marked superiority of the wines of the Rheingau is ordinarily attributed.

> "Bacharach has produced another fine wine.
> 'He never has been to Heaven and back
> Who has not drunken of Bacharach.'"

And Longfellow says:—

> "At Frankfort on the Maine,
> And at Würtzburg on the Stein,
> At Bacharach on the Rhine,
> Grow the three best kinds of wine."

We know but little of the superior red wines of Walporzheimer, Ahrweiler, and Bodendorfer, which come from the valley of the Ahr. The Ahr falls into the Rhine near Sinzig, midway between Coblenz and Bonn. The wines from its beautiful vineyards are a fine deep red. The taste is astringent, somewhat like port. There is an agreeable red wine called Kreutzburger which comes from the neighbourhood of Ehrenbreitstein. Linz on the Rhine sends us a good red wine known as Dattenberger. These are all pure wines which know no doctoring.

The Liebfrauenmilch is a Riesling wine with a fine bouquet. It owes its celebrity rather to its name than its merits. It comes from the vineyards adjoining the Liebfrauen Kirche near Worms, and was named by some pious churchman.

No wines have as many poetical tributes as the Rhine wines. One of the English poets sings:—

> "O for a kingdom rocky-throned,
> Above the brimming Rhine,
> With vassals who should pay their toll
> In many sorts of wine.
> Above me naught but the blue air,
> And all below, the vine,
> I'd plant my throne, where legends say
> In nights of harvest-time
> King Charlemagne, in golden robe,—
> So runs the rustic rhyme,—
> Doth come to bless the mellowing crops
> While bells of Heaven chime."

The Steinbergers, the Hochheimers, Marcobrunners, and Rüdesheimers, sound like so many noble families. Indeed an American senator, hearing these fine names, remarked: "I have no doubt, sir, they are all very nice girls."

There is a famous Hochheimer, no less than a hundred and sixty-seven years old, the vintage of that year when the Duke of Marlborough gained the Battle of Ramillies. Let us hope that he and Prince Eugene moistened their clay and labours with some of this famous wine. These wines do not last, however. The best age is ten years, and those which have been stored in the antique vaulted cellar of the Bernardine Abbey of Eberbach, world-renowned as the Grand-ducal Cabinet wine of the ruler of Nassau, are now completely run out. Even Rudesheimer of 1872 is no longer good.

It must be remembered, however, that these wines are never fortified. To put extraneous alcohol into their beloved Rhine wine would rouse Rudolph of Hapsburg and Conrad of Hotstettin from the sleep of centuries.

The Steinberger Cabinet of 1862 is the most superb. Of Rhine wines for bouquet, refined flavour, combined richness and delicacy. We do not except Schloss Johannisberger, because that is not in the market. A Marcobrunner and a Rüdesheimer are not to be despised.

Prince Metternich sent to Jules Janin for his autograph, and the witty poet editor sent a receipt for twelve bottles of Imperial Schloss Johannisberger. The Prince took the hint and had a dozen of the very best cabinet wine forwarded, every bottle being sealed and every cork duly branded with the Prince's crest! The Johannisberger wine is excessively sweet, singularly soft, and gives forth a delicious perfume, a rich, limpid, amber-coloured wine, with a faint bitter flavour; it is as beautiful to look at as it is luscious to the taste, and it possesses a bouquet which the Empress Eugénie compared to that of heliotrope, violets, and geranium leaves combined.

The refined pungent flavour of a good Hock, its slight racy sharpness, with an after almond flavour, make it an admirable appetizer. The staircase vineyards, in which the grapes grow on the Rhine, seem to catch all the revivifying influences of sunshine. Their splendid golden colour is caught from those first beams of the sun as he greets his bride, the Earth, after he has been separated from her for twelve dark hours.

Some very good wine comes from the Rochusberg, immediately opposite Rüdesheim. Goethe heard a sermon here once in which the preacher glorified God in proportion to the number of bottles of good wine it was daily vouchsafed to him to stow away under his waistband.

It was here that the rascal lived who drank wine out of a boot, immortalized by Longfellow. We can hardly, however, abuse the man, for he had an incurable thirst, and no crystal goblet would have held enough for him,—not indeed the biggest German beer mug.

Longfellow, in the "Golden Legend," has a chapter devoted to wine. In this poem the old cellarer muses, as he goes to draw the fine wine for the fathers, who sit above the salt, and he utters this truth of those brothers who sit below the salt:—

> "Who cannot tell bad wine from good,
> And are much better off than if they could."

The superior wines of the Rhine, Walporzheimer, Ahrweiler and Bodendorfer, all deserve notice.

The kind of wine to be served with a dinner must depend on the means of the host. It is to be feared that, ignorantly or otherwise, many wines with high-sounding names which are not good are offered to guests.

Mr. Evarts made a witty remark on this subject. Some one said to him, "I hear that as a great diner-out you find yourself the worse for drinking so many different sorts of wine." "Oh no," said Mr. Evarts, "I do not object to the different wines, it is the indifferent wines which hurt me!"

Savarin says, sententiously, "Nothing can exceed the treachery of asking people to dinner under the guise of friendship, and then giving them to eat or drink of that which may be injurious to health." We should think so. That was the pleasant hospitality of the Borgias. In the neighbourhood of Neuwied, the dealers are accused of much doctoring of wine. During the vintage, at night, when the moon has gone down, boats glide over the Rhine freighted with a soapy substance manufactured from potatoes, and called by its owners sugar. This stuff is thrown into the vats containing the must, water is introduced from pumps and wells, chemical ferments and artificial heat are applied. This noble fluid is sent everywhere by land and water, and labelled as first-class wine. It is not bad to the taste, but does not bear transportation. This adulteration chiefly affects the wines sold at German hotels.

Heinrich Heine has left us this picture of a German dinner: "I dined at the Crown at Clausthal. My repast consisted of spring greens, parsley soup, violet blue cabbage, a pile of roast veal, which resembled Chimborazo in miniature, and a sort of smoked herring called buckings, from their inventor William Buckings, who died in 1447, and who on account of that invention was so greatly honoured by Charles V. that the great monarch in 1556 made a journey from Middelburg to Bierlied, in Zealand, for the express purpose of visiting the grave of the great fish-dryer. How exquisitely such dishes taste when we are familiar with their historical associations."

It is impossible in translation to give Heine's intense ridicule and scorn. He was a Frenchman out of place in Germany. He revolted at things German, but endeared himself to his people by his wit, universality of talent, and sincerity. The world has thanked him for his "Reisebilder." Heine gives us new ideas of the horrors of German cookery when he talks of Göttingen sausages, Hamburg smoked beef, Pomeranian goose-breasts, ox-tongues, calf's brains in pastry, gudgeon cakes, and "a wretched pig's-head in a wretcheder sauce, which has neither a Grecian nor a Persian flavour, but which tasted like tea and soft soap."

He cannot leave Göttingen without this description: "The town of Göttingen, celebrated for its sausages and its university, belongs to the King of Hanover, and contains nine hundred and ninety-nine dwellings, divers chambers, an observatory, a prison, a library, and a council chamber where the beer is excellent."

German sausages are very good. Even the great Goethe, in dying, remembered to send a sausage to his æsthetic love of a lifetime, the Frau Von Stein.

Thackeray, who was keenly alive to the horrors of German cookery, says that whatever is not sour is greasy, and whatever is not greasy is sour. The curious bill of fare of a middle-class German table is something like this: They begin with a pudding. They serve sweet preserved fruit with the meat, generally stewed cherries. They go on with dreadful dishes of cabbage and preparations of milk, curdled, soured, and cheesed.

Dr. Lieber, the learned philologist, was eloquent on the subject of the coarseness of the German appetite. He had early corrected his by a visit to Italy, and he remarked, with his usual profundity, that it was "the more incomprehensible as nature had given Germany the finest wines with which to wash down the worst cookery."

A favourite dish is potato pancakes. The raw potatoes are scraped fine, mixed with milk, and then treated like flour cakes, served with apple or plum sauce.

Sauer-kraut is ridiculed, but it is only cabbage cut fine and pickled. There are two delicious dishes in which it plays an important part: one is roast pheasant cut fine and cooked with sauer-kraut and champagne; the other is sauer-kraut cooked in the *croûte* of a Strasbourg *pâté de foie gras*.

Favourite Austro-Hungarian dishes are *bachhendl*, baked spring-chicken,—the chicken rolled into a paste of egg flour and then baked. It is rather dry to eat, but just the thing with a bottle of Hungarian wine. Also a beefsteak with plenty of *paprika*, or Hungarian red pepper, Brinsa cheese, pot cheese, made in the Carpathian mountains and baked in a hot oven.

Brook trout is never fried, but boiled in water, and then served surrounded by parsley in melted butter.

In eastern Russia grows a pea, the gray pea, which is boiled and eaten like peanuts by peeling off the hard skin, or boiled with some sort of sour-sweet sauce, which softens the skin. This pea is such a favourite with the Lithuanians that it is made the subject of poetry.

Venison, and hare soup, are deliciously gamey bouillons, which are made of the soup bone of the roast. The Polish soup *barscz* is made of bouillon with the juice of red beets, little *saucissons*, and specially made pastry, with highly spiced forced-meat balls swimming in it.

Lettuce salad is prepared in Germany with sour cream.

A favourite drink is warm beer,—beer heated with the yolk of an egg in it.

> "Fill me once more the foaming pewter up!
> Another board of oysters, ladye mine!
> To-night Lucullus with himself shall sup.
> Those mute inglorious Miltons are divine;
> And as I here in slippered ease recline,
> Quaffing of Perkins's Entire my fill,
> I sigh not for the lymph of Aganippe's rill."

Beer is the amber inspiration of the Germans, and plays its daily, hourly part in their science of entertaining.

And the pea which can be skinned, which is such a favourite with the Lithuanians, has also been immortalized by Thackeray:—

> "I give thee all! I can no more,
> Though poor the offering be;
> Stewed duck and peas are all the store
> That I can offer thee!—
> A duck whose tender breast reveals
> Its early youth full well,
> And better still, a pea that peels
> From fresh transparent shell."

But it must not be supposed that rich German citizens of the United States do not know how to give a good dinner. Cosmopolitan in everything else, these, the best colonists whom Europe has sent to us, make good soldiers, good statesmen, and good entertainers. They do not insist that we shall eat pig and prune sauce. No, they give us the most affluent bill of fare which the market affords. They give us a fine dining-room in which to eat it, and they offer as no other men can "a tankard of Assmanschausen."

They give us, as a nation, a valuable present in mineral water. The Apollinaris bubbling up near the Rhine seems sent by Heaven to avert that gout and rheumatism which are the terrible after-dinner penalties of those who like too well the noble Rhine wines.

THE INFLUENCE OF GOOD CHEER ON AU-THORS AND GENIUSES.

"The ancient poets and their learned rhymes
We still admire in these our later times,
And celebrate their fames. Thus, though they die
Their names can never taste mortality.
These had their helps. They wrote of gods and kings,
Of temples, battles, and such gallant things.
And now we ask what noble meat and drink
Can help to make man work, to make him think."

"Pray, on what meat hath this our Cæsar fed?"

We should have a higher estimate of the value of a knowledge of cookery and of all the arts of entertaining, did we sufficiently realize that the style of Carlyle was owing to dyspepsia! At the age of fifteen he entered Edinburgh University in order to fit himself for the pulpit. He studied for many months to that end, but his vocation refused to be clear. The ministry grew alien to his mind. Finally he shut himself up, and as he himself says, wrestled with the Lord and all the imps of darkness. Carlyle believed in a personal Devil, not tasting food or sleeping for three days and nights, and then terminated the struggle by resolving to pursue literature. What mental revolution he underwent, he says he never could understand; all that he knew was that he came out with that "dommed dyspepsia,"—his Scotch way of pronouncing a stronger word.

Some writer says that this anecdote solves the problem of Carlyle. The force, earnestness, and eloquence of his writings were born of a fine, free intellect. Then came despondency, rage, and bitterness, springing from dyspepsia, which had been his haunting demon from the first, releasing him at intervals only to assail and torture him the "more for each surcease."

Most of his works come under the head of the Literature of Dyspepsia, and can be as plainly traced to it as to the growth of his understanding or the sincerity of his convictions. Who does not recognize, in the oddities of the trials and spiritual agonies of Herr Teufelsdröckh, the author himself under a thin disguise, and the promotings and promptings, and phenomena of censuring indigestion? All through the "Sartor Resartus" it is evident that the gastric juices of the illustrious iconoclast are insufficient; that while he is railing at humanity he is suffering from gastritis, while he is prophesying that the race will come to naught but selfishness and stupidity he is undergoing gastrodynia, or, as it is commonly called, stomachic cramp.

I do not know who wrote that masterly criticism, but evidently some man who had had a good dinner.

But Carlyle gets better and writes his noble essay on Robert Burns, the life of John Sterling, Oliver Cromwell's letters and speeches. Then he is at his best; sees man as a brother, handicapped with circumstances, riveted to temperament perhaps, but in spite of all shortcomings and neglected opportunities, still a brother, demanding respect, deserving of help. How different Carlyle would have been, as a man and as a writer, with nutritive organs capable of continually and regularly performing their functions. Dyspepsia was his worst enemy, as it has been that of many of his readers. Every mouthful he ate must have been a gastric Nemesis for sins of opinion, and of heresies against humanity. His very style is the result of indigestion,—an excess of ill-chosen, ill-prepared German fare in a British stomach, affording a strange sustenance, which, like some diseases, keep a man alive, but which pain while they sustain.

What a different genius was Prescott, who had a good dinner every day of his life, who was brought up from boyhood in a luxurious old Boston household where was the perfection of cookery!

Sydney Smith sent word to Prescott after he wrote "Ferdinand and Isabella,"—

"Tell Prescott to come here and we will drown him in turtle soup."

"Say that I can swim in those seas," was Prescott's witty rejoinder.

Mr. Prescott was fifty-three years of age when he visited England; he was extremely handsome, courteous, and very much a man of the world.

"We grow like what we eat. Bad food depresses,
Good food exalts us like an inspiration."

Mr. Prescott had been inspired by good food, as any one can see who reads that noble work "Ferdinand and Isabella." In England this accomplished man was received by Lady Lyell, to whom he was much attached. The account of English hospitality which he gives throws a rosy light on the history of the art of entertaining:

"I returned last night from the Horners, Lady Lyell's parents and sisters, a very accomplished and happy family circle. They have a small house, with a pretty lawn stretching between it and the Thames, that forms a silver edging to the close-shaven green. The family gather under the old trees on the little shady carpet, which is sweet with the perfume of flowery shrubs. And you see sails gliding by and stately swans, of which there are hundreds on the river. The next Sunday, after dinner, which we took at four o'clock, we strolled through Hampton Court and its royal park. The next day we took our picnic at Box Hill. On Friday to dinner at Sir Robert Peel's and to an evening party at Lady S——'s. I went at eleven and found myself in a brilliant saloon filled with people amongst whom I did not recognize a familiar face. You may go to ten parties in London, be introduced to a score of persons in each, and on going to the eleventh not see a face that you have ever seen before, so large is the society of the great metropolis. I was soon put at my ease, however, by the cordial reception of Lord and Lady C——, who introduced me to a great number of persons."

This alone would prove how great was Prescott's popularity, for in London, people, as a rule, are not introduced.

"In the crowd I saw an old gentleman, nicely made up, stooping a good deal, covered with orders, and making his way easily along, as all, young and old, seemed to treat him with deference. It was the Duke of Wellington, the old Iron Duke. He likes the attention he receives in this social way. He wore round his neck the order of the Golden Fleece, on his coat the order of the Garter. He is, in truth, the lion of England, not to say of all Europe."

This beautiful little *genre* picture of the Iron Duke was written in the year 1850. Forty years later General Grant was received at Apsley House by the son of the great Duke of Wellington, the second Duke, who opened the famous Waterloo room and toasted the modest American as the greatest soldier of modern times. Mr. Prescott goes on to say,—

"We had a superb dinner at Sir Robert Peel's, four and twenty guests. It was served in the long picture-gallery. The windows of the gallery look out upon the Thames, its beautiful stone bridges with lofty arches, Westminster Abbey with its towers, and the living panorama on the water. The opposite windows look on the green gardens behind the Palace of Whitehall, which were laid out by Cardinal Wolsey, and near the spot where Charles I. lived, and lost his life on the scaffold. The gallery is full of masterpieces, especially Dutch and Flemish, amongst them the famous *Chapeau de Paille*, which cost Sir Robert over five thousand pounds. In his dining-room were also superb pictures, the famous one by Wilkie, of John Knox preaching, which did not come up to the idea I had formed of it from the engraving. There was a portrait of Dr. Johnson by Reynolds, the portrait owned by Mrs. Thrale and engraved for the Dictionary; what a bijou!

"We sat at dinner looking out on the moving Thames. We dined at eight, but the twilight lingers here until half-past nine at this summer season. Sir Robert was exceedingly courteous to his guests, told some good stories, showed us his autographs, amongst which was the celebrated one written by Nelson, in which he says, 'If I die "Frigate" will be found written on my heart.'"

Mr. Prescott's letter to his daughter points out the strange difference between the life of a girl in England and a girl here.

"I think on reflection, dear Lizzy, that you did well not to come with me. Girls of your age [she was then nineteen] make no great figure in society. One never, or very rarely, meets them at dinner parties, and they are not so numerous at evening parties as with us, unless it be at balls. Six out of seven women you meet are over thirty, and many of them over forty or fifty, not to say sixty; the older they are, the more they are dressed and diamonded. Young girls dress less, and wear very little ornament indeed."

What a commentary this is on our American way of doing things,—where young girls rule society, put their mothers in the background, and wear too fine clothes.

Dr. Prescott was of course presented at Court, and his account of it is delightful:—

"Well! the presentation has come off, and I will give you some account of it before going to dine with Lord Fitzwilliam. This morning I breakfasted with Mr. Monckton Milnes, where I met Macaulay the third time this week. We had also Lord Lyttleton, an excellent scholar, Gladstone, and Lord W. Germains, a sensible and agreeable person, and two or three others. We had a lively talk, but I left early for the Court affair. I was at Mr. Abbott Lawrence's at one in my costume,—a *chapeau* with gold lace, blue coat, and white trowsers, begilded with buttons and metal, a sword, and patent-leather-boots. I was a figure indeed! but I had enough to keep me in countenance. I spent an hour yesterday with Lady M. getting instructions for demeaning myself. The greatest danger was that I should be tripped up by my sword. On reaching St. James Place we passed upstairs through files of the Guard, beefeaters, and were shown into a large saloon richly hung with crimson silk, and with some fine portraits of the family of George III. It was amusing, as we waited there an hour, to see the arrival of the different persons, diplomatic, military, and courtiers, all men and women blazing in their stock of princely finery, and such a power of diamonds, pearls, emeralds, and laces, the trains of the ladies' dresses several yards in length. Some of the ladies wore coronets of diamonds, which covered the greater part of the head. I counted on Lady D——'s head two strings of diamonds rising gradually from the size of a fourpence to the size of an English shilling, and thick in proportion. The dress of the Duchess of D—— was studded with diamonds as large as nutmegs. The young ladies dressed very plainly. I tell this for Lizzy's especial benefit. The company were permitted to pass one by one into the presence-chamber, a room of about the same size as the other, with gorgeous canopy and throne, at the farther end of which stood the little Queen and her Consort, surrounded by her Court. She was rather simply dressed, but he was in Field-Marshal's uniform, and covered, I should think, with all the orders of Europe. He is a good-looking person, but by no means so good-looking as you are given to expect from his pictures. The Queen is better looking than you might expect. I was presented by our minister, by the order of the Chamberlain, as the historian of Ferdinand and Isabella and made my profound obeisance to her Majesty who made a dignified courtesy. I made the same low bow to his Princeship, and then bowed myself out of the circle without my sword tripping up my heels. As I was drawing off, Lord Carlisle, who was standing on the outer edge, called me to him and kept me by his side telling me the names of the different lords and ladies who, after paying their obeisance to the Queen, passed out before us."

Mr. Monckton Milnes became Lord Houghton, and I had great pleasure in knowing him well many years after this. He told me, what our American historian was too modest to tell, how well Mr. Prescott appeared in London. Lionized to death, as the English alone can lionize, Mr. Prescott never lost his modest self-possession. He was everywhere remarked for his beauty, his fine manner, and his knowledge of the usages of good society. But then, in 1887 the English went equally wild, even more so, over Buffalo Bill, and probably preferred him.

Mr. Prescott was entertained at Cuddeston Palace, the residence of Bishop Wilberforce, the famous "Soapy Sam," from the fact, as he said himself, that he "was always in hot water, and always came out cleaner than he went in." This witty and accomplished prelate was very much pleased with our American scholar, and gave him a hearty welcome. It will sound curiously enough now, that Mr. Prescott found his Episcopal views very high, and says, "The service was performed with a ceremony quite Roman Catholic." The Bishop of Oxford would, were he living now, be called low church,—so much do terms vary in different ages. Truly the world moves!

I was in my youth entertained at the house of Mr. Prescott, at Nahant, and allowed to see his workroom and the machinery with which he wrote. He gave me, and I have it still, a paper which he wrote for me with the wired plate which the blind use, for he could scarcely see at all.

He was master of the art of entertaining. How charming he was at dinner at his own house; how pleasantly he made one forget his greatness, except that a supreme simplicity seems always to accompany true greatness. He had a regularity in his habits which would in a less amiable man have interfered with his agreeability, but with him it was most fascinating, as it seemed like musical chords set to noble words.

It would be pleasant to record the triumphs of Mr Webster, Mr. Motley, Mr. Lowell, Mr. Phelps, Mr. Evarts, Mr. Depew, and many another great American in England, but that, while a subject for national pride, scarcely comes within the scope of this little book.

It would seem, however, that our orators, however fed, have compassed the accomplishment of after-dinner speaking, which is so much appreciated in England, and it is to be hoped that no "dommed dyspepsia" from badly cooked food will dim the oratory of the future.

It is quite true that a witty and full talker will be silenced if he is placed before a bad dinner, one which is palpably pretentious but not well cooked, and villanously served. It is impossible for the really conscientious diner-out, who respects his digestion, whose religion is his dinner, to talk much or laugh much, if his gormandize is wounded. Even if he wills to talk, in order not to lose his reputation, his speech will be a "muddy flood of saponaceous blather," instead of his usual brilliant flow of anecdote and repartee.

Not all great men have, however, felt the influence of food as an inspirer. Dr. Johnson was great although he was a horrible feeder; and at the other extreme was General Grant, so abstemious that he once told me that he did not know the sensation of hunger; that he could go three days without food. At the splendid banquets given to him he rarely ate much, but noticed the people and the surroundings, great hero that he was.

Thackeray, Disraeli, and Dickens have given us the most appreciative descriptions of the art of entertaining, and were men deeply sensible of the charms of a good dinner.

Charles Lamb has been the poet of the homely and the comfortable side of good eating; he records for us in immortal prose and poetry what roast pig and tobacco have done for him.

We claim boldly that a part of Webster's greatness, Prescott's charm, the genius of Motley and of Lowell, the oratory of Depew, the wit of Parke Godwin and Horace Porter, even the magnificent march of Sherman to the sea, the great genius of Bryant, the sparkling cup of Anacreon, O. W. Holmes, the masterly speech of our lawyers, and the unrivalled eloquence of our pulpit orators, are owing to that earlier style of domestic American cookery which was, and is, and always shall be, deserving of the highest praise, — when meats were cooked with all their juices, before a wood fire, when bread was light and feathery, when soups were soups, and broils were broils! Oh, vanished excellence!

BONBONS.

Do, child, go to it' grandam, child;
Give grandam kingdom! and it' grandam will
Give it plumb, a cherry, and a fig.

KING JOHN.

They used to call a sugar-plum a plumb in Shakspeare's time. Was it on account of its weight? Few ladies, on receiving a box of bonbons from Maillards, go into the great question of their antiquity and their manufacture. Few, even now, who at a fashionable hotel, receive on Sundays after dinner a pretty little paper box filled with candied rose-leaves and violets, remember that they are only following the fashion of Lucretia Borgia in putting them in their pocket to eat in their rooms, or at the theatre. There is nothing new under the sun.

In France, in entertaining a lady, or a party of ladies, at theatre or opera, the gentleman host always carries a box of bonbons, within which is a little imitation-silver sugar-tongs by which she can help herself to a chocolate or a *marron déguisé*, without soiling her fingers. This pampered dame does not consider that France makes annually sixty million of francs' worth of bonbons; that it exports only about one fourth of this, leaving an enormous amount for home consumption.

They send over to England alone, cheap sweets manufactured by steam, to the amount of three hundred thousand English pounds a year.

The sugar-plum came from Italy, and dates no further back than the sixteenth century as an article of commerce. But the skilful confectioners in private houses knew how to manufacture not only those which were healthful, but those which were very useful in getting rid of dreaded rivals, unfaithful lovers, and troublesome friends.

The manufacture of the antique sugar-plum, the antediluvian baked almond, and the nauseous coloured abominations whose paint-poisoned surface has long been discarded in France, received, as I read in an old chronicle, its death-blow from the Aboukir almonds, during the period of Napoleon's invasion of Egypt, which killed more people than the bullets. Next went down the cracker bonbons, called Cossacks, on account of the terror with which they inspired the *grandes dames* on their first advent in 1814.

These latter, however, have come back, in the harmless detonating powder-charged bonbons which every one hears at a dinner-party, as the fringed papers are pulled. Then come the *primaveras*, a variety of sugared bomb. Then the *marquises, orangines, marron glacé,* or sugared chestnut, *cerises pralinée,* burnt cherries, *bowles, ananas, dattes au café,* dates delightfully stuffed and covered with sugar, *diables noirs, ganaches,* and an ephemeral but delicious candy, *bonbons fondants,* with an inscription on the box that "these must be eaten within twenty-four hours." They are sometimes fruits with a creamy sugar, raspberries, currants, strawberries, and are delicious, but quite untransportable, although transporting merchandise. Their invention made the fortune of the inventor.

Formerly the preparation of bonbons was a tedious affair. Now it is almost the work of a day, but they are perishable. If you leave a box open they will devour themselves. Kept cool and air-tight, they will last for years. About the first of December the great manufacturers in the Rue de la Paix, commence their operations for New Year's, when everybody, from President Carnot down, sends his friend a box of bonbons. They tell of one confectioner who abandoned his sugar-pots to turn playwright, about the time that Alphonse Karr forsook literature to sell bouquets. The principle remains the same. He wished to sweeten the existence of *les Parisiennes.*

In visiting one of these immense establishments one descends a stone staircase, and finds one's self in a stifling atmosphere, heavily laden with the aroma of vanilla and other essences. Around are scores of workmen, in white-paper caps and aprons, their faces red with heat, as they plunge particular fruits into large cauldrons, filled with boiling syrups. More in the shade are other stalwart men, their faces pale with the heated atmosphere, piling up almonds on huge copper vessels; and so constant is the sound of metal clashing against metal that the visitor might imagine himself in an armour smithy, instead of a sugar factory; rather with Vulcan working for the gods, or some village blacksmith pounding out horseshoes, than with a party of French *ouvriers* making sugar-plums for children to crunch. On all sides one sees sugar, gallons of liqueurs, syrups, and essences, rum, aniseed, noyau, maraschino, pineapple, apricot, strawberry, cherry, vanilla, chocolate, coffee, and tea, with sacks of almonds, and baskets of chestnuts, pistachio nuts, and filberts being emptied into machines which bruise their husks, flay them, and blanch them, all ready to receive their saccharine coating.

Those bonbons which have liqueur in them are much appreciated by gourmets who find other bonbons disagree with them! A sugar-coated brandy cherry is relished by the wisest man. Most bonbons are made by hand; those only which are flat at the bottom are cast in moulds. In the hand-made bonbons, the sugar paste is rolled into shapes by the aid of an instrument formed of a stout piece of wire, one end of which is twisted, and the other fixed into a wooden handle. With this the paste is taken out of the cauldron, and worked into the desired form by a rapid *coup de main.* For bonbons of a particular form, such as those in imitation of various fruits, models are carved in wood.

Liqueur bonbons are formed of a mixture of some given liqueur and liquid sugar, which is poured into moulds, and then placed in a slow oven for the day. Long before they are removed a hard crust has formed on the outside, while the inside remains in its original liquid state. Bonbons are crystallized by being plunged into a syrup heated to thirty degrees Reamur; by the time they are dry the crystallization is complete and acts as a protection against the atmosphere. The bonbons can then be kept a certain time, although their flavour deteriorates.

I think sugar one of the most remarkable of all the gifts of nature. It submits itself to all sorts of plastic arts, and to see a confectioner pouring it through little funnels, to see him make a flower, even to its stamens, of this excellent juice of the cane or of the beet,—they use beet sugar almost entirely in France,—is to comprehend anew how many of the greatest of all curiosities are hidden in the kitchen.

One must go to Chambéry, in Savoy, to taste some of the most exquisite *pâtisserie*, to find the most delicious candied fruits; and at Montpellier, in the south of France, is another most celebrated manufactory of bonbons.

I received once from Montpellier a box holding six pounds of these marvellous sweets, which were arranged in layers. Beginning with chocolates in every form, they passed upward by strata, until they reached the candied fruit, which was to be eaten at once. I think there were fifty-five varieties of delicious sweets in that box. Such lovely colours, such ineffable flavours, such beauties as they were! The only remarkable part of this anecdote is that I survived to tell it. I can only account for it by the fact that it was sent me by a famous physician, who must have hidden his power of healing in the box. Unlike Pandora's box which sent the troop of evils out into the world, this famous *cachet* sent nothing but good-will and pleasure, barring perhaps a possible danger.

If, however, we speak of the bonbons themselves, what can we say of the *bonbonnières*! Everything that is beautiful, everything that is curious, everything that is quaint, everything that is ludicrous, everything that is timely, is utilized. I received an immense green satin grasshopper—the last *jour de l'an*, in Paris—filled to his uttermost *antennæ* with bonbons. It could be for once said that the "grasshopper had not become a burden." The *panier Watteau*, formed of satin, pearls, straw, and flowers, may be made to conceal a handkerchief worth a thousand francs under the rose-satin lining. The boxes are painted by artists, and remain a lovely belonging for a toilet table.

Beautiful metal reproductions of some antique *chef d'œuvre* are made into *bonbonnières*. Some bonbon-boxes have themselves concealed in huge bouquets of violets, fringed with lace, or hidden under roses, which are skilfully growing out of white satin; beautiful reticules, all embroidered, hold the carefully bound up packages, where tinfoil preserves the silk and satin from contact with the sugar. If France did nothing else but make *bonbonnières*, she would prove her claim to being the most ingenious purveyor for the luxury of entertaining in all the world. If luxury means, "to freight the passing hour with flying happiness," France does her "possible" as she would say herself, to help along this fairy packing.

At Easter, when sweetmeats are almost as much in request as at the New Year,—the French make very little of Christmas,—these bonbon establishments are filled with Easter eggs of the gayest colours. There are nests of eggs, baskets of eggs, cradles full of eggs, and pretty peasants carrying eggs to market; nests of eggs, with birds of brilliant plumage sitting on the nests or hovering over them, while their freight of bonbons repose on softest swan's-down, lace, and satin; or again, the egg itself of satin, with its yolk of orange creams and its white of marsh-mallow paste. There is no end to this felicitous and dulcet strain.

The best candied fruit I have ever eaten, I bought in a railway depot at Venice. The Italians understand this art to perfection. They hang the fruit by its natural stem on a long straw; and no better accompaniment for a long railway journey can be imagined.

The French do not consider bonbons unhealthful. Instead of giving her boy a piece of bread and butter as he departs for the *Lycée* the French mamma gives him two or three chocolate bonbons. The hunter takes these to the top of the Matter-horn; ladies take them in their pockets instead of a lunch-basket; and one assured me that two slabs of chocolate sufficed her for breakfast and supper on the road from Paris to Rome.

I do not know what Baron Liebig would say to this in his learned articles on the "Nutritive Value of Certain Kinds of Food," but the French children seem to be the healthiest in the world, — a tribute to chocolate of the highest. "By their fruits shall ye know them."

In the times of the Medici, and the St. Bartholomew Massacre, the French and Italian nobles had a curious custom of always carrying about with them, in the pockets of their silk doublets, costly little boxes full of bonbons. Henry IV., Ma-rie de Medici, and all their friends and foes, carried about with them little gold and Limoges enamelled boxes, very pretty and desirable articles of *vertu* now; and doubtless there was one full of red and white comfits in the pocket of Mary Queen of Scots, when she fell dead, poor, ill-used, beautiful woman, at the foot of the block, at Fotheringay. Doubtless there was one in the pouch of the grisly Duc de Guise, with his close-cropped bullet head, and long, spidery legs, when he fell, done to death by treacherous Catherine de Medici, dead and bleeding on the polished floor of Blois! It was a childish custom, and proved that the age had a sweet tooth; but it might have been useful for diplomatic purposes, and highly conducive to flirting. As a Lord Chief Justice once said that "snuff and snuff-boxes help to develop character," so the *bonbonnière* helps to emphasize manners; and I am always pleased when an old or new friend opens for me a little silver box and offers me a sugared violet, or a rose leaf conserved in sugar, although I can eat neither of them.

A witty writer says that dessert should be "the girandole, or cunning tableau of the dinner." It should "surprise, astonish, dazzle, and enchant." We may almost decide upon the taste of an age as we read of its desserts. The tasteless luxury and coarse pleasures of the reign of Charles II., — that society where Rochester fluttered and Buckingham flaunted, — how it is all described in one dessert! At a dinner giv-en the father (of a great many) of his subjects by Lady Dormer, was built a large gilded ship of confectionery. Its masts, cabins, portholes, and lofty poop all smart and glittering, its rigging all taut, its bunting flying, its figure-head bright as gold leaf could make it. Its guns were charged with actual powder. Its cargo was two turreted pies, one full of birds and the other of frogs. When borne in by the gay pages, to the sound of music, the guns were discharged, the ladies screamed and fainted, so as to "require to be held up and consoled by the gallants, who offered them sips of Tokay." Poor little things! Such was the Court of Charles.

Then, to sweeten the smell of powder, the ladies threw at each other egg-shells filled with fragrant waters; and "all danger being over," they opened the pies. Out of one skipped live frogs; out of the other flew live birds who put out the lights; so, what with the screams, the darkness, the frogs, and the smell of powder, we get an idea of sports at Whitehall, where blackbrowed, swarthy-visaged Charles presided, on which grave Clarendon condescended to smile, and which the gentle Evelyn and Waller were condemned to approve.

We have not entirely refrained from such sugar emblems at our own great feasts; but fortunately, they have rather gone out, excepting for some emblem-haunted dinners where we do have sugared Monitors, and chocolate torpedos. I have seen the lovely Venus of Milo in frozen cream, which gave a wit the opportunity of saying that the home for such a goddess should be the temple of Isis; and Bartholdi's immortal Liberty lends herself to chocolate and nougat now and then, but very rarely at private dinners.

The fashion of our day, with its low dishes for the sweets, is so much better, that we cannot help congratulating ourselves that we do not live even in the days of the first George, when, as one witty author again says, "the House of Brunswick brought over sound protestantism, but German taste." Horace Walpole, great about trifles, incomparable decider of the width of a shoe-buckle, keen despiser of all meannesses but his own, neat and fastidious tripper along a flowery path over this vulgar planet, derided the new fashion in desserts. The ambitious confectioners, he says, "aspired to positive statuary, spindle-legged Venus, dummy Mars, all made of sugar;" and he mentions a confectioner of Lord Albemarle's who loudly complained that his lordship would not break up the ceiling of his dining-room to admit the heads, spear-points and upraised thunderbolts of a middle dish of Olympian deities eighteen feet high, all made of sugar.

The dishes known in France as *Les Quatres Mendiants*, one of nuts, one of figs or dried fruit, one of raisins, and another of oranges, still to be seen on old-fashioned dinner-tables, was, I supposed, so called because it is seldom touched, — in fact, goes a-begging.

But I have found this pretty little legend, which proves that it was far more poetical in origin. The name in French for aromatic vinegar is also connected with it. It is called "The Vinegar of the Four Thieves." So runs the legend: "Once four thieves of Marseilles, rubbing themselves with this vinegar during the plague, defied infection and robbed the dead." Who were these wretches? All that we know of them is that they dined beneath a tree on stolen walnuts and grapes, and imagined the repast a feast. We can picture them, Holbein men with slashed sleeves, as old soldiers of Francis I. who had wrestled with the Swiss. We can imagine them as beaten about by Burgundian peasants; and we know that they were grim, brown, scarred rascals, cutting purses, snatching silken cloaks, — sturdy, resolute, heartless, merry, desperate, God-forsaken scoundrels, living only for the moment. We can imagine Callot etching their rags, or Rembrandt putting in their dark shadows and high lights. We can see Salvator Rosa admiring them as they sleep under the green oak-tree, their heads on a dead deer, and the high rock above. Or we may get old Teniers to draw them for us, gambling with torn and greasy cards for a gold crucifix or a brass pot, or revelling at the village inn, swaggering, swearing, drunk, or tipsy, playing at shuffle-board. The only point in their history worth recording is that they were destined to be asked to every dinner party for four hundred years!—simply preceding the bonbons, as we see by the following verses:—

> "Once on a time, in the brave Henry's age,
> Four beggars dining underneath a tree
> Combined their stores; each from his wallet drew
> Handfuls of stolen fruit, and sang for glee.
>
> "So runs the story,—'Garçon, bring the carte,
> Soup, cutlets—stay—and mind, a matelotte.'
> And 'Charles,—a pint of Burgundy's best Beanne;
> In our deep glasses every joy shall float!'
>
> "And 'Garçon, bring me from the woven frail
> That turbaned merchants from fair Smyrna sent,
> The figs with golden seeds, the honeyed fruit,
> That feast the stranger in the Syrian tent.
>
> "'Go fetch us grapes from all the vintage rows
> Where the brave Spaniards gaily quaff the wine,
> What time the azure ripple of the waves
> Laughs bright beneath the green leaves of the vine!
>
> "'Nor yet, unmindful of the fabled scrip,
> Forget the nuts from Barcelona's shore,
> Soaked in Iberian oil from olives pressed,
> To the crisp kernels adding one charm more.
>
> "'The almonds last, plucked from a sunny tree,
> Half way up Lybanus, blanched as snowy white
> As Leila's teeth, and they will fitly crown
> The beggars' four-fold dish for us to-night.
>
> "'Beggars are happy! then let us be so;
> We've buried care in wine's red-glowing sea.
> There let him soaking lie—he was our foe;
> Joy laughs above his grave—and so will we!'"

It was from that love of contrast, then, was it, which is a part of all luxury, that the fable of the *Quatre Mendiants* was made to serve like the olives at dessert. Perhaps the fillip which walnuts give to wine suggested it. It was a modern French rendering of the skull made to do duty as a drinking-cup. It is a part of the five kernels of corn at a Pilgrim dinner, without that high conscientiousness of New England. It is a part, perhaps, of the more melancholy refrain, "Be merry, be merry, for to-morrow ye die!" It is that warmth is warmer when we remember cold; it is that food is good when we remember the starving; it is that *bringing in* of the pleasant vision of the four beggars under the tree, as a picture perhaps; at any rate there it is, moral at your pleasure.

The desserts of the middle ages were heavy and cumbrous affairs, and had no special character. There would be a good deal of Cellini cup and Limoges plate, and Palissy dish, and golden chased goblet about it, no doubt. How glad the collectors of to-day would be to get them! And we picture the heavy indigestible cakes, and poisonous bonbons. The taste must have been questionable if we can believe Ben Jonson, who tells of the beribboned dwarf jester who, at a Lord Mayor's dinner, took a flying header into a dish of custard, to the infinite sorrow of ladies' dresses; he followed, probably, that dish in which the dwarf Sir Geoffrey Hudson was concealed, and they both are after Tom Thumb, who was fishing about in a cup of posset a thousand years ago.

The dessert is allowed by all French writers to be of Italian origin; and we read of the *maîtres d'hotel*, before the Italian dessert arrived, probably introduced by Catherine de Medici and the Guises, that they gloried in mountains of fruit, and sticky hills of sweetmeats. The elegance was clumsy and ostentatious; there was no poetry in it. Paul Veronese's picture of the "Marriage of Cana" will give some idea of the primeval French dessert. The later fashion was of those trees and gardens and puppets abused by Horace Walpole; but Frenchmen delighted in seas of glass, flower-beds formed of coloured sand, and little sugar men and women promenading in enamelled bowling-greens. We get some idea of the magnificent fêtes of Louis XIV. at Versailles from the glowing descriptions of Molière.

Dufoy in 1805 introduced "frizzled muslin into a slice of fairyland;" that is, he made extraordinary pictures of temples and trees, for the centre of his dessert. And these palaces and temples were said to have been of perfect proportions; his trees of frizzled muslin were admirable. It sounds very much like children's toys just now.

He went further, Dufoy; having ransacked heaven and earth, air and water, he thrust his hand into the fire, and made harmless rockets shoot from his sugar temples. Sugar rocks were strewn about with precipices of nougat, glaciers of vanilla candy, and waterfalls of spun sugar. A confectioner in 1805 had to keep his wits about him, for after every victory of Napoleon he was expected to do the whole thing in sugar. He was decorator, painter, architect, sculptor, and florist—icer, yes, until after the Russian campaign, and then—they had had enough of ice. Thus we see that the dessert has always been more for the eye than for the stomach.

The good things which have been said over the walnuts and the wine! The pretty books written about claret and olives! One author says that if all the good things which have been said about the gay and smiling dessert could be printed, it would make a pleasant anecdotic little pamphlet of four thousand odd pages!

We must not forget all the absurdities of the dessert. The Prince Regent, whose tastes inclined to a vulgar and spurious Orientalism, at one of his costly feasts at Carleton House had a channel of real water running around the table, and in this swam gold and silver fish. The water was only let on at dessert.

These fancies may be sometimes parodied in our own time, as the bonbon makers of Paris now devote their talents to the paper absurdities of harlequins, Turks, Chinamen, and all the vagaries of a fancy-dress ball with which the passengers of steamships amuse themselves after the Captain's dinner. This is not that legitimate dessert at which we now find ices disguised as natural fruits, or copying a rose. All the most beautiful forms in the world are now reproduced in the frozen water or cream, as healthful as it is delicious, in the famous jelly with maraschino, or the delicate bonbon with the priceless liqueur, or, better still, that *eau de menthe* cordial, our own green peppermint, which, after all, saves as by one mouthful from the horrors of indigestion and adds that "thing more exquisite still" to the perfect dessert,—a good night's sleep.

FAMOUS MENUS AND RECIPES.

Gather up the fragments that remain that nothing be lost.

JOHN vi. 12.

This is not intended to be a cookery book; but in order to help the young housekeeper we shall give some hints as to *menus* and a few rare recipes.

The great line of seacoast from New York to Florida presents us with some unrivalled delicacies, and the negroes of the State of Maryland, which was founded by a rich and luxurious Lord Baltimore, knew how to cook the terrapin, the canvas-back duck, oysters, and the superb wild turkey,—not to speak of the well-fattened poultry of that rich and luxurious Lorraine of America, "Maryland, my Maryland," which Oliver Wendell Holmes calls the "gastronomical centre of the universe."

Here is an old Virginia recipe for cooking terrapin, which is rare and excellent:—

> Take three large, live, diamond-backed terrapin, plunge them in boiling water for three minutes, to take off the skin, wipe them clean, cook them in water slightly salted, drain them, let them get cold, open and take out everything from the shell. In removing the entrails care must be taken not to break the gall. Cut off the head, tail, nails, gall, and bladder. Cut the meat in even-size pieces, put them in a sauce-pan with four ounces of butter, add the terrapin eggs, and moisten them with a half pint of Madeira wine. Let the mixture cook until the moisture is reduced one-half. Then add two spoonfuls of cream sauce. After five minutes add the yolks of four raw eggs diluted with a half-cup of cream. Season with salt and a pinch of red pepper. The mixture should not boil after the yolk of egg is added. Toss in two ounces of butter before serving. The heat of the mess will cook egg and butter enough. Serve with quartered lemon.

This is, perhaps, if well-cooked, the most excellent of all American dishes.

A chicken gumbo soup is next:—

> Cut up one chicken, wash and dry it, dip it in flour, salt and pepper it, then fry it in hot lard to a delicate brown.
>
> In a soup kettle place five quarts of water and your chicken, let it boil hard for two hours, cut up twenty-four okra pods, add

them to the soup, and boil the whole another hour. One large on-ion should be put in with the chicken. Add red pepper to taste, also salt, not too much, and serve with rice. Dried okra can be used, but must be soaked over night.

Another Maryland success was the tomato catsup:—

Boil one bushel of tomatoes until soft, squeeze through a sieve, add to the juice half a gallon of vinegar, 1½ pints salt, 3 ounces of whole cloves, 1 ounce of allspice, 2 ounces of cay-enne pepper, 3 tablespoonfuls of black pepper, 3 heads of garlic, skinned and separated; boil three hours or until the quantity is reduced one-half, bottle without skimming. The spices should be put in a muslin bag, which must be taken out, of course, before bottling. If desired 1 peck of onions can be boiled, passed through a sieve, and the juice added to the tomatoes.

Green pepper pickles: Half a pound of mustard seed soaked over night, 1 quart of green pepper chopped, 2 quarts of onions chopped, 4 quarts of cucumbers also chopped, 8 quarts of green tomatoes chopped, 6 quarts of cabbage chopped; mix and mea-sure. To every gallon of this mixture add one teacup of salt, let it stand until morning, then squeeze perfectly dry with the hands. Then add 8 pounds of sugar, and cover with good vinegar and boil five minutes. After boiling, and while still hot, squeeze per-fectly dry, then add 2 ounces of cloves, 2 ounces of allspice, 3 ounces of cinnamon and the mustard seed.

The peppers should be soaked in brine thirty-six or forty-eight hours. After soaking, wipe dry and stuff, place them in glass jars, and cover with fresh vinegar.

This was considered the triumph of the Southern housekeeper.

Chicken with spaghetti: Stir four sliced onions in two ounces of butter till very soft, add one quart of peeled tomatoes; stew chicken in water until tender, and pick to pieces. Add enough of the gravy to make a quart, put with the onions and tomatoes. Let it stew fifteen minutes gently. Put into boiling water 2½ pounds of spaghetti and a handful of salt, boil twenty minutes or until tender; drain this and put in a layer on a platter sprinkled with grated cheese, and pour the stew on it. Fill the platter with these layers, reserving the best of the chicken to lay on top.

The old negro cooks made a delicious confection known as confection cake. Those who lived to tell of having eaten it declared that it was a dream. It certainly leads to dreams, and bad ones, but it is worth a nightmare:—

1½ cups of sugar, 2½ cups of flour, ½ cup of butter, ½ cup of sweet milk, whites of six eggs, 3 small teaspoons of baking pow-der. Bake in two or three layers on a griddle.

Filling: 1 small cocoanut grated, 1 pound almonds blanched, and cut up not too fine, 1 teacup of raisins chopped, 1 teacup of citron chopped, 4 eggs, whites only, 7 tablespoonfuls of pulverized sugar to each egg.

Mix this destructive substance well in the froth of egg, and spread between the layers of cake when they are hot; set it a few minutes in the oven, but do not burn it, and you have a delicious and profoundly indigestible dessert. You will be able to write Sartor Resartus, after eating of it freely.

Walnut Cake: 1 cup of butter, 2 cups of sugar, 6 eggs, 4 cups of flour, 1 cup of milk, 2 teaspoonfuls of yeast powder.

This is also baked in layers, and awaits the dynamite filling which is to blow you up:—

Walnut Filling: 2 cups of brown sugar, 1 cup of cream, a piece of butter the size of an egg. Cook twenty minutes, stirring all the time; when ready to take off the stove put in one cup of walnut meats. After this has cooked a few minutes longer, spread between the layers, and while both cake and filling are hot.

Perhaps a few *menus* may be added here to assist the memory of her "who does not know what to have for dinner:"—

<table>
<tr><td></td><td>Tomato Soup.</td><td></td></tr>
<tr><td>Golden Sherry.</td><td>Whitefish broiled.</td><td>Claret.</td></tr>
<tr><td></td><td>Mashed potatoes.</td><td></td></tr>
<tr><td></td><td>Round of beef *braisé,*</td><td>Madeira.</td></tr>
<tr><td></td><td>with glazed onions.</td><td></td></tr>
<tr><td>Champagne.</td><td>Roast plover with cress.</td><td>Château Yquem.</td></tr>
<tr><td></td><td>Chiccory Salad.</td><td></td></tr>
<tr><td></td><td>Custard flavoured with vanilla.</td><td></td></tr>
<tr><td></td><td>Cheese.</td><td>Cordials.</td></tr>
<tr><td>Chambertin.</td><td>Fruit.</td><td></td></tr>
<tr><td></td><td>Coffee.</td><td></td></tr>
</table>

Or a plain dinner:—

<table>
<tr><td>Sherry.</td><td>Oxtail Soup.</td><td>Claret.</td></tr>
<tr><td></td><td>*Filet of lobster à la Mazarin.*</td><td></td></tr>
<tr><td></td><td>Turkey rings with *purée* of chestnuts.</td><td></td></tr>
<tr><td></td><td>Salad of fresh tomatoes.</td><td></td></tr>
<tr><td>Cream tart with meringue.</td><td></td><td>Cheese.</td></tr>
</table>

This last dinner is perhaps enough for only a small party, but it is very well composed. A much more elaborate *menu* follows:—

Oysters on the half-shell.

Soup:

Consommé royale.

Fish: Rudesheimer.

Fried smelts, sauce Tartare,

Duchess *potatoes.*

Sherry. Releves:

Boned capon.

Roast ham. Champagne.

Madeira, *Entreés:*

Sweetbreads *braisé.*

Quails. Claret.

Sorbet au *kirsch.*

Game:

Port, Broiled woodcock, Chambertin.

Canvas-back duck.

Vegetables:

Cauliflower, Spinach, French peas,

Stewed tomatoes. Château Yquem.

Dessert:

Frozen pudding, *Biscuits Diplomats.*

Meringues Chantilly, Assorted Cake.

Fruit.

Brandy. Coffee. Cordials.

An excellent bill of fare for eight persons, in the month of October, is the following:—

Soup.
Bisque of crayfish.
Fish.
Baked smelts, *à la Mentone,*
Potato balls, *à la Rouenaise,*
Ribs of beef braised, stewed with vegetables.
Brussels sprouts.
Roast birds, or quail on toast.
Celery salad.

To make a bisque of crayfish is a very delicate operation, but it is worth trying:—

Have three dozen live crayfish, wash them well, and take the intestines out by pinching the extreme end of the centre fin, when with a sudden jerk the gall can be withdrawn. Put in a stewpan two ounces of butter, with a carrot, an onion, two stalks of celery, two ounces of salted pork, all sliced fine, and a bunch of parsley; fry ten minutes, add the crayfish, with a pint of French white wine and a quart of veal broth. Stir and boil gently for an hour, then drain all in a large strainer, take out the bunch of parsley and save the broth; pick the shells off the crayfish tails, trim them neatly and keep until wanted. Cook separately a pint and a half of rice, with three pints of veal broth, pound the rest of the crayfish and vegetables, add the rice, pound again, dilute with the broth of the crayfish, and add more veal broth if too thick. Pass forcibly through a fine sieve with a wooden presser, put the residue in a saucepan, warm without boiling, and stir all the while with a wooden spoon. Finish with three ounces of table butter, a glass of Madeira wine, and a pinch of cayenne pepper; serve hot in soup tureen with the crayfish tails.

To prepare baked smelts à la Mentone: Spread in a large and narrow baking-dish some fish forcemeat half an inch thick, have two dozen large, fresh, well-cleaned smelts, lay them down in a row on the forcemeat, season with salt, pepper, and grated nutmeg, pour over a thick white Italian sauce, sprinkle some bread crumbs on them, put a small pat of butter on each one and bake for half an hour in a pretty hot oven, then squeeze the juice of a lemon over and serve in a baking-dish.

To make potato balls à la Rouenaise: Boil the potatoes and rub them fine, then roll each ball in white of egg, lay them on a floured table, roll into shape of a pigeon's egg, dip them in melted butter, and fry a light brown in clear hot grease. Sprinkle fine salt over and serve in a folded napkin.

To prepare braised ribs of beef: Have a small set of three ribs cut short, cook it as *beef à la mode*, that is, stew it with spices and vegetables, dish it up with carrots, turnips, and onions, pour the reduced gravy over.

To prepare Brussels sprouts, demi-glacé: Trim and wash the sprouts, soak them in boiling salted water about thirty minutes, cool them in cold water, and drain them. Put six ounces of butter in a large frying-pan, melt it and put the sprouts in it, season with salt and pepper, fry on a brisk fire until thoroughly hot, serve in a dish with a rich drawn-butter sauce with chopped parsley.

A diplomatic supper was once served at the White House, of which the following *menu* is an accurate report:—

Salmon with green sauce.

Cold boned turkey, with truffles.

Pâtés of game, truffled.

Ham cooked in Madeira sauce.

Aspic of chicken.

Pâté de foie gras.

Salads of chicken and lobster in forms, surrounded by jelly.

Pickled oysters.   Sandwiches.

Scalloped oysters.

Stewed terrapin.

Chicken and lobster croquettes.

Chocolat à la crème.   Coffee.

Dessert:

Ices.	Fancy meringue baskets filled with cream.
Pancakes.	Large cakes.
Fancy jellies.	Charlotte Russe.

Fruits.

Cake.   Wafers.   Nougat.

One could have satisfied an appetite with all this.

General Grant was probably the most *fêted* American who ever visited Europe. He was entertained by every monarch and by many most distinguished citizens. The Duke of Wellington opened the famous Waterloo Room in Apsley House in his honour, and toasted him as the first soldier of the age. But it is improbable that he ever had a better dinner than the following:—

It was given to him in New York, in 1880, at the Hotel Brunswick. It was for ten people only, in a private parlour, arranged as a dining-room *en suite* with the Venetian parlour. The room was in rich olive and bronze tints. The buffet glittered with crystal, and Venetian glass. On the side tables were arranged the coffee service and other accessories. The whole room was filled with flowers, the chandelier hung with smilax, dotted with carnations. The table was arranged with roses, heliotrope, and carnations, the deep purple and green grapes hanging over gold dishes. The dinner service was of white porcelain with heliotrope border, the glass of iridescent crystal. The furnishing of the Venetian parlour, the rich carvings, the suits of armour, the antique chairs were all mediæval; the dinner was modern and American:—

Oysters.

Soup, *Consommé Royale.*

Fish:

Fried smelts, sauce Tartare.

Releves:

Boned capon.

Entrées:

Sweetbreads, braisé,   Quails, à la Perig-
                                                                ord.

Sorbet au kirsch.

Game.

Broiled woodcock,   Canvas-back duck.

Terrapin.

Vegetables:

Cauliflower,   Spinach, Artichokes,   French peas.

Dessert:

Biscuits Diplomatiques,   Frozen pudding,

Meringue Chantilly,   Assorted cakes.

Fruit.   Coffee.   Cigars.

Liqueurs.

Probably the last item interested and amused the General, who was no *gour-met*, much more than even the terrapin.

This *menu* for a November dinner cannot be surpassed.

COOKERY AND WINES OF THE SOUTH OF EUROPE.

Aufidius for his morning beverage used
Honey in strong Falernian wine infused;
But here methinks he showed his want of brains:
Drink less austere best suits the empty veins.

. . . . . .

Shell fish afford a lubricating slime!
But then you must observe both place and time.
They're caught the finest when the moon is new;
The Lucrine far excel the Baian too.
Misenum shines in cray fish; Circe most
In oysters; scollops let Tarentum boast.
The culinary critic first should learn
Each nicer shade of flavour to discern:
To sweep the fish stalls is mere show at best

. . . . . .

Unless you know how each thing should be drest.
Let boars of Umbrian game replete with mast,
If game delights you, crown the rich repast.

SATIRES OF HORACE.

Italian cookery is excellent at its best. The same drift of talent, the same due sense of proportion which showed itself in all their art, which built St. Mark's and the Duomo, the Ducal Palace, the Rialto, and the churches of Palladio, comes out in their cookery. Their cooks are Michel Angelo and Leonardo da Vinci in a humbler sphere.

They mingle cheese in cookery, with great effect; nothing can be better than their cauliflower covered with Parmesan cheese, and baked. Macaroni in all its forms is of course admirable. They have mastered the use of sweet oil, which in their cookery never tastes oily; it is simply a lambent richness.

The great dish, wild boar, treated with a sweet and a sour sauce, with pine cones, is an excellent dish. Wild boar is a lean pork with a game flavour. All sorts of birds, especially *becafico*, are well cooked, they lose no juice or flavour over the fire.

They make a dozen preparations of Indian meal, which are very good for breakfast. One little round cake, like a muffin, tastes almost of cocoanut; this is fried in oil, and is most delicious.

The *frittala* is another well-known dish, and is composed of liver, bacon, and birds, all pinned on a long stick, or iron pin.

In an Italian palace, if you have the good luck to be asked, the dinner is handsome. It is served in twelve courses in the Russian manner, and if national dishes are offered they are disguised as inelegant. But at an ordinary farmhouse in the hills near Florence, or at the ordinary hotels, there will be a good soup, trout fresh from the brooks, fresh butter, macaroni with cheese, a fat capon, and a delicious omelette, enriched with morsels of kidney or fat bacon, a *frittala*, a bunch of grapes, a bottle of Pogio secco, or the sweet Italian straw wine.

The Italians are very frugal, and would consider the luxurious overflow of American munificent hospitality as vulgar. At parties in Rome, Naples, and Florence it is not considered proper to offer much refreshment. At Mr. Story's delightful receptions American hospitality reigned at afternoon tea, as it did in all houses where the hostess was American, but at the houses of the Princes nothing was offered but weak wine and water and little cakes.

Many travellers have urged that the cookery of the common Italian dinner is too much flavoured with garlic, but in a winter spent in travelling through Italy I did not find it so. I remember a certain leg of lamb with beans which had a slight taste of onions, but that is all. They have learned, as the French have, that the onion is to cookery what accent is to speech. It should not be *trop prononcée*. The lamb and pistachio nuts of the Arabian Nights is often served and is delicious.

They give you in an Italian country house for breakfast, at twelve o'clock, a sort of thick soup, very savoury, probably made of chicken with an herb like okra, one dish of meat smothered in beans or tomatoes, followed by a huge dish of macaroni with cheese, or with morsels of ham through it. Then a white curd with powdered cinnamon, sugar, and wine, a bottle of *vino santo*, a cup of coffee or chocolate, and bread of phenomenal whiteness and lightness.

Alas, for the poor people! They live on the chestnuts, the frogs, or nothing. The porter at the door of some great house is seen eating a dish of frogs, which are, however, so well cooked that they send up an appetizing fragrance more like a stew of crabs than anything else. One sees sometimes a massive ancient house, towering up in mediæval grandeur, with shafts of marble, and columns of porphyry, lonely, desolate, and beautiful, infinitely impressive, infinitely grand. Some member of a once illustrious family lives within these ruined walls, on almost nothing. He would have to kill his pet falcon to give you a dinner, while around his time-honoured house cluster his tenants shaking with malaria, — pale, unhappy, starved people. It is not a cheerful sight, but it can be seen in southern Italy.

The prosperous Italians will give you a well-cooked meal, an immense quantity of bonbons, and the most exquisite candied fruits. Their *confetti* are wonderful, their cakes and ices, their candied fruit, their *tutti frutti*, are beyond all others. They crown every feast with a Paradise in spun sugar.

But they despise and fear a fire, and foreigners are apt to find the old Italian palaces dreary, and very cold. A recent traveller writes from Florence: "I have been within the walls of five Italian houses at evening parties, at three of them, music and no conversation; all except one held in cold rooms, the floors black, imperfect-ly covered with drugget, and no fire; conversation, to me at least, very dull; the topics, music, personal slander,—for religion, government, and literature, were generally excluded from polite society. In only one house, of which the mistress was a German, was tea handed around; sometimes not even a cup of water was passed." We learn from the novels of Marion Crawford that the Italians do not often eat in each others' houses.

Victor Emmanuel, the mighty hunter, had a mighty appetite. He used to dine alone, before the hour for the State dinner. Then with sword in hand, leaning on its jewelled hilt, in full uniform, his breast covered with orders, the King sat at the head of his table, and talked with his guests while the really splendid dinner was served.

Royal banquets are said to be dull. The presence of a man so much above the others in rank has a depressing effect. The guest must console himself with the glorious past of Italy, and fix his eyes on the magnificent furniture of the table, the cups of Benvenuto Cellini, the vases of Capo di Monti, the superb porcelain, and the Venetian glass, or he must devote himself to the lamb and pistachio nuts, the *choux fleurs aux Parmesan*, or the truffles, which are nowhere so large or so fine as at an Italian dinner. Near Rome they are rooted out of the oak forests by the king's dogs, and are large and full of flavour.

King Humbert has inherited his father's taste for hunting, and sends presents of the game he has shot to his courtiers.

The housekeeping at the Quirinal is excellent; a royal supper at a royal ball is something to remember. And what wines to wash them down with!—the de-licious Lacryma Christi, the Falerno or Capri, the Chianti, the Sestio Levante or Asti. Asti is a green wine, rich, strong, and sweet. It makes people ill if they drink it before it is quite old enough—but perhaps it is not often served at royal banquets.

Verdeaux was a favourite wine of Frederic the Great, but Victor Emmanuel's wine was the luscious *Monte Pulciano*.

"Monte Pulciano d'ogni vino e il Re."

The brilliant purple colour, like an amethyst, of this noble wine is unlike any other. The aromatic odour is delicious; its sweetness is tempered by an agreeable sharpness and astringency; it leaves a flattering flavour on the tongue.

These best Italian wines have a deliciousness which eludes analysis, like the famous Monte Beni, which old Tommaso produced in a small straw-covered flask at the visit of Kenyon to Donatello. This invaluable wine was of a pale golden hue, like other of the rarest Italian wines, and if carelessly and irreligiously quaffed, might have been mistaken for a sort of champagne. It was not, however, an effer-vescing wine, although its delicate piquancy produced a somewhat similar effect upon the palate. Sipping, the guest longed to sip again, but the wine demanded so deliberate a pause in order to detect the hidden peculiarities, and subtle exquisiteness of its flavour, that to drink it was more a moral than a physical delight. There was a deliciousness in it which eluded description, and like whatever else that is superlatively good was perhaps better appreciated by the memory than by present consciousness. One of its most ethereal charms lay in the transitory life of the wine's richest qualities; for while it required a certain leisure and delay, yet if you lingered too long in the draught, it became disenchanted both of its fragrance and flavour. The lustre and colour should not be forgotten among the other good qualities of the Monte Beni wine, for "as it stood in Kenyon's glass, a little circle of light glowed on the table around about it as if it were really so much golden sunshine."

There are few wines worthy of this beautiful eloquence of Hawthorne. The description bears transportation; the wine did not. The transportation of even a few miles turned it sour. That is the trouble with Italian wines. Monte Pulciano and Chianti do bear transportation. Italy sends much of the latter wine to New York. Italy has, however, never produced a really good dry wine, with all its vineyards.

The dark Grignolino wine grown in the vineyards of Asterau and Monferrato possesses the remarkable quality of keeping better if diluted with fresh water.

The Falernian from the Bay of Naples, is the wine of the poets, nor need we remind the classical scholar that the hills around Rome were formerly supposed to produce it.

The loose, volcanic soil about Mount Vesuvius grows the grapes from which Lacryma Christi is produced. It is sometimes of a rich red colour, though white and sparkling varieties are produced.

The Italians are supremely fond of *al fresco* entertainments, — their fine climate making out-of-door eating very agreeable. How many a traveller remembers the breakfast or dinner in a vine-covered *loggia* overhanging some splendid scene! It forms the subject of many a picture, from those which illustrate the stories of Boccaccio up to the beautiful sketch of Tasso, at the court of the Duc d'Este. The dangers of these feasts have been immortalized in verse and prose from Dante down, and Shakspeare has touched upon them twice. George Eliot describes one in a "*loggia* joining on a garden, with all one side of the room open, and with numerous groups of trees and statues and avenues of box, high enough to hide an assassin," in her wonderful novel of Romola. In modern days, since the Borgias are all killed, no one need fear to eat out-of-doors in Italy.

Not much can be said of the cookery of Spain. In the principal hotels of Spain one gets all the evils of both Spanish and Gascon cookery. Garlic is the favourite flavour, and the bad oil expressed from the olive, skin, seed and all, allowed to stand until it is rancid, is beloved of the Spanish, but hated by all other nations. I believe, however, that an *olla podrida* made in a Spanish house is very good. It may not be inappropriate here to give two recipes for macaroni. The first, *macaroni au gratin* is very rarely found good in an American house: —

> Break two ounces of best Italian macaroni into a pint of highly
> seasoned stock, let it simmer until very tender. When done, toss it
> up with a small piece of butter, and add pepper and salt to taste;

put in a large meat dish, sift over it some fried bread-crumbs, and serve. It will take about an hour to cook, and should be covered with the stock all the time.

Macaroni with Parmesan cheese: Boil two ounces of macaroni in half a pint of water, with an ounce of butter, until perfectly tender. If the water evaporates add a little more, taking care that the macaroni does not stick to the stewpan, or become broken. When it is done, drain away the water and stir in two ounces of good cheese grated, cayenne pepper and salt to taste. Keep stirring until the cheese is dissolved. Pour on to a hot dish and serve. A little butter may be stirred into the macaroni before the cheese, and is an improvement.

Through the Riviera, and indeed in the south of France, one meets with many peculiar dishes. No one who has read Thackeray need be reminded of *bouillabaise*, that famous fish chowder of Marseilles. It is, however, only our chowder with much red pepper. A cook can try it if she chooses, and perhaps achieve it after many failures.

There are so many very good dishes awaiting the efforts of a young American housewife, that she need not go out of her way to extemporize or explore. The best cook-book for foreign dishes is still the old Francatelli.

The presence in our midst of Italian warehouses, adds an infinite resource to the housewife. Those stimulants to the appetite called *hors d'œuvres*, we call them relishes, are much increased by studying the list of Italian delicacies. Anchovy or caviar, potted meat, grated tongue, potted cheese, herring salad, the inevitable olive, and many other delicacies could be mentioned which aid digestion, and make the plainest table inexpensively luxurious. The Italians have all sorts of delicate vegetables preserved in bottles, mixed and ready for use in a *jardinière* dressing; also the best of cheeses, *gargonzala*, and of course the truffle, which they know how to cook so well.

The Italians have conquered the art of cooking in oil, so that you do not taste the oil. It is something to live for, to eat their fried things.

Speaking of the south of Europe reminds us of that wonderful bit of orientalism out of place, which is called Algiers, and which France has enamelled on her fabulous and many-coloured shield. Algiers has become not only a winter watering-place, high in favour with the traveller, but it is a great wine-growing country. The official statement of Lieut. Col. Sir R. L. Playfair, her Majesty's consul-general, may be read with interest, dated 1889:

"Viticulture in Algeria, was in 1778 in its infancy; now nearly one hundred and twenty-five thousand acres are under cultivation with vines, and during the last year about nine hundred thousand hectolitres of wine were produced. In 1873 Mr. Eyre Ledyard, an English cultivator of the vine in Algeria, bought the property of Chateau Hydra near Algiers. He found on it five acres of old and badly planted vineyards, which produced about seven hogsheads of wine. He has extended this vineyard and carried on his work with great intelligence and industry. He cultivates the following varieties: the Mourvedie, of a red colour resembling Burgundy, Cariguan, giving a wine good, dark, and rough, Alicante or Grenache, Petit Bouschet, Cabernot and Côt, a Burgundy, Perian Lyra, Aramen, and St. Saux.

Chasselas succeeds well; the grapes are exported to France for the table.

Clairette produces abundantly and makes a good dry wine. Ainin Kelb, more correctly Ain Kelb, dog's-eye, is an Arab grape which makes a good strong wine, but which requires keeping. Muscat is a capricious bearer. From the two last-named varieties, sweet as well as dry wines are produced by adding large quantities of alcohol to the juice of the grape, and thus preventing fermentation. The crops yield quantities varying from seven hundred gallons per acre in rich land to four hundred on the hillside, except Cariguan which yields more. Aramen yields as much, but the quality is inferior.

The red wines are sent to Bordeaux and Burgundy, to give strength and quality to the French clarets, as they are very useful for blending. The dry, white wine is rather stronger and fuller than that of France or Germany, and is much used to give additional value to the thinner qualities of Rhine wine.

The cellars of Château Hydra, are now probably the best in the colony. They are excavated in the soft rock here incorrectly called tufa, in reality an aggregation of minutely pulverized shells; it is soft and sandy, and easily excavated. The surface becomes harder by exposure to the atmosphere, and it is not subject to crumbling.

Mr. Ledyard has excavated extensive cells in this rock, in which extreme evenness of temperature is ensured,—a condition most necessary for the proper manufacture of wine.

Mr. Eyre Ledyard's vineyards and cellars of the Chateau Hydra estate are now farmed by the *Société Anonyme Viticole et Vinicole d'Hydra*, of which Mr. Ledyard is chairman. These wines have been so successfully shipped to England and other countries that the company now buys grapes largely from the best vineyards, in order to make sufficient wines to meet the demand. The Hydra Company supplies wine to all vessels of the Ocean Company going to India and China. A very carefully prepared quinine white wine is made for invalids, and for use in countries where there is fever. I especially recommend a trial of this last excellent wine to Americans, as it is most agreeable as well as healthful. The postal address is M. Le Gerant, Hydra Caves, Birmandreis, Algiers.

All the stories of Algiers read like tales of the Arabian Nights, and none is more poetic than the names and the story of these delicious wines.

The Greek wines are well spoken of in Europe: Santorin, and Zante, and St. Elié, and Corinth, and Mount Hymettus, Vino Santo, and Cyprus, while from Magyar vineyards come Visontaè, Badescony, Dioszeg, Bakator, Rust, Szamorodni, Oedenburger, Ofner, and Tokay.

The Hungarian wines are very heady. He must be a swashbuckler who drinks them. They are said to make the drinker grow fat. To this unhappy class Brillat Savarin gives the following precepts:—

"Drink every summer thirty bottles of seltzer water, a large tumbler the first thing in the morning, another before lunch, and the same at bedtime.

"Drink white wines, especially those which are light and acid, and avoid beer as you would the plague. Ask frequently for radishes, artichokes with hot sauce, asparagus, celery; choose veal and fowl rather than beef and mutton, and eat as little of the crumb of bread as possible.

"Avoid macaroni and pea soup, avoid farinaceous food under whatever form it assumes, and dispense with all sweets. At breakfast take brown bread, and chocolate rather than coffee."

Indeed Brillat Savarin seems to have inspired this later poet:—

"Talk of the nectar that flowed for celestials
Richer in headaches it was than hilarity!
Well for us animals, frequently bestials,
Hebe destroyed the recipe as a charity!
Once I could empty my glass with the best of 'em,
Somehow my system has suffered a shock o' late;
Now I shun spirits, wine, beer, and the rest of 'em,
Fill me, then fill me, a bumper of chocolate.

"Once I drank logwood, and quassia and turpentine,
Liqueurs with coxcubes, aloes, and gentian in,
Sure, 't is no wonder my path became serpentine,
Getting a state I should blush now to mention in.
Farewell to Burgundy, farewell to Sillery,
I have not tasted a drop e'en of Hock o' late,
Long live the kettle, my dear old distillery,
Fill me, oh fill me, a bumper of chocolate."

As we cannot all drink chocolate, I recommend the carefully prepared white wine, with quinine in it, which comes from Chateau Hydra in Algiers, or some of the Italian wines, Barolo for instance, or the excellent native wines which are produced in Savoy.

About Aix les Bains, where the cuisine is the best in Europe, many wines are manufactured which are honest wines with no headaches in them.

SOME ODDITIES IN THE ART OF ENTER-
TAINING.

"Comparisons are odorous."

I prithee let me bring thee where crabs grow;
And I with my long nails will dig thee pig nuts;
Show thee a jay's nest, and instruct thee how
To snare the nimble marmozet; I'll bring thee
To clustering filberds, and sometimes I'll get thee
Young staniels from the rocks. Wilt thou go with me?

THE TEMPEST.

In the lamb roasted whole we have one of the earliest dishes on record in the history of cookery. Stuffed with pistachio nuts, and served with pilaf, it illustrates the antiquity of the art, and at the same time gives an example of the food upon which millions of our fellow creatures are sustained.

At a dinner of the Acclimatization Society in London, all manner of strange and new dishes were offered, even the meat of the horse. A roast monkey filled with chestnuts was declared to be delicious; the fawn of fallow deer was described as good; buffalo meat was not so highly commended; a red-deer ham was considered very succulent; a sirloin of bear was "tough, glutinous, and had, besides, a dreadful, half-aromatic, half-putrescent flavour, as though it had been rubbed with assafœtida and then hung for a month in a musk shop."

We will not try bear unless we are put to it. However, at this same dinner—we read on—haunch of venison, saddle of mutton, roast beef of old England, which is really the roast beef which is of old Normandy now, all gave way to a Chinese lamb roasted whole, stuffed with pistachio nuts, and served with *consousson*, a preparation of wheat used among the Moors, Africans, and other natives of the north of Africa littoral, in place of rice. The Moorish young ladies are, it is said, fattened into beauty by an enforced meal of this strengthening compound. The *consousson* is made into balls and stuffed into the mouths of the marriageable young lady, until she grows as tired of balls as a young belle of three seasons.

In Spain, in those damp swamps near Valencia, where the poor are old before forty and die before forty-five, the best rice sells at eleven farthings, the poorest at eight farthings per pound. This, cooked with the ground dust of *pimientos*, or capsicums, is the foundation of every stew in the south of Spain. It is of a rich brick-dust hue, and is full of fire and flavour. Into this stew the cook puts the "reptiles of the sea" known as "spotted cats," "toads" and other oily fish, sold at two pence a pound, or the *vogar*, a silvery fish, or the *gallina*, a coarse fish, chick peas, garlic, pork, and sausages. If rich she will make an *olla podrida* with bacon, fresh meat, potatoes, cabbages, and she will pour off the soup, calling it *caldo*, then the lumps of meat and bacon, called *cocida*, will be served next. Then the cigarette is smoked. If you are a king she will add a quince and an apple to the stew.

Of puddings and pies they know nothing; but what fruit they have! — water-melons weighing fifteen pounds apiece; lemon pippins called *perillons*; crimson, yellow, and purple plums; purple and green figs; tomatoes by the million; carob beans, on which half the nation lives; small cucumbers and gourds; large black grapes, very sweet; white grapes and quinces; peaches in abundance; and all the chestnuts and filberts in the world. In the summer they eat goat's flesh; and on All Saints' Day they eat pork and chestnuts and sweet *babatas* of Malaga. In exile, in Mexico and Florida, the Spaniard eats alligator, which could scarcely be called a game bird; but the flesh of young alligators' tails is very fair, and tastes like chicken if the tail is cut off immediately after death, and stewed.

The frost fish of the Adirondacks is seldom tasted, except by those who have spent a winter in the North Woods. They are delicious when fried. There is a European fish as little known as this, the *Marena*, caught in Lake Moris in the province of Pomerania, also in one lake in southern Italy, which is very good.

There are two birds known in Prussia, the bustard, and the kammel, the former a species of small ostrich, once considered very fine eating, the latter very tough, except under unusual conditions.

The Chinese enjoy themselves by night. All their feasts and festivals are kept then, generally by moonlight. When a Chinaman is poor he can live on a farthing's worth of rice a day; when he gets rich he becomes the most luxurious of sybarites, indulges freely in the most *recherché* delicacies of the table, and becomes, like any Roman voluptuary, corpulent and phlegmatic. A lady thus describes a Chinese dinner: —

"The hour was eleven A. M., the *locale* a boat. Having heard much of the obnoxious stuff I was to eat, I adopted the prescription of a friend. 'Eat very little of any dish, and be a long time about it.'

"We commenced with tea, and finished with soup. Some of the intermediate dishes were shark's-fin; birds' nests brought from Borneo, costing nearly a guinea a mouthful, fricassee of poodle, a little dog almost a pig; the fish of the conch-shell, a substance like wax or india rubber, which you might masticate but never mash; peacock's liver, very fine and *recherché*; putrid eggs, nevertheless very good; rice, of course, salted shrimps, baked almonds, cabbage in a variety of forms, green ginger, stewed fungi, fresh fish of a dozen kinds, onions *ad libitum*, salt duck cured like ham, and pig in every form, roast, boiled, and fried, Foo-Chow ham which seemed to me equal to Wiltshire. In fact, the Chinese excel in pork, though the English there never touch it, under the supposition that the pigs are fed on little babies.

"But this is a libel. Of course a pig would eat a baby, as it would a rattlesnake if it came across one; but the Chinese are very particular about their swine and keep them penned up, rivalling the Dutch in their scrubbing and washing. They grow whole fields of taro and herbs for their pigs. And I do not believe that one porker in a million ever tastes a baby."

This traveller's sympathies appear to be with the pig.

"About two o'clock we arose from the table, walked about, looked out of the window. Large brass bowls were brought with water and towels. Each one proceeded to perform ablutions, the Chinese washing their heads; after which refreshing operation we resumed our seats and re-commenced with another description of tea.

"Seven different sorts of Samchou we partook of, made from rice, from peas, from mangoes, cocoa-nut, all fermented liquors, and the mystery remained,—I was not inebriated. The Samchou was drunk warm in tiny cups, during the whole course of the dinner.

"The whole was cooked without salt and tasted very insipid to me. The bird's-nest seemed like glue or isinglass, but the coxcombs were palatable. The dog-meat was like some very delicate gizzards well-stewed, and of a short, close fibre. The dish which I most fancied turned out to be rat. Upon taking a second help, after the first taste I got the head, which made me rather sick; but I consoled myself that when in California we ate ground squirrels which are first cousins to the flat-tailed rats; and travellers who would know the world must go in for manners and customs. We had tortoise and frogs,—a curry of the latter was superior to chicken; we had fowls' hearts, and the brains of some birds, snipe, I think. We had a chow-chow of mangoes, rambustan preserved, salted cucumber, sweet potatoes, yams, taro, all sorts of sweets made of rice sugar, and cocoa-nuts; and the soup which terminated the entertainment was certainly boiled tripe or some other internal arrangement; and I wished I had halted some little time before. The whole was eaten with chop-sticks or a spoon like a small spade or shovel. The sticks are made into a kind of fork, being held crosswise between the fingers. It is not the custom for the sexes to meet at meals; I dined with the ladies."

This dinner has one suggestion for our hostesses,—it was in a boat, on a river, by torchlight. We can, however, give a better one on a yacht at Newport, or at New London, or down on the Florida coast; but it would be a pretty fancy to give it on our river. It is curious to see what varieties there are in the art of entertaining; and it is useful to remember, when in Florida, "that alligators' tails are as good, when stewed, as chicken."

The eating of the past included, under the Romans, the ass, the dog, the snail, hedge-hogs, oysters, asparagus, venison, wild-boar, sea-nettles. In England, in 1272, the hostess offered strange dishes: mallards, herons, swans, crane, and peacock. The peacock was, of old, a right royal bird which figured splendidly at the banquets of the great, and this is how the mediæval cooks dished up the dainty:—

"Flay off the skin, with the feathers, tail, neck, and head thereon. Then take the skin and all the feathers and lay it on the table, strewing thereon ground cumin; then take the peacock and roast him, and baste him with raw yolks of eggs, and when he is roasted take him off and let him cool awhile. Then sew him in his skin, and gild his comb, and so send him forth for the last course."

Our Saxon ancestors were very fond, like the Spaniards, of putting everything into the same pot; and we read of stews that make the blood boil. Travellers tell us of dining with the Esquimaux, on a field of ice, when tallow candles were considered delicious, or they found their plates loaded with liver of the walrus. They vary their dinners by helping themselves to a lump of whale-meat, red and coarse and rancid, but very toothsome to an Esquimau, notwithstanding.

If they should sit down to a Greenlander's table they would find it groaning under a dish of half-putrid whale's tail, which has been lauded as a savoury matter, not unlike cream cheese; and the liver of a porpoise makes the mouth water. They may finish their repast with a slice of reindeer, or roasted rat, and drink to their host in a bumper of train oil.

In South America the tongue of a sea-lion is esteemed a great delicacy. Fashion in Siam prescribes a curry of ants' eggs as necessary to every well-ordered banquet. The eggs are not larger than grains of pepper, and to an unaccustomed palate have no particular flavour. Besides being curried, they are brought to table rolled in green leaves mingled with shreds or very fine slices of pork.

The Mexicans make a species of bread of the eggs of insects which frequent the fresh water of the lagoons. The natives cultivate in the lagoon of Chalco a sort of carex called *tonte*, on which the insects deposit their eggs very freely. This carex is made into bundles and is soon covered. The eggs are disengaged, beaten, dried, and pounded into flour.

Penguins' eggs, cormorants' eggs, gulls' eggs, the eggs of the albatross, turtles' eggs are all made subservient to the table. The mother turtle deposits her eggs, about a hundred at a time, in the dry sand, and leaves them to be hatched by the genial sun. The Indian tribes who live on the banks of the Orinoco procure from them a sweet and limpid oil which is their substitute for butter. Lizards' eggs are regarded as a *bonne bouche* in the South Sea Islands, and the eggs of the *guana*, a species of lizard, are much favoured by West Indians. Alligators' eggs are eaten in the Antilles and resemble hens' eggs in size and shape.

We have spoken of horse-flesh as introduced at the dinner of the Acclimatization Society, but it is hardly known that the Frenchmen have tried to make it as common as beef. Isidore St. Helain says of it, that it has long been regarded as of a sweetish, disagreeable taste, very tough, and not to be eaten without difficulty; but so many different facts are opposed to this prejudice that it is impossible not to perceive the slightness of the foundation. The free or wild horse is hunted as game in all parts of the world where it exists, — Asia, Africa, and America, and perhaps even now in Europe. The domestic horse is itself made use of for alimentary purposes in all those countries.

"Its flesh is relished by races the most diverse, — Negro, Mongol, Malay, American, Caucasian. It was much esteemed until the eighth century amongst the ancestors of some of the greatest nations of Western Europe, who had it in general use and gave it up with regret. Soldiers to whom it has been served out and people who have bought it in markets, have taken it for beef; and many people buy it daily in Paris for venison."

During the commune many people were glad enough to get horse-flesh for the roast.

Locusts are eaten by many tribes of North American Indians, and there is no reason why they should not be very good. The bushmen of Africa rejoice in roasting spiders; maggots tickle the palates of the Australian aborigines; and the Chinese feast on the chrysalis of a silk-worm.

If this is what they ate, what then did they drink? No thin potations, no half-filled cups for the early English. Wine-bibbers and beer-bibbers, three-bottle men they were down to one hundred years ago. Provocatives of drink were called "shoeing horses," "whetters," "drawers off and pullers on."

Massinger puts forth a curious test of these provocatives:—

> "I asked
> Such an unexpected dainty bit for breakfast
> As never yet I cooked; 'tis red botargo,
> Fried frogs, potatoes marroned, cavear,
> Carps' tongues, the pith of an English chine of beef,
> Now one Italian delicate wild mushroom,
> And yet a drawer on too; and if you show not
> An appetite, and a strong one, I'll not say
> To eat it, but devour it, without grace too,
> For it will not stay a preface. I am shamed,
> And all my past provocatives will be jeered at."

Ben Jonson affords us many a glimpse of the drinking habits of all classes in his day.

After the Restoration, England seems to have abandoned herself to one great saturnalia, and men drank deeply, from the king down. The novels of Fielding and Smollett are full of the wildest debauchery and drunken extravagance. Statesmen drank deep at their councils, ladies drank in their boudoirs, the criminal on his way to Tyburn stopped to drink a parting glass. Hogarth in his wonderful pictures has held the mirror up to society to show how general was the shame, how terrible the curse.

In Germany the *Baierisch bier*, drunk out of *biergläschen* ornamented as they are with engraved wreaths, *"Zum Andenken," "Aus Freundschaft,"* and other little bits of national harmless sentiment, has come down from the remotest antiquity, and has never failed to provoke quiet and decorous, if sleepy hilarity.

We are afraid that the "Dew of Ben Nevis" is not so peaceful, nor the juice of the juniper, nor New England rum, nor the *aquadiente* of the Mexican, nor the *vodka* of the Russian. All these have the most terrible wild madness in them. To the honour of civilization, it is no longer the fashion to drink to excess. The vice of drunkenness rarely meets the eye of a refined woman; and let us hope that less and less may it be the bane of society, the disgrace of the art of entertaining.

THE SERVANT QUESTION.

Verily
I swear, 't is better to be lowly born,
And range with humble livers in content,
Than to be perked up in a glistering grief
And wear a golden sorrow.

HENRY VIII.

It is impossible to do much with the art of entertaining without servants, and where shall we get them? In a country village, not two hundred miles from New York, I have seen well-to-do citizens going to a little restaurant in the main street for their dinners during an entire summer, because they could not get women to stay in their houses as servants. They are willing to pay high wages, they are generous livers, but such a thing as domestic service is out of the question. If any lady comes from the city bringing two or three maids, they are of far more interest in the village than their mistress, and are besieged, waited upon, intrigued with, to leave their place, to come and serve the village lady.

What is the reason? The American farmer's daughter will not go out to service, will not be called a servant, will not work in another person's house as she will in her own. The Irish maid prefers the town, and dislikes the country, where there is no Catholic church. Such a story repeated all over the land is the story of American service.

We have, however, every day, ships arriving in New York harbour which pour out on our shores the poor of all nations. The men seem to take readily enough to any sort of work. Italians shovel snow and work on railroads, but their wives and daughters make poor domestic servants.

The best that we can get are the Irish who have been long in the country. Then come the Germans, who now outnumber the Irish. French, Swedes, Danes, Norwegians, all come in shoals.

Of all these the French are by far the best. Of course, as cooks they are unrivalled; as butler, waiter, footman, a well-trained French serving-man is the very best. He is neat, economical, and respectful. He knows his value and he is very expensive. But if you can afford him, take him and keep him.

French maids are admirable as seamstresses, and in all the best and highest walks of domestic service, but they are difficult as to the other servants. They make trouble about their food; they do not tell the truth, as a rule.

A good Irish nurse is the best and most tender, the most to be relied on. Children love Irish servants; it is the best recommendation we can give them. They are not good cooks as a rule, and are wanting in head, management, and neatness; but they are willing; and a wise mistress can make of them almost anything she desires.

The Germans surpass them very much in thrift and in concentration, but the Germans are stolid, and very far from being as gentle and willing as the Irish. If a housekeeper gets a number of German servants in training and thinks them perfect, she need not be astonished if some fine morning she rises and finds them gone off to parts unknown.

The Swedes are more reliable up to a certain point; they are never stupid, they are rather fantastic, and very eccentric. They are also full of poetry, and indulge in sublime longings. The Swedish language is made up of eloquence and poetry as soft as the Italian; it has also something of the flow and the magnificence of the Spanish. It is freighted with picturesque and brilliant metaphor, and is richer than ours in its expressions of gentleness, politeness, and courtesy. They have a great talent for arguing with gentleness and courtesy, and of protesting with politeness, and they learn our language with singular ease. I once had a Swedish maid who argued me out of my desire to have the dining-room swept, in better language than I could use myself. One must, in hiring servants, take into account all these national characteristics. The Swedes are full of talent, they can do your work if they wish to, but ten chances to one they do not wish to.

Gustavus Adolphus and Charles XII. were two types of Swedish character. The Swedes of to-day, like them, are full of dignity and lofty aspiration; they love brilliant display; they have audacious and adventurous spirits; one can imagine them marching to victory; but all this makes them, in this country, "too smart" to be servants.

They are excellent cooks. A Swedish woman formerly came to my house to cook for dinner parties, and she was equal to any French *chef*. Her price was five dollars; she would do all my marketing for me, and serve the dinner most perfectly,—that is, render it up to the men waiters. I rarely had any fault to find; if I had, it was I who was in the wrong. She came often to instruct my Irish cook; but had I attempted any further intercourse, I felt that it would have been I who would have had to leave the house, and not my excellent cook. They have every qualification for service excepting this: they will not obey,—they are captains.

The Norwegians are very different. We must again remember that at home they are poor, frugal, religious, and capable of all sacrifice; they will work patiently here for seven years in order to go back to Norway, to that poetical land, whose beauty is so unspeakable. These girls who come from the herds, who have spent the summer on the plains in a small hut and alone, making butter and cheese, are strong, patient, handsome, fresh creatures, with voices as sweet as lutes, and most obedient and good,—their thoughts ever of father and mother and home. Would there were more of them. If they were a little less awkward in an American house they would be perfect.

As for the men, they are the best farm-laborers in the world. They have a high, noble, patient courage, a very slow mind, and are fond of argument. The Norwegian is the Scotchman of Scandinavia, as the Swede is the Irishman. There are no better adopted citizens than the Norwegians, but they live here only to go back to Norway when they have made enough. Deeply religious, they are neither narrow nor ignoble. They would be perfect servants if well trained.

The Danes are not so simple; they are a mercantile people, and are desperately fond of bargaining. They are also, however, most interesting. Their taste for art is vastly more developed than that of either the Swedes or the Norwegians. A Danish parlour-maid will arrange the *bric-à-brac* and stand and look at it. To go higher in their home history, they are making great painters. As servants they are hardly known enough amongst us to be criticised; those I have seen have been neat, faithful, and far more obedient than their cleverer Swedish sisters.

Could I have my choice for servants about a country house they should be Norwegians, in a city house, French.

In Chicago, the ladies speak highly of the German servants, if they do not happen to be Nihilists, which is a dreadful possibility. At the South they still have the negro, most excellent when good, most objectionable when bad. Certainly freedom has not improved him as to manners, and a coloured coachman in Washington can be far more disagreeable than an Irishman, or a French cabby during the Exposition, which is saying a great deal.

The excellence, the superiority, the respectful manners of English servants at home has induced many ladies to bring over parlour maids, nurses, cooks, from England, with, however, but small success. I need but copy the following from the "London Queen," to show how different is the way of speaking of a servant, and to a servant in London from that which obtains in New York. It is *verbatim:*—

"The servants should rise at six-thirty, and the cook a little earlier; she then lights the kitchen fire, opens the house, sweeps the hall, cleans the steps, prepares upstairs and downstairs breakfast. Meantime the house parlourmaid does the dining-room, takes up hot water to bedrooms, lays the table, and so forth, while the housemaid dusts the day nursery and takes up the children's breakfast. Supposing the family breakfast is not wanted before eight-thirty, that meal should be taken, in both kitchen and nursery, before eight o'clock. As soon as this is over the cook must tidy her kitchen, look over her stores, contents of pantry, etc., and be ready by nine-thirty to take her orders for the day. She will answer the kitchen bell at all times, and perhaps the front door in the morning, and will be answerable besides for ordinary kitchen work, for the hall, kitchen stairs, all the basement, and according to arrangement possibly the dining-room. She must have fixed days for doing the above work, cleaning tins, etc. The cook also clears away the breakfast. As soon as the housemaid has taken up the family breakfast, she, the housemaid, must begin the bedrooms, where the second scullery-maid may help her as soon as she has done helping the cook. The house parlour-maid will be responsible for the drawing-room and sitting-room and all the bedrooms, also stairs and landing, having regular days for cleaning out one of each weekly, being helped by the second scullery-maid. She should be dressed in time for lunch, wait on it, and clear away. She will answer the front door in the afternoon, take up five o'clock tea, lay the table and wait at dinner. The scullery maid must clear the kitchen meals and help in all the washing up, take up nursery tea, help the cook prepare late dinner, carry up the dishes for late dinner, clear and wash up kitchen supper. The nurse has her dinner in the kitchen. Servants' meals should be breakfast, before the family, dinner directly after upstairs lunch, tea at five, supper at nine. They should go to bed regularly at ten o'clock. Now as to their fare. For breakfast a little bacon or an egg, or some smoked fish; for dinner, meat, vegetables, potatoes, and pudding. If a joint has been sent up for lunch, it is usual for it to go down to the servants' table.

"Allow one pint and a half of beer to each servant who asks for it, or one bottle. Tea, butter, and sugar are given out to them. The weekly bills for the servants shall be about two dollars and a half."

The neatness of all this careful housekeeping would be delightful if it could be carried out with us, or if the servant would accept it. But imagine a New York mistress achieving it! The independent voter would revolt, his wife would never accept it. English servants lose all their good manners when they come over here, and do not appear at all as they do in London.

American servants are always expected to eat what goes down from the master's table, and there is no such thing as making one servant wait upon another in our free and independent country. There are households in America where many servants are kept in order by a very clever mistress, but it is rarely an order which lasts for long. It is a vexed question, and the freedom with which we take a servant, without knowing much of her character, must explain a great deal of it. Foreign servants find out soon their legal rights, and their importance. Here where labour is scarce, it is not so easy to get a good footman, parlour maid, or cook; the great variety and antipathy of race comes in. The Irishman will not work on a railroad with the Italian, and we all know the history of the "Heathen Chinee." That is repeated in every household.

Mr. Winans, in Scotland, hires a place which reaches from the North Sea to the Atlantic; he spends two hundred thousand dollars a year on it. He has perhaps three hundred servants, every one of them perfect. Imagine his having such a place here! How many good servants could he find; how long would they stay? How long does a French *chef*, at ten thousand dollars a year, stay? Only one year. He prefers to return to France.

Indeed, French servants, poorly paid and very poorly fed at home, are the hardest to keep in this country; they all wish to go back. It is a curious fact that they grow impertinent and do not seem to enjoy the life. They go back to Europe, and resume their good manners as if nothing had happened. It must be in the air.

It is, however, possible for a lady to get good servants and to keep them for a while, if she has great executive ability and a natural leadership; but the whole question is one which has not yet been at all mastered.

There is no "hook and eye" between the ship loaded down with those who want work and those who want work done. The great lack of respect in the manners of servants in hotels is especially noticeable to one returning from Europe. A woman, a sort of care-taker on a third-story floor, will sing while a lady is talking to her, not because she wishes to sing at all, but to establish her independence. In Europe she would say, "Yes, my Lady," or "No, my Lady" when spoken to.

It is to be feared that the Declaration of Independence is between us and good service. We must be content if we find one or two amiable Irish, or old negroes, who will serve us because of the love they bear us, and for our children's sake, whom they love as if they were their very own.

This is, however, but taking the seamy side, and the humbler side. Many opulent people in America employ thirty servants, and their house goes on with much of European elegance. It is not unusual in a fine New York house to find a butler and four men in the dining-room; a *chef* and his assistants in the kitchen; a head groom and his men in the stables; a coachman, who is a very important functionary; and three women in the nursery besides the nursery governess, who acts as the amanuensis of the lady; the lady's maid, whose sole duty is to wait on her lady, and perhaps her young lady; a parlour maid or two; and two chambermaids, a laundress and her assistants.

Of course the men in such a vast establishment do not sleep in the house, perhaps with one or two exceptions; the valet and the head footman may be kept at home, as they may be needed in the night, for errands, etc. But our American houses are not built to accommodate so many. One lady, the head of such an establishment, said that she had "never seen her laundress." A different staircase led to the servants' room; her maid did all the interviewing with this important personage.

If a lady can find a competent housekeeper to direct this large household, it is all very well, but that is yet almost impossible, and the life of a fashionable woman in New York, who is the head of such a house, is apt to be slavery. The housekeeper and the butler are seldom friends, therefore the hostess has to reconcile these two conflicting powers before she can give a dinner; the head footman walks off disgusted and leaves a vacant place, etc.

The households of men of foreign birth, who understand dealing with different nationalities, are apt to get on very well with thirty servants; doubtless such men import their own servants.

In a household where one man alone is kept, he is expected to open the front door and to do all the work of the dining-room, and must have an assistant in the pantry. The cook, if a woman, generally demands and needs one; if a man, he demands two, for a *chef* will not do any of the menial work of cookery. He is a pampered official.

In England, the housekeeper engages the servants and supervises them. She has charge of the stores and the house linen, and in general is responsible for the economical and exact management of all household details, and for the comfort of guests and the family. She is expected to see that her employers are not cheated, and this in our country makes her unpopular. A bad housekeeper is worse than none, as of course her powers of stealing are endless.

The butler is responsible for the silver and wine. He must be absolute over the footman. It is he who directs the carving and passing of dishes, and then stands behind the chair of his mistress. All the men-servants must be clean shaven; none are permitted to wear a mustache, that being the privilege of the gentlemen.

A lady's maid is not expected to do her own washing, or make her own bed in Europe; but in this country, being required to do all that, and to eat with the other servants, she is apt to complain. A French maid always complains of the table. She must dress hair, understand dress-making, and clear starching, be a good packer, and always at hand to dress her lady and to sit up for her when she returns from parties. Her wages are very high and she is apt to become a tyrant.

It is very difficult to define for an American household the duties of servants, which are so well defined in England and on the continent. Every lady has her own individual ideas on this subject, and servants have *their* individual ideas, which they do not have in Europe. I heard an opulent gentleman who kept four men-servants in his house, and three in his stable, complain one snowy winter that he had not one who would shovel snow from his steps, each objecting that it was not his business; so he wrote a note to a friendly black man, who came around, and rendered it possible for the master of the house to go down to business. This was an extreme case, but it illustrates one of the phases of our curious civilization.

The butler is the important person, and it will be well for the lady to hold him responsible; he should see to it that the footmen are neat and clean. Most servants in American houses wear black dress-coats, and white cravats, but some of our very rich men have now all their flunkies in livery, a sort of cut-away dress-coat, a waistcoat of another colour, small clothes, long stockings, and low shoes. Powdered footmen have not yet appeared.

If we were in England we should say that the head footman is to attend the door, and in houses where much visiting goes on he could hardly do anything more. Ladies, however, simplify this process by keeping a "buttons," a small boy, who has, as Dickens says, "broken out in an eruption of buttons" on his jacket, who sits the livelong day the slave of the bell.

The second man seems to do all the work, such as scrubbing silver, sweeping, arranging the fireplaces, and washing dishes; and what the third man does, except to black boots, I have never been able to discover. I think he serves as valet to the gentlemen and the growing boys, runs with notes, and is "Jeames Yellowplush" generally. I was once taken over her vast establishment by an English countess, who was most kind in explaining to me her domestic arrangements; but I did not think she knew herself what that third man did. I noticed that there were always several footmen waiting at dinner.

"They also serve who only stand and wait."

One thing I do remember in the housekeeper's room. There sat a very grand dame carving, and giving the servants their dinner. She rose and stood while my lady spoke to her, but at a wave of the hand from the countess all the others remained seated. The butler was at the other end of the table looking very sheepish. The dinner was a boiled leg of mutton, and some sort of meat pie, and a huge Yorkshire pudding,—no vegetables but potatoes; pitchers of ale, and bread and cheese, finished this meal. The third footman, I remember, brought in afternoon tea; perhaps he filled that place which is described in one of Miss Mulock's novels:—

"Dolly was hired as an off maid, to do everything which the other servants would not do."

The etiquette of the stable servants was also explained to me in England. The coachman is as powerful a person in the equine realm as is the butler in the house. The head groom and his assistants always raise their finger to their hats when spoken to by master, or mistress, or the younger members of the family, or visitors, and in the case of royalty all stand with hats off, the coachman on the box slightly raising his, until the Prince of Wales, or his peers, are seated.

In some houses I was told that the upper servants had their meals prepared by a kitchen maid, and that they had a different table from the scullery maids.

The nursery governess was a person to be pitied; she was an educated girl, still the servant of the head nurse. She passed her entire life with the children, yet ate by herself, unless perhaps with the very young children. The head governess ate luncheon with the family, and came in to the parlour with the young ladies in the evening. Generally this personage was expected to sing and play for the amusement of the company. Now, imagine a set of servants thus trained, brought to America. The men soon learn that their vote is as good as the master's, and if they are Irishmen it is a great deal better. They soon cease to be respectful. This is the first break in the chain. A man, a Senator, was asked out to dinner in Albany; the lady of the house said, "I have a great respect for Senator — —; he used to wait on this table."

That is a glorious thing for the flag, for the United States, but there is a missing link in the golden chain of household order. It is a difficult task to produce here the harmony of an English household. Our service at home is like our diplomatic service; we have no trained diplomats, no gradation of service, but in the case of our foreign ministers, they have risen to be the best in the world. We have plenty of talent at top; it is the root of the tree which puzzles us.

We may make up our minds that no longer will the American girl go out to service. It is a thousand pities that she will not. It is not ignoble to do household work well. The châtelaines of the Middle Ages cooked and served the meals with their own fair hands. Training-schools are greatly needed; we should follow the nurses' training-school.

Our dinner-tables in America are generally long and narrow, fitted to the shape of the dining-room. Once I saw in England, in a great house, a table so narrow that one could almost have shaken hands with one's opposite neighbour. The ornaments were high, slender vases filled with grasses and orchids, far above our heads. One or two matchless ornaments of Dresden, the gifts of monarchs, alone ornamented the table. This was a very sociable dinner-table and rather pleasing. Then came the round table, so vast that the footmen must have mounted up on it to place the centre piece, like poor distraught Lady Caroline Lamb, whose husband came in to find her walking up and down the table, telling the butler to "produce pyramidal effects." There is also the fine broad parallelogram, suited to a baronial hall; and this is copied in our best country houses. As no conversation of a confidential character is ever allowed at an English table until all the servants have left the room, so it is not considered good-breeding to allow a servant to talk to the mistress or the young ladies of what she hears in the servants' hall. The gossip of couriers and maids at a foreign watering-place reaches American ears, and unluckily gets into American newspapers sometimes. It is a wise precaution on the part of the English never to listen to this. As we have conquered everything else in America, perhaps we shall conquer the servant question, to the advantage of both parties. We should try to keep our servants a longer time with us.

There are some houses where the law of change goes on forever, and there are some where the domestic machine runs without friction. The hostess may be a person with a talent for governing, and may be inspired with a sixth sense. If she is she can make her composite family respectful, helpful, and happy; but it must be confessed that it is as yet a vexed question, one which gives us trouble and will give us more. Those people are the happiest who can get on with three or four servants, and very many families live well and elegantly with this number, while more live well with two.

To mark the difference in feeling as between those who employ and those who serve, one little anecdote may apply. At a watering-place in Europe I once met an English family, of the middle class. The lady said to her maid, "Bromley, your master wishes you to be in at nine o'clock this evening."

Bromley said, "Yes, my lady."

An American lady stood near with her maid, who flushed deeply.

"What is the matter, Jane?" asked her lady.

"I never could stand having any one called my master," said the American.

This intimate nerve of self-love, this egotism, this false idea of independence affects women more than men, and in a country where both can go from the humblest position to the highest, it produces a "glistering grief." The difficulty of getting good servants prevents many families from keeping house. It brings on us the foreign reproach that we live in hotels and boarding-houses. It is at this moment the great unsolved American Question. What shall we do with it?

SOMETHING ABOUT COOKS.

"Last night I weighed, quite wearied out,
The question that perplexes still;
And that sad spirit we call doubt
Made the good naught beside the ill.

"This morning, when with rested mind,
I try again the selfsame theme,
The whole is altered, and I find
The balance turned, the good supreme."

What amateur cook has not had these moments of depression and exaltation as she has weighed the flour and sugar, stoned the raisins, and mixed the cake, or, even worse in her young novitiate, has attempted to make a soup and has begun with the formula which so often turns out badly:—

"Take a shin of beef and put it in a pot with three dozen carrots, a dozen onions, two dozen pieces of celery, twelve turnips, a fowl, and two partridges. It must simmer six hours, etc." Yes, and last week and the week before her husband said, "it was miserable." How willingly would she allow the claim of that glorious old coxcomb, Louis Eustache Ude, who had been cook to two French kings and never forgave the world for not permitting him to call himself an artist.

"Scrapers of catgut," he says, "call themselves artists, and fellows who jump like a kangaroo claim the title; yet the man who has under his sole direction the great feasts given by the nobility of England to the allied sovereigns, and who superintended the grand banquet at Crockford's on the occasion of the coronation of Victoria, was denied the title prodigally showered on singers, dancers, and comedians, whose only quality, not requiring the microscope to discern, is vanity."

Ude was the most eccentric of cooks. He was *maître d'hôtel* to the Duke of York, who delighted in his anecdotes and mimicry. In his book, which he claims is the only work which gives due dignity to the great art, he says: "The chief fault in all great peoples' cooks is that they are too profuse in their preparations. Suppers are after all only ridiculous proofs of the extravagance and bad taste of the givers." He mentions great wastes which have seared his already seared conscience thus:

"I have known balls where the next day, in spite of the pillage of a pack of footmen, which was enormous, I have seen thirty hams, one hundred and fifty to two hundred carved fowls, and forty or fifty tongues given away. Jellies melt on all the tables; pastries, patties, aspics, and lobster salads are heaped up in the kitchen and strewed about in the passages; and all this an utter waste, for not even the footmen would eat this; they do not consider it a legitimate repast to dine off the remnants of a last night's feast. Footmen are like cats; they only like what they steal, but are indifferent to what is given them."

This was written by the cook of the bankrupt Duke of York, noted for his extravagance; but how well it would apply to-day to the banquet of many a *nouveau riche*, to how many a hotel, to how much of our American housekeeping. Ude was a poet and an enthusiast. Colonel Damer met him walking up and down at Crockford's in a great rage, and asked what was the matter. "Matter! *Ma foi!*" answered he; "you saw that man just gone out? Well he ordered red mullet for his dinner. I made him a delicious little sauce with my own hand. The mullet was marked on the carte two shillings. I added sixpence for the sauce. He refuses to pay sixpence for the sauce. The imbecile! He seems to think red mullets come out of the sea with my sauce in their pockets."

Carême, one of the greatest of French cooks, became eminent by inventing a sauce for fast-days. He then devoted several years to the science of roasting in all its branches. He studied design and elegance under Robert Lainé. His career was one of victory after victory. He nurtured the Emperor Alexander, kept alive Talleyrand through "that long disease, his life," fostered Lord Londonderry, and delighted the Princess Belgratine. A salary of a thousand pounds a year induced him to become *chef* to the Regent; but he left Carlton House, he would return to France. The Regent was inconsolable, but Carême was implacable. "No," said the true patriot, "my soul is French, and I can only exist in France." Carême, therefore, overcome by his feelings, accepted an unprecedented salary from Baron Rothschild and settled in Paris.

Lady Morgan, dining at the Baron's villa in 1830, has left us a sketch of a dinner by Carême which is so well done that, although I have already alluded to it, I will copy *verbatim*: "It was a very sultry evening, but the Baron's dining-room stood apart from the house and was shaded by orange trees. In the oblong pavilion of Grecian marble refreshed by fountains, no gold or silver heated or dazzled the eye, but porcelain beyond the price of all precious metals. There was no high-spiced sauce in the dinner, no dark-brown gravy, no flavour of cayenne and allspice, no tincture of catsup and walnut pickle, no visible agency of those vulgar elements of cooking of the good old times, fire and water. Distillations of the most delicate viands had been extracted in silver, with chemical precision. Every meat presented its own aroma," — it was not cooked in a gas stove, — "every vegetable its own shade of verdure. The mayonnaise was fixed in ice, like Ninon's description of Sevigné's heart, '*une citronille frité à la neige.*' The tempered chill of the *plombière* which held the place of the eternal *fondus* and *soufflets* of our English tables, anticipated and broke the stronger shock of the exquisite avalanche, which, with the hue and odour of fresh-gathered nectarines, satisfied every sense and dissipated every coarser flavour. With less genius than went to the composition of that dinner, men have written epic poems."

Comparing Carême with the great Beauvilliers, the greatest restaurant cook in Paris from 1782 to 1815, a great authority in the matter says: "There was more *aplomb* in the touch of Beauvilliers, more curious felicity in Carême's. Beauvilliers was great in an *entrée*, Carême sublime in an *entremet*; we should put Beauvilliers against the world for a *rôti*, but should wish Carême to prepare the sauce were we under the necessity of eating an elephant or our great grandfather."

Vatel was the great Condé's cook who killed himself because the turbot did not arrive. Madame de Sevigné relates the event with her usual clearness. Louis XIV. had long promised a visit to the great Condé at Chantilly, the very estate which the Duc d'Aumale has so recently given back to France, but postponed it from time to time fearing to cause Condé trouble by the sudden influx of a gay and numerous retinue. The old château had become a trifle dull and a trifle mouldy, but it got itself brushed up. Vatel was cook, and his first mortification was that the roast was wanting at several tables. It seemed to him that his great master the captain would be dishonoured, but the king had brought a larger retinue than he had promised. "He had thought of nothing but to make this visit a great success." Gourville, one of the prince's household, finding Vatel so excited, asked the prince to reassure him, which he did very kindly, telling him that the king was delighted with his supper. But Vatel mournfully answered: "Monseigneur, your kindness overpowers me, but the roast was wanting at two tables." The next morning he arose at five to superintend the king's dinner. The purveyor of fish was at the door with only two baskets. "And is this all?" asked Vatel. "Yes," said the sleepy man. Vatel waited at the gates an hour; no more fish. Two or three hundred guests, and only two packages. He whispered to himself, "The joke in Paris will be that Vatel tried to save the prince the price of two red mullets a month." His hand fell on his rapier hilt, he rushed up-stairs, fell on the blade; as he expired the cart loaded with turbot came into the yard. Voila!

Times have changed. Cooks now prefer living on their masters to dying for them.

The Prince de Loubise, inventor of a sauce the discovery of which has made him more glorious than twenty victories, asked his cook to draw him up a bill of fare, a sort of rough estimate for a supper. Bertrand's first estimate was fifty hams. "What, Bertrand! Are you going to feast the whole army of the Rhine? Your brains are surely turning." Bertrand was blandly contemptuous. "My brains are surely turning? No, Monseigneur, only one ham will appear on the table, but the rest are indispensable for my *espagnoles*, my garnishing."

"Bertrand, you are plundering me," stormed the prince. "This article shall not pass." The blood of the cook was up. "My lord," said he, sternly, "you do not understand the resources of our art. Give the word and I will so melt down these hams that they will go into a little glass bottle no bigger than my thumb." The prince was abashed by the genius of the spit, and the fifty hams were purchased.

The Duke of Wellington liked a good dinner, and employed an artist named Felix. Lord Seaforth, finding Felix too expensive, allowed him to go to the Iron Duke, but Felix came back with tears in his eyes.

"What is the matter," said Lord Seaforth; "has the Duke turned rusty?"

"No, no, my lord! but I serve him a dinner which would make Francatelli or Ude die of envy, and he say nothing. I go to the country and leave him to try a dinner cooked by a stupid, dirty cook-maid, and he say nothing; that is what hurt my feelings."

Felix lived on approbation; he would have been capable of dying like Vatel.

Going last winter to see *le Bourgeoise Gentilhomme* at the Comédie Française, I was struck with the novelty of the dinner served by this hero of Molière's who is so anxious to get rid of his money. All the dishes were brought in by little fellows dressed as cooks, who danced to the minuet.

In a later faithful chronicle I learn that a certain marquis of the days of Louis XVI. invented a musical spit which caused all the snowy-garbed cooks to move in rhythmical steps. All was melody and order. "The fish simmered in six-eight time, the ponderous roasts circled gravely, the stews blended their essences to solemn anthems. The ears were gratified as the nose was regaled; this was an idea worthy of Apecius."

So Molière, true to the spirit of his time, paid this compliment to the Marquis.

Béchamel was cook to Louis XIV., and invented a famous sauce.

Durand, who was cook to the great Napoleon, has left a curious record of his tempestuous eating. Francatelli succeeded Ude in England, was the *chef* at Chesterfield House, at Lord Kinnaird's, and at the Melton Club. He held the post of *maître d'hôtel* for a while but was dismissed by a cabal.

The gay writer from whose pages we have gathered these desultory facts winds up with an advice to all who keep French cooks. "Make your *chef* your friend. Take care of him. Watch over the health of this man of genius. Send for the physician when he is ill."

Imagine the descent from these poets to the good plain cook, — you can depend upon the truth of this description, — with a six weeks' reference from her last place. Imagine the greasy soups, the mutton cutlets hard as a board, the few hard green peas, the soggy potatoes. How awful the recollections of one who came in "a week on trial!" Whose trial? Those who had to eat her food. It is bad to be without a cook, but ten times worse to have a bad one.

But if Louis Eustache Ude, the cook *par excellence* of all this little study, lamented over the waste in great kitchens, how much more should he revolt at that wholesale destruction of food which might go to feed the hungry, nourish and sustain the sick, and perhaps save many a child's life. What should be done with the broken meats of a great household? The cook is too apt to toss all into a tub or basket, to swell her own iniquitous profits. The half-tongues, ends of ham, roast beef, chicken-legs, the real honest relics of a generous kitchen would feed four or five poor families a week. What gifts of mercy to hospitals would be the half of a form of jelly, the pudding, the blanc mange, which are thrown away by the careless!

In France the Little Sisters of the Poor go about with clean dishes and clean baskets, to collect these morsels which fall from the rich man's table. It is a worthy custom.

While studying the names of these great men like Ude and Carême, Vatel and

Francatelli, what shades of dead *pâtissiers*, spirits of extinct *confiseurs*, rise around us in savoury streams and revive for us the past of gastronomic pleasure! Many a Frenchman will tell you of the iced meringues of the Palais Royal and the *salades de fraises au marasquin* of the Grand Seize as if they were things of the past. The French, gayer and lighter handed at the moulding of pastry, are apt to exceed all nations in this delicate, delicious *entremet*. The *vol au vent de volaille*, or chicken pie, with its delicate filling of chicken, mushroom, truffles, and its enveloping pastry, is never better than at the Grand Hôtel at Aix les Bains, where one finds the perfection of good eating. "Aix les Bains," says a resident physician, "lies half-way between Paris and Rome, with its famous curative baths to correct the good dinners of the one, and the good wines of the other." Aix adds a temptation of its own.

The French have ever been fond of the playthings of the kitchen,—the tarts, custards, the frothy nothings which are fashioned out of the evanescent union of whipped cream and spun sugar. Their politeness, their brag, their accomplishments, their love of the external, all lead to such dainties. It was observed even so long ago as 1815, when the allies were in Paris, that the fifteen thousand *pâtés* which Madame Felix sold daily in the *Passage des Panoramas* were beginning to affect the foreign bayonets; and no doubt the German invasion may have been checked by the same dulcet influence.

There is romance and history even about pastry. The *baba*, a species of savoury biscuit coloured with saffron, was introduced into France by Stanislaus, the first king of Poland, when that unlucky country was alternately the scourge and the victim of Russia. The dish was perhaps oriental in origin. It is made with *brioche* paste, mixed with madeira, currants, raisins, and potted cream.

French jellies are rather monotonous as to flavour, but they look very handsome on a supper-table. A *macédoine* is a delicious variety of dainty, and worthy of the French nation. It is wine jelly frozen in a mould with grapes, strawberries, green-gages, cherries, apricots, or pineapple, or more economically with slices of pears and apples boiled in syrup coloured with carmine, saffron, or cochineal, the flavour aided by angelica or brandied cherries. An invention of Ude and one which we could copy here is jelly *au miroton de pêche*:—

> Get half a dozen peaches, peel them carefully and boil them, with their kernels, a short time in a fine syrup, squeeze six lemons into it, and pass it through a bag. Add some clarified isinglass and put some of it into a mould in ice; then fill up with the jelly and peaches alternately and freeze it.

Fruit cheeses are very pleasant, rich conserves for dessert. They can be made with apricots, strawberries, pineapple, peaches, or gooseberries. The fruit is powdered with sugar and rubbed through a colander; then melted isinglass and thick cream is added, whipped over ice and put into the mould.

The French prepare the most ornamental ices, both water and cream, but they do not equal in richness or flavour those made in New York.

Pancakes and fritters, although English dishes, are very popular in France and very good. Apple fritters with sherry wine and sugar are very comforting things.

The French name is *beignet de pomme*. Thackeray immortalizes them thus:—

> "Mid fritters and lollypops though we may roam,
> On the whole there is nothing like beignet de pomme.
> Of flour half a pound with a glass of milk share,
> A half-pound of butter the mixture will bear.
> Pomme! Pomme! Beignet de pomme!
> Of beignets there's none like the beignet de pomme!
>
> "A beignet de pomme you may work at in vain
> If you stir not the mixture again and again.
> Some beer just to thin it may into it fall,
> Stir up that with three whites of eggs added to all.
> Pomme! Pomme! Beignet de pomme!
> Of beignets there's nothing like beignet de pomme!
>
> "Six apples when peeled you must carefully slice,
> And cut out the cores if you'll take my advice;
> Then dip them in butter and fry till they foam,
> And you'll have in six minutes your beignet de pomme.
> Pomme! Pomme! Beignet de pomme!
> Of beignets there's nothing like beignet de pomme!"

In the *Almanach de Gourmands* there appeared a philosophical treatise on pastry and pastry cooks, probably by the learned Giedeaud de la Reynière himself. Pastry, he says, is to cooking what rhetorical metaphors are to oratory,—life and ornament. A speech without metaphors, a dinner without pastry, are alike insipid; but, in like manner, as few people are eloquent, so few can make perfect pastry. Good pastry-cooks are as rare as good orators.

This writer recommends the art of the rolling-pin to beautiful women as being at once an occupation, a pleasure, and a sure way of recovering embonpoint and freshness. He says: "This is an art which will chase *ennui* from the saddest. It offers varied amusement and sweet and salutary exercise for the whole body; it restores appetite, strength, and gayety; it gathers around us friends; it tends to advance an art known from the most remote antiquity. Woman! lovely and charming woman, leave the sofas where *ennui* and hypochondria prey upon the springtime of your life, unite in the varied moulds sugar, jasmine, and roses, and form those delicacies that will be more precious than gold when made by hands so dear to us." What woman could refuse to make a pudding and any number of pies after that?

There seems to be nothing left to eat after all this perilous sweet stuff but a devilled biscuit at ten o'clock.

> "'A well devilled biscuit!' said Jenkins, enchanted,
> 'I'll have after dinner,—the thought is divine!'
> The biscuit was brought and he now only wanted,
> To fully enjoy it, a glass of good wine.
> He flew to the pepper and sat down before it,
> And at peppering the well-buttered biscuit he went;
> Then some cheese in a paste mixed with mustard spread o'er it,

And down to the kitchen the devil was sent.

"'Oh, how!' said the cook, 'can I thus think of grilling?
When common the pepper, the whole will be flat;
But here's the cayenne, if my master be willing
I'll make if he pleases a devil with that.'
So the footman ran up with the cook's observation
To Jenkins, who gave him a terrible look;
'Oh, go to the devil!'—forgetting his station—
Was the answer that Jenkins sent down to the cook."

A slice of *pâté de foie gras*, olives stuffed with anchovy, broiled bones, anchovy on toast, Welsh rarebit, devilled biscuit, devilled turkey-legs, devilled kidneys, *caviare*, devilled crabs, soft-shell crabs, shrimp salad, sardines on toast, broiled sausages, etc., are amongst the many appetizers which *gourmets* seek at ten or twelve o'clock, to take the taste of the sweets out of their mouths, and to prepare the pampered palate perhaps for punch, whiskey, or brandy and soda.

THE FURNISHING OF A COUNTRY HOUSE.

The hostess should, in furnishing her house, provide a number of bath-tubs. The tin ones, shaped like a hat, are very convenient, as are also india-rubber portable baths. If there is not a bath-room belonging to every room, this will enable an Englishman to take his tub as cold as he pleases, or allow the American to take the warmer sponge bath which Americans generally prefer.

The house should also be well supplied with lunch-baskets for picnics and for the railway journey. These can be had for a small sum, and are well fitted up with drinking-cups, knives, forks, spoons, corkscrews, sandwich-boxes, etc. These and a great supply of unbreakable cups for the lawn-tennis ground are very useful.

There should be also any number of painted tin pails, and small pitchers to carry hot water; several services of plain tea things, and Japanese waiters, on which to send tea to the bedrooms; and in every room should be placed a table, thoroughly furnished with writing-materials, and with all the conveniences for writing and sealing a letter.

Shakspeare's bequest to his wife of his second-best bed has passed as a bit of post-mortem ungallantry, which has dimmed his fame as a model husband; but to-day that second-best bed would be a very handsome bequest, not only because it was Shakspeare's, but because it was doubtless a "tester," for which there is a craze. All the old four-posters, which our grandmothers sent to the garret, are on their way back again to the model bedroom. With all our rage for ventilation and fresh air, we no longer fear the bed curtains which a few years ago were supposed to foster disease and death; because the model bedroom can now be furnished with a ventilator for admitting the fresh, and one permitting the egress of the foul air. Each gas bracket is provided with a pipe placed above it, which pierces the wall and through which the product of combustion is carried out of the house. This is a late sanitary improvement in London, and is being introduced in New York.

As for the bed curtains, they are hung on rods with brass rings, no canopy on top, so that the curtains can be shaken and dusted freely. This is a great improvement on the old upholstered top, which recalls Dickens's description of Mrs. Todger's boarding-house, where at the top of the stairs "the odour of many generations of dinners had gathered and had never been dispelled." In like manner the unpleasant feeling that perhaps whole generations of sleepers had breathed into the same upholstery overhead, used to haunt the wakeful, in old English inns, to the murdering of sleep.

There is a growing admiration, unfortunately, for tufted bedsteads. They are in the long run neither clean nor wholesome, and not easily kept free from vermin; but they are undeniably handsome, and recall the imperial beds of state apartments, where kings and queens are supposed to seek that repose which comes so unwillingly to them, but so readily to the plough-boy. These upholstered, tufted, satin-covered bedsteads should be fitted with a canopy, and from this should hang a baldachin and side curtains. Certain very beautiful specimens of this regal arrangement, bought in Italy, are in the Vanderbilt palaces in New York. Opulent purchasers can get copies at the great furnishing-houses, but it is becoming difficult to get the real antiques. Travellers in Brittany find the most wonderful carved bedsteads built into the wall, and are always buying them of the astonished fisher-folk, who have no idea how valuable is their smoke-stained, carved oak.

But as to the making up of the bed. There are nowadays cleanly springs and hair mattresses, in place of the old feather-beds; and as to stiff white bedcovers, pillowslips and shams, false sheets and valenciennes trimmings, monogrammed and ruffled fineries, there is a truce. They were so slippery, so troublesome, and so false withal, that the beds that have known them shall know them no more forever. They had always to be unpinned and unhooked before the sleeper could enter his bed; and they were the torment of the housemaid. They entailed a degree of washing and ironing which was endless, and yet many a young housekeeper thought them indispensable. That idea has gone out completely. The bed now is made up with its fresh linen sheets, its clean blankets and its Marseilles quilt, with square or long pillow as the sleeper fancies, with bolster in plain linen sheath. Then over the whole is thrown a light lace cover lined with Liberty silk. This may be as expensive or as cheap as the owner pleases. Or the spreads may be of satin covered with Chinese embroidery, Turkish Smyrniote, or other rare things, or of the patchwork or decorative art designs now so fashionable. One light and easily aired drapery succeeds the four or five pieces of unmanageable linen. If the bed is a tester and the curtains of silk or chintz, the bed-covering should match in tint. In a very pretty bedroom the walls should be covered with chintz or silk.

The modern highly glazed tile paper for walls and ceiling is an admirable covering, as it refuses to harbour dirt, and the housemaid's brush can keep it sweet and clean. Wall papers are so pretty and so exquisite in design that it seems hardly necessary to do more than mention them. Let us hope the exasperating old rectangular patterns, which have confused so many weary brains and haunted so many a feverish pillow, are gone forever.

The floors should be of plain painted wood, varnished, than which nothing can be cleaner; or perhaps of polished or oiled wood of the natural colour, with parquetried borders. If this is impossible cover with dark-stained mattings, which are as clean and healthful as possible. These may remain down all winter, and rugs may be laid over them at the fireplace and near the bed, sofa, etc. Readily lifted and shaken, rugs have all the comfort of carpets, and none of their disadvantages.

Much is said of the unhealthfulness of gas in bedrooms, but if it does not escape, it is not unhealthful. The prettiest illumination is by candles in the charming new candlesticks in tin and brass, which are as nice as Roman lamps.

On the old bedsteads of Cromwell's time we find a shelf running across the head of the bed, just above the sleeper's head,—placed there for the posset cup. This is now utilized for a safety lamp, for those who indulge in the pernicious practice of reading in bed; but it is even better used as a receptacle for the book, the letter-case, the many little things which an invalid may need, and it saves calling a nurse.

All paint used in a model bedroom should be free from poison. The fireplace should be tiled, and the windows made with a deep beading on the sill. This is a piece of wood like the rest of the frame, which comes up two or three inches in front of the lower part of the window. The object of this is to admit of the lower sash being raised without causing a draught. The room is thus ventilated by the air which filters through the slight aperture between the upper and lower sashes. Above all things have an open fireplace in the bedroom. Abolish stoves from that sacred precinct. Use wood for fuel if possible; if not, the softest of cannel-coal.

Have brass rods placed, on which to hang portières in winter. Portières and curtains may be cheaply made of ingrain carpet embroidered; or of Turkish or Indian stuffs; splendid Delhi pulgaries, a mass of gold silk embroidered, with bits of looking-glass worked in; of velvet; camel's-hair shawls; satin, chintz, or cretonne. Costly thy portières as thy purse can buy; nothing is so pretty and so ornamental.

Glazed chintzes may be hung at the windows, without lining, as the light shines through the flowers, making a good effect. Chenille curtains of soft rich colours are appropriate for the modern bedroom. Madras muslin curtains will do for the windows, but are not heavy enough for portières.

There are hangings made of willow bamboo, which can be looped back, or left hanging, which give a window a furnished look, without intercepting the light. Low wooden tables painted red, tables for writing materials, brackets on the walls for vases, candlesticks, and photograph screens, a long couch with many pillows, a Shaker rocking-chair, a row of hanging book-shelves,—these, with bed and curtains in fresh tints, make a pretty room in a country house.

If possible, people who entertain much should have a suite of bedrooms for guests, so that no one need be turned out of one's room to make way for a guest.

Brass beds are to be recommended as cleanly, handsome, and durable. Many ladies have, however, found fault with them because they show the under mattress, where the clothes are tucked in over the upper one. This can be remedied by making a valance which is finished with a ruffle at the top, which can be fluted, the whole tied on by tapes. Two or three of these in white will be all that a housekeeper needs, and if made of pretty coloured merino to match the room, they will last clean a long time.

Every bedroom should have, if possible, a dressing-room, where the washstand, wardrobe, bath-tub, box for boots and shoes, box for soiled clothes, and toilet-table, perhaps, can be kept. In the new sanitary houses in London, the water cistern is placed in view behind glass in these rooms, so that if anything is the matter with the water supply, it can be remedied immediately. However, in old fashioned houses, where dressing-rooms cannot be evoked, screens can be so placed as to conceal the unornamental objects.

A toilet-table should be ornamental and not hidden, with its curtains, pockets, looking-glasses, little bows, shelves for bottles, devices for secret drawers for love letters, and so on. Ivory brushes with the owner's monogram, all sorts of pretty Japanese boxes, and dressing-cases, silver-backed brushes and mirrors, button-hooks, knives, scissors can be neatly laid out.

A little table for afternoon tea should stand ready, with a tray of Satsuma or old Worcester, with cups and tea equipage, and a copper kettle with alcohol lamp should stand on a bracket on the wall. In the heating of water, a trivet should be attached to the grate, and a little iron kettle might sing forever on the hob. Ornamental ottomans in plush covers, which open and disclose a wood box, should stand by the fireplace. Chameleon glass lamps with king-fisher stems are pretty on the mantel-piece, which can be upholstered to match the bed; and there may be vases in amber, primrose, cream-colour, pale blue, and ruby. No fragrant flowers or growing plants should be allowed in a bedroom. There should be at least one clock in the room, to strike the hour with musical reiteration.

As for baths, the guest should be asked if he prefers hot or cold water, and the hour at which he will have it. If a tin hat-bath, or an india-rubber tub is used, the maid should enter and arrange it in this manner: first lay a rubber cloth on the floor and then place the tub on it. Then bring a large pail of cold water, and a can of hot. Place near the tub a towel-rack hung with fresh towels, both damask and Turkish, and if a full-length Turkish towel be added it will be a great luxury. If the guest be a gentleman, and no man-servant be kept, this should all be arranged the night before, with the exception of course of the hot water, which can be left out-side the door at any hour in the morning when it is desired. If it is a stationary tub, of course the matter is a simple one, and depends on the turn of a couple of faucets.

Some visitors are very fussy and dislike to be waited on; to such the option must be given: "Do you prefer to light your own fire, to turn on your bath, to make your own tea, or shall the maid enter at eight o'clock and do it for you?" Such questions are often asked in an English country house. Every facility for doing the work would of course be supplied to the visitor.

The bedroom being nowadays made so very attractive, the guest should stay in it as much as possible, if he or she find that the hostess likes to be alone; in short, absent yourself occasionally. Do your letter-writing and some reading in your room. Most people prefer this freedom and like to be let alone in the morning.

At a country house, gentlemen should be very particular to dress for dinner. If not in the regulation claw-hammer, still with a change of garment. There is a very good garment called a smokee, which is worn by gentlemen in the summer, a sort of light jacket of black cloth, which goes well with either black or white cravat; but with all the *laisser aller* of a country visit, inattention to the proprieties of dress is not included.

A guest must go provided with a lawn-tennis costume, if he plays that noble game which has become the great consolation of our rising generation. No doubt the hostess blesses the invention of this great time killer, as she sees her men and maidens trooping out to the ground, under the trees. This suggests the subject of out-of-door refreshment, the claret cup, the champagne cup, the shandy gaff, the fresh cider, and the thousand and one throat-coolers, for which our American genius seems to have been inspired to meet the drain of a very dry climate, and which we shall consider elsewhere.

ENTERTAINING IN A COUNTRY HOUSE.

We who love the country salute you who love the town.
I praise the rivulets, the rocks overgrown with moss, and the
groves of the delightful country. And do you ask why? I live and
reign as soon as I have quitted those things which you extol to the
skies with joyful applause, and like a priest's fugitive-slave I re-
ject luscious wafers; I desire plain bread, which is more agreeable
than honied cakes.

HORACE, *Ode* X.

Poets have been in the habit of praising a country life since the days of Homer,
but Americans have not as a people appreciated its joys. As soon as a countryman
was able to do it, he moved to the largest city near him, presumably New York, or
perhaps Paris. The condition of opulence, much desired by those who had been
bred in poverty, suggested at once the greater convenience of a town life, and the
busy work-a-day world, to which most Americans are born, necessitates the near-
ness to Wall Street, to banks, to people, and to the town.

City people were content formerly to give their children six weeks of country
air, and old New Yorkers did not move out of the then small city, even in the hot
months. The idea of going to the country to live for pleasure, to find in it a place in
which to spend one's money and to entertain, has been, to the average American
mind, a thing of recent growth. Perhaps our climate has much to do with this. People bred in the country feared to meet that long cold winter of the North, which
even to the well-to-do was filled with suffering. Who does not remember the ice in
the pitcher of a morning, which must be broken before even faces were washed?

Therefore the furnace-heated city house, the companionship, the bustle, the
stir, and convenience of a city has been, naturally enough, preferred to the loneliness of the country. As Hawthorne once said, Americans were not yet sufficiently
civilized to live in the country. When he went to England, and saw a different
order of things, he understood why.

England, a small place with two thousand years of civilization, with admirable roads, with landed estates, with a mild winter, with a taste for sport, with dogs,
horses, and well-trained servants, was a very different place.

It may be years before we make our country life as agreeable as it is in En-
gland. We have to conquer climate first. But the love of country life is growing in
America. Those so fortunate as to be able to live in a climate like that of southern
California can certainly quote Horace with sympathy. Those who live so near to a

great city as to command at once city conveniences and country air and freedom, are amongst the fortunate of the earth. And to hundreds, thousands of such, in our delightfully prosperous new country, the art of entertaining in a country house assumes a new interest.

No better model for a hostess can be found than an Englishwoman. There is, when she receives her guests, a quiet cordiality, a sense of pleasurable expectancy, an inbred ease, grace, suavity, composure, and respect for her visitors, which seems to come naturally to a well-bred Englishwoman; that is to say, to the best types of the highest class. To be sure they have had vast experience in the art of entertaining; they have learned this useful accomplishment from a long line of well-trained predecessors. They have no domestic cares to worry them. At the head of her own house, an Englishwoman is as near perfection as a human being can be.

There is the great advantage of the English climate, to begin with. It is less exciting than ours. Nervous women are there almost unknown. Their ability to take exercise, the moist and soft air they breathe, their good appetite and healthy digestion give English women a physical condition almost always denied to an American.

Our climate drives us on by invisible whips; we breathe oxygen more intoxicating than champagne. The great servant question bothers us from the cradle to the grave; it has never entered into an English woman's scheme of annoyance, so that in an English hostess there is a total absence of fussiness.

English women spend the greater part of the year in travelling, or at home in the country. Town life is with them a matter of six weeks or three months at the most. They are fond of nature, of walking, of riding; they share with the men a more vigorous physique than is given to any other race. A French or Italian woman dreads a long walk, the companionship of a dozen dogs, the yachting and the race course, the hunting-field and the lawn tennis pursued with indefatigable vigilance; but the fair English girl, with her blushing cheeks, her dog, her pony, and her hands full of wild flowers, is a character worth crossing the ocean to see. She is the product of the highest civilization, and as such is still near the divine model which nature furnishes. She has the underlying charm of simplicity, she is the very rose of perfect womanhood. She may seem shy, awkward, and reserved, but what the world calls pride or coldness may turn out to be hidden virtue, or reserve, or modesty.

English home education is a seminary of infinite importance; a girl learns to control her speech, to be always calm and well-bred. She has been toned down from her youth. She has been carefully taught to respect the duties of her high position; she has this advantage to counterbalance the disadvantage which we freeborn citizens think may come with an overpride of birth, — she has learned the motto *noblesse oblige*. The English fireside is a beacon light forever to the soldier in the Crimea, to the colonist in Australia, to the grave official in India, to the missionary in the South Seas, to the English boy wherever he may be. It sustains and ennobles the English woman at home and abroad.

As a hostess, the English woman is sure to mould her house to look like home.

She has soft low couches for those who like them, high-backed tall chairs for the tall, low chairs for the lowly. She has her bookcases and pretty china scattered everywhere, she has work-baskets and writing-tables and flowers, particularly wild ones, which look as if she had tossed them in the vases herself. Her house looks cheerful and cultivated.

I use the word advisedly, for all taste must be cultivated. A state apartment in an old English house can be inexpressibly dreary. High ceilings, stiff old girandoles, pictures of ancestors, miles of mirrors, and the Laocoön or other specimens of Grecian art, which no one cares for except in the Vatican, and the ceramic and historical horrors of some old collector, who had no taste, — are enough to frighten a visitor. But when a young or an experienced English hostess has smiled on such a house, there will be some delightful lumber strewn around, no end of pretty brackets and baskets and curtains and screens, and couches piled high with cushions; and then the quaint carvings, the rather affected niches, the mantelpiece nearly up to the ceiling, as in Hogarth's picture, — all these become humanized by her touch. The spirit of a hostess should aim at the combination of use and beauty. Some finer spirits command both, as Brunelleschi hung the dome at Florence high in air, and made a thing of beauty, which is a joy forever, but did not forget to build under it a convenient church as well. As for the bedrooms in an English country house, they transcend description, they are the very apotheosis of comfort.

The dinners are excellent, the breakfast and lunch comfortable, informal, and easy, the horses are at your disposal, the lawn and garden are yours for a stroll, the chapel lies near at hand, where you can study architecture and ancient brass. There are pleasant people in the house, you are let alone, you are not being entertained. That most dreadful of sensations, that somebody has you on his mind, and must show you photographs and lift off your *ennui* is absent; you seem to be in Paradise.

English people will tell you that house parties are dull, — not that all are, but some are. No doubt the jaded senses lose the power of being pleased. A visit to an English house, to an American who brings with her a fresh sense of enjoyment, and who remembers the limitations of a new country, one who loves antiquity, history, old pictures, and all that time can do, one who is hungry for Old World refinements, to such an one a visit to an English country house is delightful. To a worn-out English set whose business it has been for a quarter of a century to go from one house to another, no doubt it is dull. Some unusual distraction is craved.

"To relieve the monotony and silence and the dull, depressing cloud which sometimes settles on the most admirably arranged English dinner-party, even an American savage would be welcomed," says a modern novel-writer. How much more welcome then is a pretty young woman who, with a true enthusiasm and a wild liberty, has found her opportunity and uses it, plays the banjo, tells fortunes by the hand, has no fear of rank, is in her set a glacier of freshness with a heart of fire, like Roman punch.

How much more gladly is a young American woman welcomed, in such a house, and how soon her head is turned. She is popular until she carries off the eldest son, and then she is severely criticised, and by her spoiled caprices becomes a heroine for Ouida to rejoice in, and the *fond* of a society novel.

But the glory is departing from many a stately English country house. Fortune is failing them; they are, many of them, to rent. Rich Americans are buying their old pictures. The Gainsboroughs, the Joshua Reynoldses, the Rembrandts, which have been the pride of English country houses, are coming down, charmed by the silver music of the almighty dollar; the old fairy tale is coming true,—even the furniture dances.

We have the money and we have the vivacity, according to even our severest critics; we have now to cultivate the repose of an English hostess, if we would make our country houses as agreeable as she does.

We cannot improvise the antiquity, or the old chapel, or the brasses; we cannot make our roads as fine as those which enable an English house party to drive sixteen miles to a dinner; in fact we must admit that they have been nine hundred years making a lawn even. But we must try to do things our own way, and use our own advantages so that we can make our guests comfortable.

The American autumn is the most glorious of seasons for entertaining in a country house. Nature hangs our hillsides then with a tapestry that has no equal even at Windsor. The weather, that article which in America is so apt to be good that if it is bad we apologize for it, is more than apt to be good in October, and makes the duties of a hostess easy then, for Nature helps to entertain.

It is to be feared that we have not yet learned to be guests. Trusting to that boundless American hospitality which has been apt to say, "Come when you please and stay as long as you can," we decline an invitation for the 6th, saying we can come on the 9th. This cannot be done when people begin to give house-parties. We must go on the 6th or not at all.

We should also define the limits of a visit, as in England; one is asked on Wednesday to arrive at five, to leave at eleven on Saturday. Then one does not overstay one's welcome. Host and hostess and guest must thoroughly understand one another on this point, and then punctuality is the only thing to be considered.

The opulent, who have butler, footman, and French cooks, need read no further in this chapter, the remainder of which will be directed to that larger class who have neither, and who have to help themselves. No lady should attempt to entertain in the country who has not a good cook, and one or two attendant maids who can wait well and perform other duties about the house. With these three and with a good deal of knowledge herself, a hostess can make a country house attractive.

The dining-room should be the most agreeable room in the house, shaded in the morning and cool in the afternoon,—a large room with a hard-wood floor and mats, if possible, as these are clean and cool.

Carving should be done by one of the servants at a side table. There is nothing more depressing on a warm evening than a smoking joint before one's plate. A light soup only should be served, leaving the more substantial varieties for cold weather.

Nowadays the china and glass are so very pretty, and so very cheap, that they can be bought and used and left in the house all winter without much risk. If people are living in the country all winter a different style of furnishing, and a different style of entertaining is no doubt in order.

It is well to have very easy laws about breakfast, and allow a guest to descend when he wishes. If possible give your guest an opportunity to breakfast in his room. So many people nowadays want simply a cup of tea, and to wait until noon before eating a heavy meal; so many desire to eat steaks, chops, toast, eggs, hot cakes, and coffee at nine o'clock, that it is difficult for a hostess to know what to do. Her best plan, perhaps, is to have an elastic hour, and let her people come down when they feel like it. In England the maid enters the bedroom with tea, excellent black tea, a toasted muffin, and two boiled eggs at eight o'clock, a pitcher of hot water for the wash-stand, and a bath. No one is obliged to appear until luncheon, nor even then if indisposed so to do. Dinner at whatever hour is a formal meal, and every one should come freshly dressed and in good form, as the English say.

The Arab law of hospitality should be printed over every lintel in a country house: "Welcome the coming, speed the parting guest;" "He who tastes my salt is sacred; neither I nor my household shall attack him, nor shall one word be said against him. Bring corn, wine, and fruit for the passing stranger. Give the one who departs from thy tents the swiftest horse. Let him who would go from thee take the fleet dromedary, reserve the lame one for thyself." If these momentous hints were carried out in America, and if these children of the desert, with their grave faces, composed manners, and noble creed, could be literally obeyed, we fear country-house visiting would become almost too popular.

But if we cannot give them the fleet dromedary, we can drive them to the fast train, which is much better than any dromedary. We can make them comfortable, and enable them to do as they like. Unless we can do that, we should not invite any one.

Unless a guest has been rude, it is the worst taste to criticise him. He has come at your request. He has entered your house as an altar of safety, an ark of refuge. He has laid his armour down. Your kind welcome has unlocked his reserve. He has spoken freely, and felt that he was in the presence of friends. If in this careless hour you have discovered his weak spot, be careful how you attack it. The intimate unreserve of a guest should be respected.

And upon the guest an equal, nay, a superior conscientiousness should rest, as to any revelation of the secrets he may have found out while he was a visitor. No person should go from house to house bearing tales. We do not go to our friend's house to find the skeleton in the closet. No criticisms of the weaknesses or eccentricities of any member of the family should ever be heard from the lips of a guest. "Whose bread I have eaten, he is henceforth my brother," is another Arab proverb.

Speak well always of your entertainers, but speak little of their domestic arrangements. Do not violate the sanctity of the fireside, or wrong the shelter of the roof-tree which has lent you its protection for even a night.

The decorations for a country ballroom, in a rural neighbourhood, have called forth many an unknown genius in that art which has become the well-known profession of interior decoration. The favourite place in Lenox, and at many a summer resort, has been the large floor of a new barn. Before the equine tenants begin to champ their oats, the youths and maids assume the right to trip the light fantastic toe on the well-laid hard floor. The ornamentations at such a ball at Lenox were candles put in pine shields, with tin holders, and decorations of corn and wheat sheaves, tied with scarlet ribbons, surrounding pumpkins which were laid in improvised brackets, hastily cut out of pine, with hatchets, by the young men. Magnificent autumn leaves were arranged with ferns as garlands, and many were the devices for putting candles and kerosene lamps behind these so as to give almost the effect of stained glass, without causing a general conflagration.

The effect of a pumpkin surrounded by autumn leaves recalls the Gardens of the Hesperides. No apple like those golden apples which we call pumpkins was ever seen there. To be sure they are rather large to throw to a goddess, and might bowl her down, but they look very handsome when tranquilly reposing.

A sort of Druidical procession might be improvised to help along this ball, and the hostess would amuse her company for a week with the preparations.

First, get a negro fiddler to head it, dressed like Browning's Pied Piper in gay colours, and playing his fiddle. Then have a procession of children, dressed in gay costumes; following them, "two milk-white oxen garlanded" with wreaths of flowers and ribbons, driven by a boy in Swiss costume; then a goat-cart with the baby driving two goats, also garlanded; next a lovely Alderney cow, also decorated, accompanied by a milkmaid, carrying a milking-stool; then another long line of children, followed by the youths and maids, bearing the decorations for the ballroom. Let all these parade the village street and wind up at the ballroom, where the cow can be milked, and a surprise of ice cream and cake given to the children. This is a Sunday-school picnic and a ball decoration, all in one, and the country lady who can give it will have earned the gratitude of neighbours and friends. It has been done.

In the spring the decorations of a ballroom might be early wild flowers and the delicate ground-pine, far more beautiful than smilax, and also ferns, the treasures of the nearest wood.

Wild flowers, ferns, and grasses, the ground-pine, the checkerberry, and the partridge berry make the most exquisite garlands, and it is only of late—when a few great geniuses have discovered that the field daisy is the prettiest of flowers, that the best beauty is that which is at our hands wherever we are, that the greatest rarity is the grass in the meadow—that we have reached the true meaning of interior decoration.

Helen Hunt, in one of her prettiest papers, describes the beauty of kinnikinick, a lovely vine which grows all over Colorado. Although we have not that, we can even in winter find the hemlock boughs, the mistletoe, the holly, for our decorations. Of course, hot-house flowers and smilax, if they can be obtained, are very beautiful and desirable, but they are not within the reach of every purse, or of every country house.

Sheaves of wheat, tied with fine ribbons and placed at intervals around a room, can be made to have the beauty of an armorial bearing. These, alternating with banners and hemlock boughs, are very effective. All these forms which Nature gives us have suggested the Corinthian capital, the Ionic pillar, the most graceful of Greek carvings. The acanthus leaf was the inspiration of the architect who built the Acropolis.

Vine leaves, especially after they begin to turn, are capable of infinite suggestion, and we all remember the recent worship of the sunflower. Hop vines and clematis, especially after the last has gone to seed, remain long as ornaments.

As for the refreshments to be served,—the oyster stew, the ice cream, the good home-made cake, coffee, and tea are within the reach of every country housekeeper, and are in their way unrivalled. Of course, if she wishes she can add chicken salad, boned turkey, *pâté de foie gras*, and punch, hot or cold.

If it is in winter, the coachmen outside must not be forgotten. Some hot coffee and oysters should be sent to these patient sufferers, for our coachmen are not dressed as are the Russians, in fur from head to foot. If possible, there should be a good fire in the kitchen, to which these attendants on our pleasure could be admitted to thaw out.

A PICNIC.

"Come hither, come hither, the broom was in blossom all over
yon rise,
There went a wild murmur of brown bees about it with songs
from the wood.
We shall never be younger, O Love! let us forth to the world
'neath our eyes—
Ay! the world is made young, e'en as we, and right fair is her
youth, and right good."

Appetites flourish in the free air of hills and meadows, and after drinking in
the ozone of the sea, one feels like drinking something else. There is a very good
story of a reverend bishop who with a friend went a-fishing, like Peter, and being
very thirsty essayed to draw the cork of a claret bottle. In his zeal he struck his bottle against a stone, and the claret oozed out to refresh the thirsty earth, instead of
that precious porcelain of human clay of which the bishop was made. His remark
to his friend was, "James, you are a layman, why don't you say something?"

Now to avoid having our layman or our reverend wish to say something, let
us try to suggest what they should eat and what they should drink.

There are many kinds of picnics,—fashionable ones at Newport and other watering-places, where the French waiters of the period are told to get up a repast
as if at the Casino; there are clam-bakes which are ideal, and there are picnics at
Lenox and at Sharon, where the hotel keeper will help to fill the baskets.

But the real picnic, which calls for talent and executive ability, should emanate
from some country house, where two or three other country houses co-operate
and help. Then what jolly drives in the brakes, what queer old family horses and
antediluvian wagons, what noble dog-carts, and what prim pony phaetons can
join in the procession. The day should be fine, and the place selected a hillside with
trees, commanding a fine view. This is at least desirable. The necessity for a short
walk, a short scramble after leaving the horses, should not be disregarded.

The night before the picnic, which presumably starts early, the lady of the
house should see to it that a boiled ham of perfect flavour is in readiness, and
she may flank it with a boiled tongue, four roasted chickens, a game pie, and any
amount of stale bread to cut into sandwiches.

Now a sandwich can be at once the best and the worst thing in the world, but
to make it the best the bread should be cut very thin, the butter, which must be as
fresh as a cowslip, should be spread with deft fingers, then a slice of ham as thin

as a wafer with not too much fat must be laid between, with a *soupçon* of mustard. The prepared ham which comes in cans is excellent for making sandwiches. Cheese sandwiches, substituting a thin slice of American fresh cheese for the ham, are delicious, and some rollicking good-livers toast the cheese.

Tongue, cold beef, and even cold sausages make excellent varieties of sandwich. To prevent their becoming the "sand which is under your feet" cover them over night with a damp napkin.

Chicken can be eaten for itself alone, but it should be cut into very convenient fragments, judiciously salted and wrapped in a very white napkin.

The game or veal pie must be in a strong earthen dish, and having been baked the day before, its pieces will have amalgamated with the crust, and it will cut into easily handled slices.

All must be packed in luncheon baskets with little twisted cornucopias holding pepper and salt, hard-boiled eggs, the patty by itself, croquettes, if they happen to be made, cold fried oysters, excellent if in batter and well-drained after cooking; no article must be allowed to touch another.

If cake and pastry be taken, each should have a separate basket. Fruit also should be carefully packed by itself, for if food gets mixed and mussy, even a mountain appetite will shun it.

A bottle of olives is a welcome addition, and pickles and other relishes may be included. Sardines are also in order.

Now what to drink? Cold tea and iced coffee prepared the night before, the cream and sugar put in just before starting, should always be provided. They are capital things to climb on, to knit up the "ravelled sleeve of care," and if somewhat exciting to the nerves, will be found the best thirst-quenchers.

These beverages should be carefully bottled and firmly corked,—and don't forget the corkscrew. Plenty of tin cups, or those strong glass beer-mugs which you can throw across the room without breaking, should also be taken.

Claret is the favourite wine for picnics, as being light and refreshing. Ginger ale is excellent and cheap and compact. "Champagne," says Walter Besant in his novel "By Celia's Arbour" is a wine as Catholic as the Athanasian Creed, because it goes well with chicken and with the more elaborate *pâté de foie gras*.

Some men prefer sherry with their lunch, some take beer. If you have room and a plentiful cellar, take all these things. But tea and coffee and ginger ale will do for any one, anywhere.

It has been suggested by those who have suffered losses from mischievous friends, that a composite basket containing everything should be put in each carriage, but this is refining the matter.

Arrived at the picnic-ground, the whole force should be employed by the hostess as an amiable body of waiters. The ladies should set the tables, and the men bring water from the spring. The less ceremony the better.

Things have not been served in order, they never are at a picnic, and the cunning hostess now produces some claret cup. She has made it herself since they reached the top of the mountain. Two bottles of claret to one of soda water, two lemons, a glass of sherry, a cucumber sliced in to give it the most perfect flavour, plenty of sugar and ice; and where had she hidden that immense pitcher, a regular brown toby, in which she has brewed it?

"I know," said an *enfant terrible*; "I saw her hiding it under the back seat."

There it is, filled with claret cup, the most refreshing drink for a warm afternoon. Various young persons of opposite sexes, who have been looking at each other more than at the game pie, now prepare to disappear in the neighbouring paths, under a pretence but feebly made of plucking blackberries,—artless dissemblers!

Mamma shouts, "Mary, Caroline, Jane, Tom, Harry, be back before five, for we must start for home." May she get them, even at half-past six. From a group of peasants over a bunch of sticks in the Black Forest, to a queen who delighted to picnic in Fontainebleau, these *al fresco* entertainments are ever delicious. We cannot put our ears too close to the confessional of Nature. She has always a new secret to tell us, and from the most artificial society to that which is primitive and rustic, they always carry the same charm. It is the Antæus trying to get back to Mother Earth, who strengthens him.

In packing a lunch for a fisherman, or a hunter, the hostess often has to explain that brevity is the soul of wit. She must often compress a few eatables into the side pocket, and the bottle of claret into the fishing-basket. If not, she can palm off on the man one of those tin cases which poor little boys carry to school, which look like books and have suggestive titles, such as "Essays of Bacon," "Crabbe's Tales," or "News from Turkey," on the back. If the fisherman will take one of these his sandwiches will arrive in better order.

The Western hunter takes a few beans and some slices of pork, some say in his hat, when he goes off on the warpath. The modern hunter or fisher, if he drive to the meet or the burn, can be trusted with an orthodox lunch-basket, which should hold cold tea, cold game-pie, a few olives, and a bit of cheese, and a large reserve of sandwiches. When we grow more celestial, when we achieve the physical theory of another life, we may know how to concentrate good eating in a more portable form than that of the sandwich, but we do not know it yet.

Take an egg sandwich,—hard-boiled eggs chopped, and laid between the bread and butter. Can anything be more like the sonnet?—complete in only fourteen lines, and yet perfection! Only indefinite chicken, wheaten flour, the milk of the cow, all that goes to make up our daily food in one little compact rectangle! Egg sandwich! It is immense in its concentration.

Some people like to take salads and apple pies to picnics. There are great moral objections to thus exposing these two delicacies to the rough experiences of a picnic. A salad, however well dressed, is an oily and slippery enjoyment. Like all great joys, it is apt to escape us, especially in a lunch basket. Apple pie, most delicate of pasties, will exude, and you are apt to find the crust on the top of the basket, and the apple in the bottom of the carriage.

If you will take salad, and will not be taught by experience, make a perfect *jardinière* of all the cold vegetables, green peas, beans, and cauliflower, green peppers, cucumbers, and cold potatoes, and take this mixture dry to the picnic. Have your mayonnaise in a bottle, and dress the salad with it after sitting down, on a very slippery, ferny rock, at the table. Truth compels the historian to observe, that this is delicious with the ham, and you will not mind in the least, until the next day, the large grease-spot on the side breadth of your gown.

As for the apple pie, that is taken at the risk of the owner. It had better be left at home for tea.

Of course, *pâté de foie gras*, sandwiches, boned turkey, jellied tongue, the various cold birds, as partridges, quails, pheasant, and chicken, and raw oysters, can be taken to a very elaborate picnic near a large town. Salmon dressed with green sauce, lobster salad, every kind of salad, is in order if you can only get it there, and "*caviare* to the general." Cold terrapin is not to be despised; eaten on a bit of bread it is an excellent dainty, and so is the cold fried oyster.

Public picnics, like Sunday-school picnics, fed with ice cream and strawberries; or the clam bake, a unique and enjoyable affair by the sea, are in the hands of experts, and need no description here. The French people picnic every day in the *Bois de Boulogne*, the woods of Versailles, and even on their asphalt, eating out of doors when they can. It is a very strange thing that we do not improve our fine climate by eating our dinners and breakfasts with the full draught of an unrivalled ozone.

PASTIMES OF LADIES.

Her feet beneath her petticoat,
Like little mice, stole in and out,
As if they feared the light;
But oh, she dances such a way!
No sun upon an Easter day
Is half so fine a sight.

Sir John Suckling.

The "London Times" says that the present season has seen "driving jump to a great height of favour amongst fashionable women."

It is a curious expression, but enlightens us as to the liberty which even so great an authority takes with our common language. There is no doubt of the fact that the pony phaeton and the pair of ponies are becoming a great necessity to an energetic woman. The little pony and the Ralli cart, as a ladies' pastime, is a familiar figure in the season at Newport, at a thousand country places, at the seaside, in our own Central Park, and all through the West and South.

It has been much more the custom for ladies in the West and South to drive themselves, than for those at the North; consequently they drive better. Only those who know how to drive well ought ever to attempt it, for they not only endanger their own lives, but a dozen other lives. Whoever has seen a runaway carriage strike another vehicle, and has beheld the breaking up, can realize for the first time the tremendous force of an object in motion. The little Ralli cart can become a battering-ram of prodigious force.

No form of recreation is so useful and so becoming as horseback exercise. No English woman looks so well as when turned out for out-of-door exercise. And our American women, who buy their habits and hats in London, are getting to have the same *chic*. Indeed, so immensely superior is the London habit considered, that the French circus-women who ride in the Bois, making so great a sensation, go over to London to have their habits made, and thus return the compliment which English ladies pay to Paris, in having all their dinner gowns and tea gowns made there. Perhaps disliking this sort of copy, the Englishwomen are becoming careless of their appearance on horseback, and are coming out in a straw hat, a covert coat, and a cotton skirt.

The soft felt hat has long been a favourite on the Continent, at watering-places for the English; and it is much easier for the head. Still, in case of a fall it does not save the head like a hard, masculine hat.

We have not yet, as a nation, taken to cycling for women; but many English-women go all over the globe on a tricycle. A husband and wife are often seen on a tricycle near London, and women who lead sedentary lives, in offices and schools, enjoy many of their Saturday afternoons in this way.

Boating needs to be cultivated in America. It is a superb exercise for developing a good figure; and to manage a punt has become a common accomplishment for the riverside girls. Ladies have regattas on the Thames.

Fencing, which many actresses learn, is a very admirable process for developing the figure. The young Princesses of Wales are adepts in this. It requires an outfit consisting of a dainty tunic reaching to the knees, a fencing-jacket of soft leather with tight sleeves, gauntlet gloves, a mask, a pair of foils, and costing about fifteen dollars.

American women as a rule are not fond of walking. There must be something in the nature of an attraction or a duty to rouse our delicate girls to walk. They will not do it for their health alone. Gymnastic teaching is, however, giving them more strength, and it would be well if in every family of daughters there were some calisthenic training, to develop the muscles, and to induce a more graceful walk.

To teach a girl to swim is almost a duty, and such splendid physical exercises will have a great influence over that nervous distress which our climate produces with its over-fulness of oxygen.

If girls do not like to walk, they all like to dance, and it is not intended as a pun when we mention that "a great jump" has been made back to the old-fashioned dancing, in which freedom of movement is allowed. Those who saw Mary Anderson's matchless grace in the Winter's Tale all tried to go and dance like her, and to see Ellen Terry's spring, as the pretty Olivia, teaches one how entirely beautiful is this strong command of one's muscles. From the German cotillion, back to the Virginia reel, is indeed a bound.

Our grandfathers knew how to dance. We are fast getting back to them. The traditions of Taglioni still lingered fifty years ago. The earliest dancing-masters were Frenchmen, and our ancestors were taught to *pirouette* as did Vestris when he was so obliging as to say after a royal command, "The house of Vestris has always danced for that of Bourbon."

The galop has, during the long langour of the dance, alone held its own, in the matter of jollity. The glide waltz, the redowa, the stately minuet, give only the slow and graceful motions. The galop has always been a great favourite with the Swedes, Danes, and Russians, while the redowa reminds one of the graceful Viennese who dance it so well. The mazourka, danced to wild Polish music, is a poetical and active affair.

The introduction of Hungarian bands and Hungarian music is another reason why dancing has become a "hop, skip and a bound," without losing dignity or grace. Activity need not be vulgar.

The German cotillion, born many years ago at Vienna to meet the requirements of court etiquette, is still the fashionable dance with which the ball closes.

Its favours, beginning with flowers and ribbons and bits of tinsel, have now ripened into fans, bracelets, gold scarf-pins and pencil-cases, and many things more expensive. Favours may cost five thousand dollars for a fashionable ball, or dance, as they say in London.

The German is a dance of infinite variety, and to lead it requires a man of head. One such leader, who can construct new figures, becomes a power in society. The waltz, galop, redowa, and polka step can all be utilized in it. There is a slow walk in the quadrille figure, a stately march, the bows and courtesies of the old minuet, and above all, the *tour de valse*, which is the means of locomotion from place to place. The changeful exigencies of the various figures lead the forty or fifty, or the two hundred to meet, exchange greetings, dance with each other, and change their geographical position many times. Indeed no army goes through more evolutions.

A pretty figure is *La Corbeille, l'Anneau, et la Fleur*. The first couple performs a *tour de valse*, after which the gentleman presents the lady with a basket, containing a ring and a flower, then resumes his seat. The lady presents the ring to one gentleman, the flower to another, and the basket to the third. The gentleman to whom she presents the ring selects a partner for himself, the gentleman who receives the flower dances with the lady who presents it, while the other gentleman holds the basket in his hand and dances alone.

The kaleidoscope is one of the prettiest figures. The four couples perform a *tour de valse*, then form as for a quadrille; the next four couples in order take positions behind the first four couples, each of the latter couples facing the same as the couples in front. At a signal from the leader, the ladies of the inner couples cross right hands, move entirely round and turn into places by giving left hands to their partners. At the same time the outer couples waltz half round to opposite places. At another signal the inner couples waltz entirely round, and finish facing outward. At the same time the outer couples *chassent croisé* and turn at corners with right hands, then *dechassent* and turn partners with left hands. Valse *générale* with *vis à vis*.

La Cavalier Trompé is another favourite figure. Five or six couples perform a *tour de valse*. They afterwards place themselves in ranks of two, one couple behind the other. The lady of the first gentleman leaves him and seeks a gentleman of another column. While this is going on the first gentleman must not look behind him. The first lady and the gentleman whom she has selected separate and advance on tip-toe on each side of the column, in order to deceive the gentleman at the head, and endeavour to join each other for a waltz. If the first gentleman is fortunate enough to seize his lady, he leads off in a waltz; if not, he must remain at his post until he is able to take a lady. The last gentleman remaining dances with the last lady.

To give a German in a private house, a lady has all the furniture removed from her parlours, the floor covered with crash over the carpet, and a set of folding-chairs for the couples to sit in. A bare wooden floor is preferable to the carpet and crash.

It is considered that all taking part in a German are introduced to one another, and on no condition whatever must a lady, so long as she remains in the German, refuse to speak or to dance with any gentleman whom she may chance to receive as a partner. Every American should learn that he can speak to any one whom he meets at a friend's house. The roof is an introduction, and, for the purpose of making his hostess comfortable, the guest should, at dinner-party and dance, speak to his next neighbour.

The laws of the German are so strict, and to many so tiresome, that a good many parties have abjured it, and merely dance the round dances, the lancers and quadrilles, winding up with the Sir Roger de Coverley or the Virginia Reel.

The leader of the German must have a comprehensive glance, a quick ear and eye, and a great belief in himself. General Edward Ferrero, who made a good general, declared that he owed all his success in war to his training as a dancing-master. With all other qualities, the leader of the German must have tact. It is no easy matter to get two hundred people into all sorts of combinations and mazes and then to get them out again, to offend nobody, and to produce that elegant kaleidoscope called the German.

The term *tour de valse* is used technically, meaning that the couple or couples performing it execute the round dance designated by the leader once round the room. Should the room be small, they make a second tour. After the introductory *tour de valse* care must be taken by those who perform it not to select ladies and gentlemen who are on the floor, but from among those who are seated. When the leader claps his hands to warn those who are prolonging the valse, they must immediately cease dancing.

The favours for the German are often fans, and this time-honoured, historic article grows in beauty and expense every day. And what various memories come in with the fan! It was created in primeval ages. The Egyptian ladies had fans of lotus leaves; and lately a breakfast was given all in Egyptian fashion, except the eating. The Roman ladies carried immense fans of peacocks' feathers. They did not open and shut like ours, opening and shutting being a modern invention. The *flabilliferaor* or fan-bearer, was some young attendant, generally female, whose common business it was to carry her mistress's fan. There is a Pompeian painting of Cupid as the fan-bearer of Ariadne, lamenting her desertion by Theseus. In Queen Elizabeth's day the fan was usually made of feathers, like that still used in the East. The handle was richly ornamented and set with stones. A fashionable lady was never without her fan, which was held to her girdle by a jewelled chain. That fashion, with the large feathers, has returned in our day. Queen Elizabeth dropped a silver-handled fan into the moat at Arnstead Hall, which occasioned many madrigals. Sir Francis Drake presented to his royal mistress a fan of feathers, white and red, enamelled with a half-moon of mother-of-pearl. Poor Leicester gave her, as his New Year's gift in 1574, a fan of white feathers set in a handle of gold, adorned on one side with two very fair emeralds, and fully garnished with rubies and diamonds, and on each side a white bear,—his cognizance,—and two pearls hanging, a lion rampant and a white, muzzled bear at his foot. Just before Christmas in 1595 Elizabeth went to Kew, and dined at my Lord Keeper's house, and there was handed her a fine fan with a handle garnished with diamonds.

Fans in Shakspeare's time seem to have been composed of ostrich and other feathers, fastened to handles. Gentlemen carried fans in those days, and in one of the later figures of the German they now carry fans. According to an old manuscript in the Ashmolean Museum, Sir Edward Cole rode the circuit with a prodigious fan, which had a long stick with which he corrected his daughters. Let us hope that that custom will not be reintroduced.

The vellum fans painted by Watteau, and the lovely fans of Spain enriched with jewels are rather too expensive for favours for the German; one very rich entertainer gave away tortoise-shell fans with jewelled sticks, two years ago, at Delmonico's. Fans of silk, egg-shaped, and painted with birds, were used for an Easter German.

Ribbons were used for a cotillon dinner with very good effect. "From the chandelier in the centre of the dining room," we read, "depended twenty scarfs of grosgrain ribbon, each three and a half yards long and nine inches wide, heavily fringed and richly adorned at both ends with paintings of flowers and foliage. These scarfs were so arranged that an end of each came down to the place one of the ladies was to occupy at the table, and care was taken in their selection to have colours harmonizing with the ladies' dress and complexion."

These cotillion dinners have been a pretty fashion for two or three winters, as they enable four or five young hostesses to each give a dinner, the whole four to meet with their guests at one house for a small German, after the dinner. Each hostess compares her list with that of her neighbour, that there shall be no confusion. It is believed that this device was the invention of the incomparable Mr. McAllister, to whom society owes a great deal. Fashionable society like the German must have a leader, some one who will take trouble, and think out these elaborate details. Nowhere in Europe is so much pains taken about such details as with us.

The *menus* of these cotillion dinners are often water-colour paintings, worthy of preservation; sometimes a scene from one of Shakspeare's plays, sometimes a copy of some famous French picture, — in either case something delightfully artistic.

For a supper after a dance the dishes are placed on the table, and it is served *en buffet*; but for a sit-down supper, served at little tables, the service should be exactly like a dinner except that there is no soup or fish.

The manner of using flowers in America at such entertainments is simply bewildering. A climbing rose will seem to be going everywhere over an invisible trellis; delicate green vines will depend from the chandelier, dropping roses; roses cover the entire table-cloth; or perhaps the flowers are massed, all of yellow, or of white, or red, or pink.

Nothing could exceed the magnificence of the great baskets of white and yellow chrysanthemums, roses, violets, and carnations, at a breakfast given to the Comte de Paris, at Delmonico's on October 20th, and at the subsequent dinner given him by his brother officers of the Army of the Potomac. His royal arms were in white flowers, the *fleur de lis* of Joan of Arc, on a blue ground of flowers. Jacqueminot Roses went up and down the table, with the words "Grand Army of the

Potomac" in white flowers.

The orchid, that most regal and expensive of all flowers, a single specimen often costing many dollars, was used by a lady to make an imitation fire, the wood, the flames, and all consisting of flowers placed in a most artistic chimney-piece.

Indeed, the cost of the cut flowers used in New York in one winter for entertaining is said to be five millions of dollars. Orchids have this advantage over other flowers—they have no scent; and that in a mixed company and a hot room is an advantage, for some people cannot bear even the perfume of a rose.

A large lump of ice, with flowers trained over it, is a delightfully refreshing adornment for a hot ballroom. In grand party decorations, like one given by the Prince of Wales to the Czarina of Russia, ten tons of ice were used as an ornamental rockery. In smaller rooms the glacier can be cut out and its base hidden in a tub, lights put behind it and flowers and green vines draped over it. The effect is magical. The flowers are kept fresh, the white column looks always well, and the coolness it diffuses is delicious. It might, by way of contrast to the Dark Continent, be a complimentary decoration for a supper to be given to Mr. Stanley, to ornament the ballroom with Arctic bowlders, around which should be hung the tropical flowers and vines of Africa.

PRIVATE THEATRICALS.

A poor thing, my masters, not the real thing at all, a base imitation, but still a good enough mock-orange, if you cannot have the real thing.

OLD PLAY.

Some of our opulent citizens in the West, particularly in that wondrous city Chicago, which is nearer to Aladdin's Lamp than anything else I have seen, have built private theatres in their palaces. This is taking time by the forelock, and arranging for a whole family of coming histrionic geniuses.

When all the arrangements for private theatricals must be improvised,—and, indeed, it is a greater achievement to play in a barn than on the best stage,—the following hints may prove serviceable.

Wherever the amateur actor elects to play, he must consider the extraneous space behind the acting arena necessary for his exits and entrances, and his theatrical properties. In an ordinary house the back parlour, with two doors opening into the dining-room, makes an ideal theatre, for the exits can be masked and the space is especially useful. At least one door opening into another room is absolutely necessary, if no better arrangement can be made. The best stage, of course, is like that of a theatre, raised, with space at the back and sides, for the players to retire to, and issue from. But if nothing better can be managed, a pair of screens and a curtain will do.

It is hardly necessary to say that all these arrangements depend on the requirements of the play and its legitimate business, which may demand a table, a bureau, a piano, or a bed. That very funny piece "Box and Cox" needs nothing but a bed, a table, and a fireplace. And here we would say to the youthful actor, Select your play at first with a view to its requiring little change of scene, and not much furniture. A young actor needs space. He is embarrassed by too many chairs and tables. Then choose a play which has so much varied incident that it will play itself.

The first thing is to build the stage. Any carpenter will lay a few stout boards on end pieces, which are simply squared joists, and for very little money will take away the boards and joists afterwards, so that a satisfactory stage can be built for a few dollars. Sometimes, ingenious boys build their own stage with a few boxes, but this is apt to be dangerous. Very few families are without an old carpet which will serve for a stage covering; and if this is lacking, green baize is very cheap. A whole stage fitting, curtains and all, can be made of green baize.

Footlights may be made of tin, with bits of candle put in; or a row of old bottles of equal height, with candles stuck in the mouth, make a most admirable and cheap set of footlights.

The curtain is always difficult to arrange, especially in a parlour. A light wooden frame should be made by the carpenter,—firm at the joints, and as high as the room allows. Attached to the stage, at the foot, this frame forms three sides of a square. The curtain must be firmly nailed to the top piece. A stiff wire should be run along the lower edge of the curtain, and a number of rings attached to the back of it, in squares,—three rows, of four rings each, extending from top to bottom. Three cords are now fastened to the wire, and passing through the rings are run over three pulleys on the upper piece of the frame. It is well for all young managers of garret theatres to get up one of these curtains, even with the help of an upholsterer, as the other draw-curtain never works so securely, and often hurts the *dénouement* of the play. When the drop curtain above described is used, one person holds all the strings, and it pulls together.

Now for the stage properties. They are easily made. A boy who can paint a little will indicate a scene, with black paint, on a white ground; tinsel paper, red flannel, and old finery will supply the fancy dresses.

A stage manager who is a natural born leader is indispensable. Certain ambitious amateurs performed the opera of "Patience" in New York. It would have been a failure but for the musical talent of the two who took the title *rôles*, and the diligent six weeks' training which the players received at the hand of the principal actor in the real operetta. This seems very dear for the whistle, when one can go and hear the real tune. It is in places where the real play cannot be heard, that amateur theatricals are of importance.

Young men at college get up the best of all amateur plays, because they are realistic, and stop at nothing to make strong outlines and deep shadows. They, too, buy many properties like wigs and dresses, and give study and observation to the make-up of the character.

If they need a comic face they have an artist from the theatre put it on with a camel's-hair pencil. An old man's face, or a brigand's is only a bit of water-colour. A pretty girl can be made out of a heavy young man by rouge, chalk, and a blond wig. For a drunkard or a villain, a few purple spots are painted on chin, cheek, forehead and nose, judiciously.

Young girls are apt, in essaying private theatricals, to sacrifice too much to prettiness. This is a fatal mistake; one must even sacrifice native bloom if the part requires it, or put on rouge, if necessary.

As amusement is the object, the plays had better be comedy than tragedy; and no such delicate wordy duels as the "Scrap of Paper," should be attempted, as that requires the highest skill of two great actors.

After reading the part and committing the lines to memory, young actors must submit to many and long rehearsals. After many of these and much study, they must not be discouraged if they grow worse instead of better. Perseverance conquers all things, and at last they reach the dress rehearsal. This is generally a disappointment, and time should be allowed for two dress rehearsals. It is a most excellent and advantageous discouragement, if it leads the actors to more study.

The stage manager has a difficult *rôle* to play, for he may discover that his actors must change parts. This nearly always excites a wounded self-love, and ill-feeling. But each one should bear in mind that he is only a part of a perfect whole, and be willing to sacrifice himself.

If, however, plays are not successful and cease to amuse, the amateur stage can be utilized for *tableaux vivants*, which are always pretty, and may be made very artistic. The principle of a picture, the pyramidal form, should be closely observed in a tableau.

There should be a square of black tarletan or gauze nailed before the picture, between the players and the footlights. The drop curtain must be outside of this, and go up and down very carefully, at a concerted signal.

Although the pure white light of candles, or lime light, is the best for such pictures, very pretty effects can be easily made by the introduction of coloured lights, such as are produced by the use of nitrate of strontia, chlorate of potash, sulphuret of antimony, sulphur, oxymuriate of potassa, metallic arsenic, and pulverized charcoal. Muriate of ammonia makes a bluish-green fire, and many colours can be obtained by a little study of chemistry.

To make a red fire, take five ounces of nitrate of strontia dry, and one and a half ounces finely powdered sulphur; also five drachms chlorate of potash, and four drachms sulphuret of antimony. Powder the last two separately in a mortar, then mix them on paper and having mixed the other ingredients, previously powdered, add these last and rub the whole together on paper. To use, mix a little spirits of wine with the powder, and burn in a flat iron plate or pan; the effect is excellent on the picture.

Sulphate of copper when dissolved in water turns it a beautiful blue. The common red cabbage gives three colours. Slice the cabbage and pour boiling water on it. When cold add a small quantity of alum, and you have purple. Potash dissolved in the water will give a brilliant green. A few drops of muriatic acid will turn the cabbage water into crimson. Put these various coloured waters in globes, and with candles behind them they will throw the light on the picture.

Again, if a ghastly look be required, and a ghost scene be in order, mix common salt with spirits of wine in a metal cup, and set it upon a wire frame over a spirit lamp. When the cup becomes heated, and the spirits of wine ignites, the other lights in the room should be extinguished, and that of the spirit lamp hidden from the observer. A light will be produced that will make the players seem like the witches in Macbeth, "that look not like the inhabitants of the earth, but yet are of it."

The burning of common salt produces a very weird effect; for salt has properties other than the conservative, preserving, hospitable qualities which legend and the daily needs of mankind have ascribed to it.

A very pretty effect for Christmas Eve may be made by throwing these lights on the highly decorated tree. A set of Christmas tableaux can be arranged, giving groups of the early Christians going into the Catacombs as the Pagans are going out, with a white shaft of light making a cross between them. A picture representing the Christmas of each nationality can be made, as for instance the Russian, the Norwegian, the Dane, the Swede, the German, the English of three hundred years ago. These are all possible to a family in which are artistic boys and girls.

The grotesque is lost in a tableau where there seems to be an æsthetic need of the heroic, the refined, and the historic. A double action may be represented with good effect, and here can be used the coloured lights. Angels above, for instance, can well be in another colour than sleeping children below.

To return for a moment to the first use of the stage, the play. It is a curious thing to see the plays which amateurs act well. The "Rivals" is one of these, and so is "Everybody's Friend." "The Follies of a Night" plays itself, and "The Happy Pair" goes very well. "A Regular Fix," one of Sothern's plays, is exceptionally funny, as is "The Liar," in which poor Lester Wallack was so very good. "Woodcock's Little Game," too, is excellent.

Cheap and unsophisticated theatricals, such as schoolboys and girls can get up in the garret or the basement, are those which give the most pleasure. But so strong is the underlying love of the drama that youth and maid will attempt the hard and sometimes discouraging work, even in cities where professional work is so very much better.

The private amateur player should study to be accurate as to costume. Pink-satin Marie Antoinette slippers must not be worn with a Greek dress; classic sandals are easily made.

It is an admirable practice to get up a play in French. It helps to conquer the *délicatesse* of the language. The French *répertoire* is very rich in easily acted plays, which any French teacher can recommend.

Imitation Negro minstrels are funny, and apt to be better than the original. A funny man, a mimic, one who can talk in various dialects, is a precious boon to an amateur company. Many of Dion Boucicault's Irish characters can be admirably imitated.

In this connection, why not call in the transcendent attraction of music? Now that we have lady orchestras, why not have them on the stage, or let them be asked to play occasional music between the acts, or while the tableaux are on? It adds a great charm.

The family circle in which the brothers have learned the key bugle, cornet, trombone, and violoncello, and the sisters the piano and harp, and the family that can sing part songs are to be envied. What a blessing in the family is the man who can sing comic songs, and who does not sing them too often.

A small operetta is often very nicely done by amateurs. We need not refer to the lamented "Pinafore," but that sort of thing. Would that Sir Arthur would write another "Pinafore!" but, alas! there was never but one.

A private theatre is a great addition to a large country house, and it can be made cheaply and well by a modern architect. It can be used as a ballroom on off evenings, as a dining-room, or for any other gathering.

Nothing can be more improving for young people than to study a play. Observe the expressions of the Oberammergau peasants, their intellectual and happy faces, "informed with thought," and contrast them with the faces of the German and Bavarian peasants about them. Their old pastor, Deisenberg, by training them in poetry and declamation, by founding his well-written play on their old traditions, by giving them this highly improving recreation for their otherwise starved lives, made another set of human beings of them. They have a motive in life besides the mere gathering in of a livelihood.

So it would be in any country neighbourhood, however rustic and remote, if some bright woman would assemble the young people at her house and train them to read and recite, lifting their young souls above vulgar gossip, and helping them to understand the older dramatists, to even attempt Shakspeare. Funny plays might be thrown in to enliven the scene, but there should be a good deal of earnest work inculcated as well. Music, that most divine of all the arts, should be assiduously cultivated. All the Oberammergau school-masters must be musicians, and all the peasants learn how to sing. What a good thing it would be if our district school-teachers should learn how to teach their scholars part songs.

When the art of entertaining has reached its apotheosis, we feel certain that we can have this influence emanating from every opulent country house, and that there will be no more complaint of dulness.

HUNTING AND SHOOTING.

My love shall hear the music of my hounds:
Uncouple in the western valley; let them go, —
Dispatch, I say, and find the Forester.
We will, fair Queen, up to the mountain's top.

MIDSUMMER NIGHT'S DREAM.

Fashion is at her best when she makes men and women love horses, dogs, boating, swimming, and all out-of-door games, — when she preaches physical culture. It is a good thing to see a man play lawn-tennis under a hot sun for hours; you feel that such a man could storm a battery. Nothing is more encouraging to the lover of all physical culture than the hunting, shooting, boating, and driving mania in the United States.

"Hunting" and "shooting" are sometimes used as synonymous terms in America; in England they mean quite different things. Hunting is riding to hounds without firearms, letting the dogs kill the fox; while shooting is to tramp over field, mountain, and through forest with dogs and gun, to kill deer, grouse, or partridge. The 12th of August is the momentous day, the first of the grouse shooting. Every one who can afford it, or who has a friend who can afford it, is off for the moors on the 11th, hoping to fill his bag. The 1st of September, partridge, and the 1st of October, pheasant shooting, are gala days, and the man is little thought of who cannot handle a gun.

In August inveterate fox-hunters meet at four or five o'clock in the morning for cub-hunting, which amusement is over by eleven or twelve. As the winter comes on the real hunting begins, and lasts until late in March. In the midland counties it is the special sport. Melton, in Leicestershire, is a noted hunting rendezvous. People, many Americans among them, take boxes there for the season, with large stables, and beguile the evenings with dinners, dancing, and card-parties. It is a sort of winter watering-place without any water, where the wine flows in streams every night, and where the brandy flask is filled every morning, "in case of accidents" while out with the hounds. An enthusiast in riding can be in the saddle ten or twelve hours out of every day, except Sunday, which is a dull day at Melton.

All the houses within such a neighbourhood are successively made the rendezvous or meet of the hunt. People come from great distances and send their horses by rail; others drive or ride in, and send their valuable hunters by a groom, who walks them the whole way. The show of "pink" is generally good. "Pink" means the scarlet hunting-coat worn by the gentlemen, the whippers-in, etc. The weather fades these coats to a pale pink very much esteemed by the older men.

They suggest the scars of a veteran warrior, hence the name. Some men hunt in black, but always in top boots. These boots are a cardinal point in a sportsman's dandyism.

Once or twice during the season a hunt breakfast is given in the house where the meet takes place. This is a pretty scene. All sorts of neat broughams, dog-carts, and old family chariots bring the ladies, who wear as much scarlet as good taste will allow.

Ladies, with their children, come to these breakfasts, which are sumptuous affairs. Great rounds of cold beef, game patties, and salads are spread out. All sorts of drinks, from beer up to champagne, are offered. One of the ladies of the house sits at the head of the table, with a large antique silver urn before her, and with tea and coffee ready for those who wish these beverages.

Some girls come on horseback, and look very pretty in their habits. These Dianas cut slices of beef and make impromptu sandwiches for their friends outside who have not dismounted. The daughters of the house stand on the steps while liveried servants hand around cake and wine, and others carry foaming tankards of ale, and liberal slices of cheese, among the farmers and attendants of the kennel.

It is an in-door and an out-door feast. The hounds are gathered in a group, the huntsman standing in the centre cracking his whip, and calling each hound by his name. Two or three masters of neighbouring packs are talking to the master of the hounds, a prominent gentleman of the county, who holds fox-hunting as something sacred, and the killing of a fox otherwise than in a legitimate manner as one of the seven deadly sins.

Twelve o'clock strikes, and every one begins to move. Generally the throw off is at eleven, but in honour of this breakfast a delay has been allowed. The huntsman mounts his horse and blows his horn; the hounds gather around him, and the whole field starts out. They are going to draw the covers at some large plantation above the park. The earths, or fox-holes, have been stopped for miles around, so that the fox once started has no refuge to make for, and is compelled to give the horses a run. It is a fine, manly sport, for with all the odds against him, the fox often gets away.

It is a pretty sight. The hounds go first, with nose to the ground, searching for the scent. The hunters and whippers-in, professional sportsmen, in scarlet coats and velvet jockey caps, ride immediately next to them, followed by the field. In a little while a confusion of rumours and cries is heard in the wood, various calls are blown on the horn, and the frequent cracking of high whips, which sound is used to keep the hounds in order, has all the effect of a succession of pistol shots. Hark! the fox has broken cover, and a repeated cry of "Tally Ho!" bursts from the wood. Away go the hounds, full cry, and what sportsmen call their music, something between a bay and a yelp, is indeed a pleasant sound, heard as it always is under circumstances calculated to give it a romantic character. Many ladies and small boys are amongst the followers of the chase. As soon as a boy can sit on his pony he begins to follow the hounds. A fox has no tail and no feet in hunting parlance, he has only a brush and pads. The lady who is in at the death receives the brush, and the man the pads, as a rule.

The hunt is a privileged institution in England, and can make gaps in hedges and break down walls with impunity. The farmer never complains if his wheat and turnip fields are ruined by the sport, nor does a lady complain if her flower garden and ornamental arbour be laid in ruins. The wily fox who has made such a skilful run must be followed at any cost.

Shooting is, however, the favourite sport of all Englishmen. Both pheasants and partridges are first carefully reared; the eggs generally purchased in large quantities, hatched by hens, and the birds fed through the summer with meal and other appropriate food. The gamekeepers take the greatest pride in the rearing of these birds. The pheasant is to the Englishman what the ibis was to the Egyptian.

They are let loose in the woods only when nearly full-grown. When the covers are full, and a good bag is to be expected, the first of October is a regular feast-day; a large party is asked, and a variety of costumes makes the scene picturesque. Red or purple stockings, knickerbockers of stout cloth or velveteen, a shooting-jacket of rough heavy material, and stout shoes make up the costume. The ladies collect after breakfast to see the party start out, a rendezvous is agreed upon, and luncheon or tea brings them together at either two or five o'clock, under a sheltering hedge on the side of a wood. The materials for an ample meal are brought to the appointed place, and a gay picnic ensues.

Though shooting is a sport in which more real personal work is done by those who join in it, and in which skill is a real ingredient, still it is neither so characteristic nor so picturesque as fox-hunting. There, a firm seat in the saddle, a good horse, and a determination to ride straight across country, are all that is needed for the majority of the field. In shooting much patience is required, besides accuracy of aim, and a judicious knowledge of when and how to shoot.

When we consider that hunting is the fashion which Americans are trying to follow, in a country without foxes, we must concede that success must be the result of considerable hard study. The fox is an anise-seed bag, but stone walls and high rail fences often make a stiffer country to ride over than any to be found abroad. In England there are no fences.

As an addition to the art of entertaining, hunting is a very great boon, and a hunt breakfast at the Westchester Hunting Club is as pretty a sight as possible.

In America, the sport began in Virginia in the last century, and no doubt in our great West and South it will some day become as recognized an institution as in England. We have room enough for it, too much perhaps. Shooting should become, from the Adirondacks to the Mississippi, a recognized sport, as it was once a necessity. If Americans could devote five months of the year to sport, as the Englishmen do, they might rival Great Britain. Unfortunately, Americans are bringing down other kinds of game. We cannot help thinking, however, that shooting a buck in the Adirondacks is a more manly sport than shooting one in England.

No one who has ever had the privilege will forget his first drive through the delights of an English park. The herds of fallow deer that haunt the ferny glades beneath the old oaks and beeches, are kept both for show and for the table; for park-fed venison is a more delicious morsel than the flesh of the Scotch red deer, that runs wild on the moor. White, brown, and mottled, with branching antlers which serve admirably for offensive and defensive weapons, the deer browse in groups; the does and fawns generally keeping apart from the more lordly bucks. The park-keeper knows them all, and when one is shot, the hides, hoofs, and antlers become his perquisites.

The method of shooting a buck is, however, this: The keeper's assistant drives the herd in a certain direction previously agreed upon. The sight is a very pretty one. The keeper stations himself, rifle in hand, in the fork of some convenient tree along the route. He takes aim at the intended victim, and at the ominous report the scared herd scampers away faster than ever, leaving their comrade to the knives of the keeper. It is very much like going out to shoot a cow. There is occasionally an attempt to renew the scenes of Robin Hood and Sherwood Forest, and the hounds are let out, but it is a sham after all, as they are trained not to kill the deer. The stag in this instance is given a start, being carried bound in a cart to a certain point, whence he is released and the chase commences. Thus the same stag may be hunted a number of times and be none the worse for it,—which is not the way they do it in the Adirondacks.

American venison is a higher flavoured meat than English, and should be only partly roasted before the fire, then cut in slices half-raw, placed on a chafing-dish with jelly and gravy, and warmed and cooked before the guest to ensure perfection.

A Polish officer of distinction has sent me the following account of hunting in his province:—

"We do not hunt the fox as in England. He is shot when met in a drive, or worried out of his subterranean castle by a special breed of dogs, the Dachshund, or Texel; or if young cubs are suspected to be in the hole the exits so far as known are closed, a shaft sunk to the centre, and the whole brood extinguished.

"We ride to hounds after hare, and the speed of a fox-hunt is nothing when compared with a cruise of the hare; for the greyhound, used for the latter, can beat any fox hound in racing. No one would ever think of water-killing deer as is done in the Adirondacks, and woe unto him who kills a doe!

"The old-fashioned way to kill the wild boar is to let him run at you, then kneel on one knee holding a hunting knife, or cutlass, double-edged. The boar infuriated by the dogs rushes at you. If well directed, the knife enters his breast and heart; if it does not, then look out. This is what is called pig-sticking in India. Old Emperor William hunted the boar in the Royal Forests near Berlin, and King Humbert does the same in the mountains near Rome.

"Bird hunting, that of snipe, woodcock, partridge, quail, and waterfowl, is done in the same way as here, excepting the use of duck batteries.

"There is very little big game to be found in Europe, that is, in the civilized parts of it, but in some forests belonging to royalty and that ilk, the elk, the stag, the bear, and the wild boar, present themselves as a target, and bison are to be found in Russia. The elk is purely royal game in Prussia.

"Southern or Upper Silesia is called the Prussian Ireland, and was famous for hunting-parties; ladies would join, and we would drive home with lighted torches attached to our sleighs."

These accounts of hunting-parties are introduced into the Art of Entertaining as they each and all contain hints which may be of use to the future American entertainer.

THE GAME OF GOLF.

As an addition to one's power of entertaining one's self, "golf affords a wide field of observation for the philosopher and the student of human nature. To play it aright requires nerve, endurance, and self-control, qualities which are essential to success in all great vocations; on the other hand, golf is peculiarly trying to the temper, although it must be said that when the golfer forgets himself his outbursts are usually directed against inanimate objects, or showered upon his own head." How it may take possession of one is well described in this little poem from the "St. James Gazette:" —

"Would you like to see a city given over,
Soul and body, to a tyrannizing game?
If you would, there's little need to be a rover,
For St. Andrews is that abject city's name.

"It is surely quite superfluous to mention,
To a person who has been here half an hour,
That Golf is what engrosses the attention
Of the people, with an all-absorbing power.

"Rich and poor alike are smitten with the fever;
'Tis their business and religion both to play;
And a man is scarcely deemed a true believer
Unless he goes at least a round a day.

"The city boasts an old and learned college,
Where you'd think the leading industry was Greek;
Even there the favoured instruments of knowledge
Are a driver, and a putter, and a cleek.

"All the natives and the residents are patrons
Of this royal, ancient, irritating game;
All the old men, all the young men, maids and matrons,
With this passion burn in hard and gem-like flame.

"In the morning, as the light grows strong and stronger,
You may see the players going out in shoals;
And when night forbids their playing any longer,
They will tell you how they did the different holes.

"Golf, golf, golf, and golf again, is all the story!
Till despair my overburdened spirit sinks;
Till I wish that every golfer was in glory,

And I pray the sea may overflow the links.

"Still a slender, struggling ray of consolation
Comes to cheer me, very feeble though it be;
There are two who still escape infatuation,
One's my bosom friend McFoozle, t'other's me.

"As I write the words McFoozle enters blushing,
With a brassy and an iron in his hand;
And this blow, so unexpected and so crushing,
Is more than I am able to withstand.

"So now it but remains for me to die, sir.
Stay! There is another course I may pursue.
And perhaps, upon the whole, it would be wiser,
I will yield to fate and be a golfer, too!"

"The game of golf," says Andrew Lang, its gifted poet and its historian, "has been described as putting little balls into holes difficult to find, with instruments which are sadly inadequate and illy adapted to the purpose." Its learned home is St. Andrews, in Scotland, although its advocates give it several classic starting-points. Learned antiquarians seem to think that the name comes from a Celtic word, meaning club. It is certainly an ancient game, and some variation of it was known on the Continent under various names.

The game requires room. A golf-course of nine holes should be at least a mile and a half long, and a hundred and twenty feet wide. It is usual to so lay out the course that the player ends where he began. All sorts of obstructions are left, or made artificially,—running water, railway embankments, bushes, ditches, etc.

The game is played with a gutta-percha ball, about an inch and a quarter in diameter, and a variety of clubs, with wooden or iron heads, whose individual use depends on the position in which the ball lies. It is usual for each player to be followed by a boy, who carries his clubs and watches his ball, marking it down as it falls. Games are either singles,—that is, when two persons play against one another, each having a ball,—or fours, when there are two on each side, partners playing alternately on one ball.

The start is made near the club house at a place called the tee. Down the course, anywhere from two hundred and fifty to five hundred yards distant, is a level space, fifty feet square, called a putting-green, and in its centre is a hole about four and a half inches in diameter and of the same depth. This is the first hole, and the contestant who puts his ball into it in the fewest number of strokes wins the hole. As the score is kept by strokes, the ball that is behind is played first. In this way the players are always together.

For his first shot from the tee, the player uses a club called the driver. It has a wooden head and a long, springy, hickory handle. With this an expert will drive a ball for two hundred yards. It is needless to say that the beginner is not so successful. After the first shot a cleek is used; or if the ball is in a bad hole, a mashie; if it is necessary to loft it, an iron, and so on,—the particular club depending, as we have said, on the position in which the ball lies.

The first hole won, the contestants start from a teeing-ground close by it, and fight for the second hole, and so on around the course,—the one who has won the most holes being the winner.

"A fine day, a good match, and a clear green" is the paradise of the golfer, but it still can be played all the year and even, by the use of a red ball, when snow is on the ground. In Scotland and athletic England it is a game for players of all ages, though in nearly all clubs children are not allowed. It can be played by both sexes.

A beginner's inclination is to grasp a golf club as he would a cricket bat, more firmly with the right hand than with the left, or at times equally firm with both hands. Now in golf, in making a full drive, the club when brought back must be held firmly with the left hand and more loosely with the right, because when the club is raised above the shoulder, and brought round the back of the neck, the grasp of one hand or the other must relax, and the hand to give way must be the right hand and not the left. The force of the club must be brought squarely against the ball.

The keeping of one's balance is another difficulty. In preparing to strike, the player bends forward a little. In drawing back his club he raises, or should raise, his left heel from the ground, and at the end of the upward swing stands poised on his right foot and the toe or ball of the left foot. At this point there is danger of his losing his balance, and as he brings the club down, falling either forward or backward, and consequently either heeling or toeing the ball, instead of hitting it with the middle of the face. Accuracy of hitting depends greatly on keeping a firm and steady hold of the ground with the toe of the left foot, and not bending the left knee too much.

To "keep your eye on the ball" sounds an injunction easy to be obeyed, but it is not always so. In making any considerable stroke, the player's body makes or should make a quarter turn, and the difficulty is to keep the head steady and the eye fixed upon the ball while doing this.

Like all other games, golf has its technical terms; the "teeing-ground," "putting," the "high-lofting stroke," the "approach shot," "hammer-hurling," "topping," "slicing," "hooking," "skidding," and "foozling" mean little to the uninitiated, but everything to the golfer.

Let us copy *verbatim* the following description of the Links of St. Andrews, the Elysium of the braw Scots:

"The Links occupy a crook-necked stretch of land bordered on the east by the sea and on the left by the railway and by the wide estuary of the Eden. The course, out and in, is some two miles and a half in length, allowing for the pursuit of balls not driven quite straight. Few pieces of land have given so much inexpensive pleasure for centuries. The first hole is to some extent carpeted by grass rather longer and rougher than the rest of the links. On the left lie some new houses and a big hotel; they can only be 'hazards' on the outward tack to a very wild driver indeed."

These "hazards" mean, dear reader, that if you and I are stopping at that big hotel, we may have our eyes put out by a passing ball; small grief would that be to a golfer!

"On the right it is just possible to 'heel' the ball over heaps of rubbish into the sea sand. The natural and orthodox hazards are few. Everybody should clear the road from the tee; if he does not the ruts are tenacious. The second shot should either cross or fall short of the celebrated Swilcan Burn. This tributary of ocean is extremely shallow, and meanders through stone embankments, hither and thither, between the tee and the hole. The number of balls that run into it, or jump in from the opposite bank, or off the old stone footbridge is enormous! People 'funk' the burn, top their iron shots, and are engulfed. Once you cross it, the hole whether to right or left is easily approached.

"The second hole, when the course is on the left, is guarded near the tee by the 'Scholar's Bunker,' a sand face which swallows a topped ball. On the right of the course are whins, much scantier now than of old; on the left you may get into long grass, and thence into a very sandy road under a wall, a nasty lie. The hole is sentinelled by two bunkers and many an approach lights in one or the other. The putting-green is nubbly and difficult.

"Driving to the third hole, on the left you may alight in the railway, or a straight hit may tumble into one of three little bunkers, in a knoll styled 'the Principal's Nose.' There are more bunkers lying in wait close to the putting-green.

"The driver to the fourth hole has to 'carry' some low hills and mounds; then comes a bunker that yawns almost across the course, with a small outpost named Sutherlands, which Englishmen profanely desired to fill up. This is impious.

"The long bunker has a buttress, a disagreeable round knoll; from this to the hole is open country if you keep to the right, but it is whinny. On the left, bunkers and broken ground stretch, and there is a convenient sepulchre of hope here, and another beyond the hole.

"As you drive to the fifth hole you may have to clear 'hell,' but 'hell' is not what it was. The first shot should carry you to the broken spurs of a table land, the Elysian fields, in which there yawn the Beardies, deep, narrow, greedy bunkers. Beyond the table land there is a gorge, and beyond it again a beautiful stretch of land and the putting-green. To the right is plenty of deep bent grass and gorse. This is a long hole and full of difficulties, the left side near the hole being guarded by irregular and dangerous bunkers.

"The sixth or heathery hole has lost most of its heather, but is a teaser. A heeled ball from the tee drops into the worst whins of the course in a chaos of steep, difficult hills. A straight ball topped falls into 'Walkinshaw's Grave,' or if very badly topped into a little spiteful pitfall; it is the usual receptacle of a well-hit second ball on its return journey. Escaping 'Walkinshaw's Grave' you have a stretch of very rugged and broken country, bunkers on the left, bent grass on the right, before you reach the sixth hole.

"The next, the high hole, is often shifted. It is usually placed between a network of bunkers with rough grass immediately beyond it. The first shot should open the hole and let you see the uncomfortable district into which you have to play. You may approach from the left, running the ball up a narrow causeway between the bunkers, but it is usually attempted from the front. Grief, in any case, is almost unavoidable."

It is evident the Scotch pleasure in "contradeectin'" is emphasized in golf.

One gets a wholesome sense of invigorating sea air, healthy exercise, and that delightful smell of the short, fresh grass. One sees "the beauty of the wild aerial landscape, the delicate tints of sand, and low, far-off hills, the distant crest of Lochnager, the gleaming estuary, and the black cluster of ruined towers above the bay, which make the charm of St. Andrews Links."

Golf has come to our country, and is becoming a passion. There is a club at Yonkers and one at Cedarhurst, but that on the Shinnecock Hills, on Long Island, will probably be the great headquarters of golf in the United States, as this club owns eighty acres beautifully adapted to the uses of the game, and has a large club-house, designed by Stanford White.

So we may expect an American historian to write an account of this fine vigorous game, in some future Badminton Library of sports and pastimes; and we shall have our own dear "fifth hole, which offers every possible facility to the erratic driver for coming to grief," if we can be as "contradeectin'" as a Scot. You never hear one word about victory; this golf literature is all written in the minor key,— but it is a gay thing to look at.

The regular golf uniform is a red jacket, which adds much to the gayety of a green, and has its obvious advantages.

"Ladies' links should be laid out on the model, though on a smaller scale, of the long round, containing some short putting-holes, some larger holes admitting of a drive or two of seventy or eighty yards, and a few suitable hazards. We venture to suggest seventy or eighty yards as the average limit of a drive, advisedly not because we doubt a lady's power to make a longer drive, but because that cannot be well done without raising the club above the shoulder. Now we do not presume to dictate, but we must observe that the posture and gestures requisite for a full swing are not particularly graceful when the player is clad in female dress.

"Most ladies put well, and all the better because they play boldly for the hole, without considering too much the lay of the ground; and there is no reason why they should not practise and excel in wrist shots with a lofting-iron or cleek. Their right to play, or rather the expediency of their playing, the long round is much more doubtful. If they choose to play at times when the male golfers are feeding or resting, no one can object; but at other times, must we say it? they are in the way, just because gallantry forbids to treat them exactly as men. The tender mercies of the golfer are cruel. He cannot afford to be merciful, because, if he forbears to drive into the party in front he is promptly driven into from behind. It is a hard lot to follow a party of ladies with a powerful driver behind you, if you are troubled with a spark of chivalry or shyness.

"As to the ladies playing the long round with men as their partners, it may be sufficient to say, in the words of a promising young player who found it hard to decide between flirtation and playing the game, 'It is mighty pleasant, but it is not business.'"

To learn this difficult game requires months of practice, and great nerve and talent for it. I shall not attempt to define what is meant by "dormy," "divot," "foozle," "gobble," "grip," or "gully." "*Mashy*, a straight-faced niblich," is one of these definitions.

Horace G. Hutchinson's book on golf is a most entertaining work,—if for no other reason than that its humour, the pleasant out-of-door atmosphere, the true enthusiasm for the game, and the illustrations, which are very well drawn, all make it an addition to one's knowledge of athletic sports.

That golf has taken its place amongst the arts of entertaining, we have no better proof than the very nice description of it in Norris's novel of "Marcia." This clever writer introduces a scene where "Lady Evelyn backs the winner" in the following sprightly manner:—

"Not many years ago all golfers who dwelt south of the Tweed were compelled, when speaking of their favourite relaxation, to take up an apologetic tone; they had to explain with humility, and with the chilling certainty of being disbelieved, that an immense amount of experience, dexterity, and self-command are requisite in order to make sure of hitting a little ball across five hundred yards of broken ground, and depositing it in a small hole in four or five strokes; but now that golf links have been established all over England there is no longer any need to make excuses for one of the finest games that human ingenuity or the accident of circumstances have ever called into existence. The theory of the game is simplicity itself,—you have only to put your ball into a hole in one or less strokes than your opponent; but the practice is full of difficulty, and what is better still, full of endless variety, so that you may go on playing golf from the age of eight to that of eighty, and yet never grow tired of it. Indeed, the circumstance that gray-haired enthusiasts are to be seen enjoying themselves thoroughly, and losing their tempers ludicrously, wherever 'the royal and ancient sport' has taken root, has caused certain ignorant persons to describe golf contemptuously as the old gentleman's game. Such criticisms, however, come only from those who have not attempted to acquire the game."

We advise all incipient golfers to read "Marcia," and to see how well golf and love-making can go together.

Golf has its poetic and humoristic literature; and as we began with its poetic side we may end with its broadest, latest joke:—

Two well-known professional golfers were playing a match. We will call them Sandy and Jock. On one side of the golf course was a railway, over which Jock drove his ball, landing it in some long grass. They both hunted for a long while for the missing ball. Sandy wanted Jock to give in and say that the ball was lost; but Jock would not consent, as a lost ball meant a lost hole. They continued to look round, and Jock slyly dropped another ball, and then came back and cried, "I've found the ba', Sandy."

"Ye're a leear," said Sandy, "for here it's in ma pooch."

We commend also "Famous Golf Links," by Hutchinson as clear and agreeable reading.

OF GAMES.

Come, thou complaisant cards, and cheat me
Of a bad night, and miserable dreams.

Shakspeare.

'Tis pleasant, through the loopholes of retreat,
To peep at such a world,—to see the stir
Of the great Babel, and not feel the crowd.

Cowper.

There is no amusement for a town or country-house, where people like to stay at home, so perfectly innocent and amusing as games which require a little brain.

It is a delightful feature of our modern civilization that books are cheap, and that the poets are read by every one. That would be a barren house where we did not find Scott, Byron, Goldsmith, Longfellow, Tennyson, Browning, Bret Harte, and Jean Ingelow.

Therefore, there would be little embarrassment should we ask the members of the circle around the evening lamp to write a parody on "Evangeline," "Lady Clara Vere de Vere," "Hervé Riel," or "The Heathen Chinee." The result is amusing.

Amongst games requiring memory and attention, we may mention Cross Purposes, The Horned Ambassador, I Love my Love with an A, the Game of the Ring, which is arithmetical, The Deaf Man, The Goose's History, Story Play, which consists in putting a word into a narrative so cleverly that it will not readily be guessed, although several may tell different stories with the word repeated. The best way to play this is to have some word which is not the word, like "ambassador," if the word be "banana" for instance, so by thus repeating "ambassador" the listener maybe baffled. The Dutch Conceit, My Lady's Toilette, Scheherazade's Ransom are also very good. This last deserves a description. Three of the company sustain the parts of the Sultan, the Vizier, and the Princess. The Sultan takes his seat at the end of the room, and the Vizier then leads the Princess before him with her hands bound behind her. The Vizier then makes an absurd proclamation that the Princess, having exhausted all her stories is about to be punished, unless a sufficient ransom be offered. All the rest of the company then advance in turn, and propose enigmas which must be solved by the Sultan or Vizier; sing the first verse of a song, to which the Vizier must answer with the second verse; or recite any well-known piece of poetry in alternate lines with the Vizier. Forfeits must be paid, either by the company when successfully encountered by the Sultan and

Vizier, or by the Vizier when unable to respond to his opponents; and the game goes on till the forfeits amount to any specified number on either side. Should the company be victorious and obtain the greater number of forfeits, the Princess is released and the Vizier has to execute all the penalties that may be imposed upon him. If otherwise, the Princess is led to execution. For this purpose she is seated on a low stool. The penalties for the forfeits, which should be previously prepared, are written on slips of paper and put in a basket, which she holds in her hands, tied behind her. The owners of the forfeits advance, and draw each a slip of paper. As each person comes forward the Princess guesses who it is, and if right, the person must pay an additional forfeit, the penalty for which is to be exacted by the Princess herself. When all the penalties have been distributed, the hands and eyes of the Princess are released, and she then superintends the execution of the various punishments that have been allotted to the company.

Another very good game is to send one of the company out, and as he comes in again to address him in the supposed character of General Scott, the Duke of Wellington, or of some Shakspearean hero. This, amongst bright people, can be very amusing. The hero thus addressed must find out who he is himself,—a difficult task for any one to discover, even with leading questions.

The Echo is another nice little game. It is played by reciting some story, which Echo is supposed to interrupt whenever the narrator pronounces certain words which recur frequently in his narrative. These words relate to the profession or trade of him who is the subject of the story. If, for example, the story is about a soldier the words which would recur most frequently would naturally be uniform, gaiters, *chapeau bras*, musket, plume, pouch, sword, sabre, gun, knapsack, belt, sash, cap, powder-flask, accoutrements, and so on. Each one of the company, with the exception of the person who tells the story, takes the name of soldier, powder-flask, etc., except the name accoutrements. When the speaker pronounces one of these words, he who has taken it for his name, ought, if the word has been said only once, to pronounce it twice; if it has been said twice, to pronounce it once. When the word "accoutrements" is uttered the players, all except the soldier, ought to repeat the word "accoutrements" either once or twice.

These games are amusing, as showing how defective a thing is memory, how apt it is to desert us under fire. It is very interesting to mark the difference of character exhibited by the players.

Another very funny game is Confession by a Die, played with cards and dice. It would look at first like a parody on Mother Church, but it does not so offend. A person takes some blank cards, and counting the company, writes down a sin for each. The unlucky sinner when called upon must not only confess, but, by throwing the dice, also confess as many sins as they indicate, and do penance for them all. These can, with a witty leader, be made very amusing.

The Secretary is another good game. The players sit at a table with square pieces of paper and pencils, and each one writes his own name, handing the paper, carefully folded down, to the secretary, who distributes them, saying, "Character." Then each one writes out an imaginary character, hands it to the secretary, who says, "Future." The papers are again distributed, and the writers forecast the future. Of course the secretary throws in all sorts of other questions, and when the game is through, the papers are read. They form a curious and heterogeneous piece of reading; sometimes such curious bits of character-reading crop out that one suspects complicity. But if honestly played it is amusing.

The Traveller's Tour is interesting. One of the party announces himself as the traveller. He is given an empty bag, and counters, with numbers on, are distributed amongst the players. Thus if twelve persons are playing the numbers must count up to twelve,—a set of ones to be given to one, twos to two, and so on. Then the traveller asks for information about the places to which he is going. The first person gives it if he can; if not, the second, and so on. If the traveller considers it correct information or worthy of notice he takes from the person one of his counters as a pledge of the obligation he is under to him. The next person in order takes up the next question, and so on. After the traveller reaches his destination he empties his bag and sees to whom he has been indebted for the greatest amount of information. He then makes him the next traveller. Of course this opens the door for all sorts of witty rejoinders, according as the players choose to exaggerate the claims of certain hotels, and to invent hits at certain watering-places.

The rhyming game is amusing. "I have a word that rhymes with game."

Interlocutor.—"Is it something statesmen crave?"

Speaker.—"No, it is not fame."

Interlocutor.—"Is it something that goes halt?"

Speaker.—"No, it is not lame."

Interlocutor.—"Is it something tigers need?"

Speaker.—"No, it is not to tame."

Interlocutor.—"Is it something we all would like?"

Speaker.—"No, it is not a good name."

Interlocutor.—"Is it to shoot at duck?"

Speaker.—"Yes, and that duck to maim." Such words as "nut," "thing," "fall," etc., which rhyme easily, are good choices. The two who play it must be quick-witted.

The game of Crambo, in which each player has to write a noun on one piece of paper, and a question on another, is curious. As, for instance, the drawer gets the word "Africa" and the question "Have you an invitation to my wedding?" He must write a poem in which he answers the question and brings in the other word.

The game of Preferences has had a long and successful career. It is a very good addition to the furniture of a country parlour to possess a blank-book which is left lying on the table, in which each guest should be asked to write out answers to the following questions:

Who is your favourite hero in history?

Who is your favourite heroine?

Who is your favourite king?

Who is your favourite queen?

What is your favourite Christian name for a man?

What is your favourite Christian name for a woman? etc.

The game of Authors, especially when created by the persons who wish to play it, is very interesting. The game can be bought and is a very common one, as perhaps every one knows, but it can be rendered uncommon by the preparation of the cards among the members of the family. There are sixty-four cards to be prepared, each bearing the name of a favourite author and any three of his works. The entire set is numbered from one to sixty-four. Any four cards containing the name and works of the same author form a book.

Or the names of kings and queens and the learned men of their reigns may be used, instead of authors; it is a very good way to study history. The popes can be utilized, with their attendant great men, and after playing the game for a season one has no difficulty in fixing the environment of the history of an epoch.

As the numbers affixed to the cards may be purely arbitrary, the count at the end will fluctuate with great impartiality. The Dickens cards may count but one, while Tupper will be named sixteen. Carlyle will only count two, while Artemas Ward will be sixty. King Henry VIII., who set no small store by himself, may be No. I in the kingly game, while Edward IV. will be allowed a higher numeral than he was allotted in life.

Now we come to a game which interests old and young. None are so apathetic but they relish a peep behind the dark curtain. The apple-paring in the fire, the roasted chestnut and the raisin, the fire-back and the stars, have been interrogated since time began. The pack of cards, the teacup, the dream-book, the board with mystic numbers, the Bible and key, have been consulted from time immemorial. The makers of games have given in their statistics, and they declare there are no games so popular as those which foretell the future.

Now this tampering with gruesome things which may lead to bad dreams is not recommended, but so long as it is done for fun and an evening's amusement it is not at all dangerous. The riches which are hidden in a pack of fortune-telling cards are very comforting while they last. They are endless, they are not taxed, they have few really trying responsibilities attached, they bring no beggars. They buy all we want, they are gained without headache or backache, they are inherited without stain, and lost without regret. Of what other fortune can we say so much?

Who is not glad to find a four-leaved clover, to see the moon over his right shoulder, to have a black cat come to the house? She is sure to bring good fortune!

The French have, however, tabularized fortune-telling for us. Their peculiar ability in arranging ceremonials and *fêtes*, and their undoubted genius for tactics and strategy, show that they might be able to foresee events. Their ingenuity, in all technical contrivances, is an additional testimony in the right direction, and we are not surprised that they have here, as is their wont, given us the practical help which we need in fortune-telling.

Mademoiselle Lenormand, the sorceress who foretold Napoleon's greatness and to many of the great people of France their downfall and misfortunes, has left us thirty-six cards in which we can read the decrees of fate. Lenormand was a clever sybil. She knew how to mix things, and throw in the inevitable bad and the possible good so as at least to amuse those who consulted her.

In this game, which can be bought at any bookstore, the *cavalier*, for instance, is a messenger of good fortune, the clover leaf a harbinger of good news, but if surrounded by clouds it indicates great pain, but if No. 2 lies near No. 26 or 28 the pain will be of short duration, and so on.

Thus Mlle. Lenormand tells fortunes still, although she has gone to the land of certainty, and has herself found out whether her symbols and emblems and her combinations really did draw aside the curtain of the future with invisible strings. Amateur sybils playing this game can be sure that they add to the art of entertaining.

The cup of tea, and the mysterious wanderings of the grounds around the cup, is used for divination by the old crone in an English farmhouse, while the Spanish gypsy uses chocolate grounds for the same purpose. That most interesting of tragic sybils, Norna of the Fitful Head, used molten lead.

Cards from the earliest antiquity have been used to tell fortunes. Fortuna, courted by all nations, was in Greek Tyche, or the goddess of chance. She differed from Destiny, or Fate, in so far as that she worked without law, giving or taking at her own good pleasure. Her symbols were those of mutability, a ball, a wheel, a pair of wings, a rudder. The Romans affirmed that when she entered their city she threw off her wings and shoes, determined to live with them forever. She seems to have thought better of it, however. She was the sister of the Parcae, or Fates, those three who spin the thread of life, measure it, and cut it off. The power to tell fortunes by the hand is easily learned from Desbarolles' book, is a very popular accomplishment, and never fails to amuse the company and interest the individual.

It must not be made, however, of too much importance. It never amuses people to be warned that they may expect an early and violent death.

Then comes Merelles, or Blind Men's Morris, which can be played on a board or on the ground, but which now finds itself reduced to a parlour game. This takes two players. American Bagatelle can be played alone or with an antagonist. Chinese puzzles, which are infinitely amusing, and all the great family of the Sphinx, known as puzzles, are of infinite service to the retired, the invalid, and weary people for whom the active business of life is at an end.

We may describe one of these games as an example. It is called The Blind Abbot and his Monks. It is played with counters. Arrange eight external cells of a square so that there may be always nine in each row, though the whole number may vary from eighteen to thirty-six. A convent in which there were nine cells was occupied by a blind abbot and twenty-four monks, the abbot lodging in the centre cell and the monks in the side cells, three in each, giving a row of nine persons on each side of the building. The abbot suspecting the fidelity of his brethren often went out at night and counted them. When he found nine in each row, the old man counted his beads, said an *Ave,* and went to bed contented. The monks, taking advantage of his failing sight, contrived to deceive him, so that four could go out at night, yet have nine in a row. How did they do it?

The next night, emboldened by success, the monks returned with four visitors, and then arranged them nine in a row. The next night they brought in four more belated brethren, and again arranged them nine in a row, and again four more. Finally, when the twelve clandestine monks had departed, and six monks with them, the remainder deceived the abbot again by presenting a row of nine. Try it with the counters, and see how they so abused the privileges of conventual seclusion!

Then try quibbles: "How can I get the wine out of a bottle if I have no corkscrew and must not break the glass or make a hole in it or the cork?"

The *raconteur,* or story-teller, is a potent force. Any one who can memorize the stories of Grimm, or Hans Christian Anderson, or Browning's "Pied Piper," or Ouida's "Dog of Flanders," or Dr. Holmes' delightful "Punch Bowl," and tell these in a natural sort of way is a blessing. But this talent should never be abused. The man who, in cold blood, fires off a long poetical quotation at a dinner, or makes a speech when he is not asked, in defiance of the goose-flesh which is creeping down his neighbours' backs, is a traitor to honour and religion, and should be dragged to execution with his back to the horses, like a Nihilist. It is only when these extempore talents can be used without alarming people that they are useful or endurable.

Perhaps we might make our Christmas Holidays a little more gay. There are old English and German customs beyond the mistletoe, and the tree, and the rather faded legend of Santa Claus. There are worlds of legendary lore. We might bring back the Leprechaun, the little fairy-man in red, who if you catch him will make you happy forever after, and who has such a strange relationship to humanity that at birth and death the Leprechaun must be tended by a mortal. To follow up the Banshee and the Brownie, to light the Yule log, to invoke the Lord of Misrule, above all to bring back the waits or singing-boys who come under the window with an old carol, and the universal study of symbolism,—all this is useful at Christmastide, when the art of entertaining is ennobled by the song "Glory to God in the highest, and on earth peace, good-will toward men."

The supper-table has unfortunately fallen into desuetude, probably on account of our exceedingly late dinners. We sup out, we sup at a ball, but rarely have that informal and delightful meal which once wound up every evening.

Mrs. Elizabeth Montague, in her delightful letters, talks about the "Whisk, and the Quadrille parties, with a light supper," which amused the ladies of her day. We still have the "Whisk," but what has become of *lansquenet,* quadrille basset, piquet, those pretty and courtly games?

Whist! Who shall pretend to describe its attractions? What a relief to the tired man of affairs, to the woman who has no longer any part in the pageant of society!

What pleasure in its regulating, shifting fortunes. We have seen, in its parody on life, that holding the best cards, even the highest ones, does not always give us the game. We have noticed that with a poor hand, somebody wins fame, success, and happiness. We have all felt the injustice of the long suit, which has baffled our best endeavours. We play our own experience over again, with its faithless kings and queens. The knave is apt to trip us up, on the green cloth as on the street.

So long as cards do not lead to gambling, they are innocent enough. The great passion for gambling is behind the game of boaston, played appropriately for beans. We all like to accumulate, to believe that we are fortune's favourite. What matter if it be only a few more beans than one's neighbour?

That is a poorly furnished parlour which has not a chess table in one corner, a whist table properly stocked, and a little solitaire table for Grandma. Cribbage and backgammon boards, cards of every variety, bezique counters and packs, and the red and white champions for the hard-fought battle-field of chess, should be at hand.

Playing cards made their way through Arabia from India to Europe, where they first arrived about the year 1370. They carried with them the two rival arts, engraving and painting. They were the *avants couriers* of engraving on wood and metal, and of the art of printing.

Cards, begun as the luxuries of kings and queens, became the necessity of the gambler, the solace of all who like games. They have been one of the worst curses and one of the greatest blessings of poor human nature.

> "When failing health, or cross event,
> Or dull monotony of days,
> Has brought us into discontent
> Which darkens round us like a haze" —

then the arithmetical progression of a game has sometimes saved the reason. They are a priceless boon to failing eyesight.

Piquet, a courtly game, was invented by Etienne Vignoles, called La Hire, one of the most active soldiers of the reign of Charles VII. This brave soldier was an accomplished cavalier, deeply imbued with a reverence for the manners and customs of chivalry. Cards continued from his day to follow the whim of the court, and to assume the character of the period, through the regency of Marie de Medicis, the time of Anne of Austria and of Louis XIV. The Germans were the first people to make a pack of cards assume the form of a scholastic treatise; the king, queen, knight, and knave tell of English customs, manners, and nomenclature.

The highly intellectual game of Twenty Questions can be played by three or four people or by a hundred. It is an unfailing delight by the wood fire in the remote house in the wood, or by the open window looking out on the lordly Hudson of a summer's night. It only needs that one bright mind shall throw the ball, and half a dozen may catch. Mr. Lowell once said there was no subject so erudite, no quotation so little known, that it could not be reached in twenty questions.

But we are not all as bright as James Russell Lowell. We can, however, all ask questions and we can all guess; it is our Yankee privilege. The game of Twenty Questions has led to the writing of several books. The best way to begin is, however, to choose a subject. Two persons should be in the secret. The questioner begins: Is it animal, vegetable or mineral? Is it a manufactured object? Ancient or modern? What is its shape, size and colour? What is its use? Where is it now? The object of the answerer is of course to baffle, to excite curiosity; it is a mental battledore and shuttlecock.

It is strange that the pretty game of croquet has gone out of favour. It is still, however, to be seen on some handsome lawns. Twenty years ago it inspired the following lines:—

CROQUET.

"A painter must that poet be
And lay with brightest hues his palette
Who'd be the bard of Croquet'rie
And sing the joys of hoop and mallet.

"Given a level lawn in June
And six or eight, enthusiastic,
Who never miss their hoops, or spoon,
And are on duffers most sarcastic;

"Given the girl whom you adore—
And given, too, that she's your side on,
Given a game that's not soon o'er,
And ne'er a bore the lawn espied on;

"Given a claret cup as cool
As simple Wenham Ice can make it,
Given a code whose every rule
Is so defined that none can break it;

"Given a very fragrant weed—
Given she doesn't mind your smoking,
Given the players take no heed
And most discreetly keep from joking;

"Given all these, and I proclaim,
Be fortune friendly or capricious,
Whether you win or lose the game,
You'll find that croquet is delicious."

ARCHERY.

"The stranger he made no muckle ado,
But he bent a right good bow,
And the fattest of all the herds he slew
Forty good yards him fro:
'Well shot! well shot!' quoth Robin Hood."

"Aim at the moon, if you ambitious are,
And failing that, you may bring down a star."

Fashion has brought us again this pretty and romantic pastime, which has filled the early ballads with many a picturesque figure. Now on many a lawn may be seen the target and the group in Lincoln green. Indeed, it looks as if archery were to prove a very formidable rival to lawn tennis.

The requirements of archery are these: First, a bow; secondly, arrows; thirdly, a quiver, pouch, and belt; fourthly, a grease pot, an arm-guard or brace, a shooting-glove, a target and a scoring-card.

The bow is the most important article in archery, and also the most expensive. It is usually from five to six feet in length, made of a simple piece of yew or of lance-wood and hickory glued together back to back. The former is better for gentlemen, the latter for ladies, as it is adapted for the short, sharp, pull of the feminine arm. The wood is gradually tapered, and at each end is a tip of horn; the one from the upper end being longer than the other or lower end. The strength of bows is marked in pounds, varying from twenty-five to forty pounds in strength for ladies, for gentlemen from fifty to eighty pounds. One side of the bow is flat, called the back, the other, called the belly, is rounded. Nearly in the middle, where the hand should take hold, it is lapped round with velvet, and that part is called the handle. In each of the tips of the horns is a notch for the string, called the nock.

Bow strings are made of hemp or flax, the former being the better material, for though at first they stretch more, yet they wear longer and stand a harder pull, and are, as well, more elastic in the shooting. In applying a fresh string to a bow, be careful in opening it not to break the composition that is on it. Cut the tie, take hold of the eye which will be found ready worked at one end, let the other part hang down, and pass the eye over the upper end of the bow. If for a lady, it may be held from two to two and a half inches below the nock; if for a gentleman, half an inch lower, varying it according to the length and strength of the bow. Then run your hand along the side of the bow and string to the bottom nock. Turn it around that and fix it by the noose, called the timber noose, taking care not to untwist the string in making it. This noose is simply a turn back and twist, without a knot.

When strung a lady's bow will have the string about five inches from the belly, and a gentleman's about half an inch more. The part opposite the handle is bound round with waxed silk in order to prevent its being frayed by the arrow. As soon as a string becomes too soft and the fibres too straight, rub it with beeswax and give it a few turns in the proper direction, so as to shorten it, and twist its strands a little tighter. A spare string should always be provided by the shooter.

Arrows are differently shaped by various makers; some being of uniform thickness throughout, while others are protuberant in the middle; some again are larger at the point than at the feather end. They are generally made of white deal, with joints of iron or brass riveted on, and have a piece of heavy wood spliced to the deal, between it and the point, by which their flight is improved. At the other end a piece of horn is inserted, in which is a notch for the string. They are armed with three feathers glued on, one of which is a different colour from the others, and is intended to mark the proper position of the arrow when placed on the string, this one always pointing from the bow. These feathers, properly applied, give a rotary motion to the arrow, which causes its flight to be straight. They are generally from the wing of the turkey or the goose. The length and weight of the arrows vary, the latter in England being marked in sterling silver coin and stamped in the arrow in plain figures. It is usual to paint a crest or a monogram or distinguishing rings on the arrow, just between the feathers by which they may be known in shooting at the target.

The quiver is merely a tin case painted green, intended for the security of the arrows when not in use. The pouch and belt are worn round the waist, the latter containing those arrows which are actually being shot. A pot to hold grease for touching the glove and string, and a tassel to wipe the arrows are hung at the belt. The grease is composed of beef suet and wax melted together. The arm is protected from the blow of the string by the brace, a broad guard of strong leather buckled on by two straps. A shooting-glove, also of thin tubes of leather, is attached to the wrist by three flat pieces, ending in a circular strap buckled around it. This glove prevents the soreness of the fingers, which soon comes after using the bow without it.

The target consists of a circular mat of straw, covered with canvas painted in a series of circles. It is usually from three feet six inches to four feet in diameter, the centre is gilt, and called the gold; the ring about it is called the red, after which comes the inner white, then the black, and finally the outer white. These targets are mounted on triangular stands, from fifty to a hundred yards apart; sixty being the usual shooting distance.

A scoring-card is provided with columns for each colour, which are marked with a pin. The usual score for a gold hit, or the bull's-eye, is 9, the red 7, inner white 5, black 3, and outer white, 1.

To string the bow properly it should be taken by the handle in the right hand. Place one end on the ground, resting in the hollow of the right foot, keeping the flat side of the bow, called the back, toward your person. The left foot should be advanced a little, and the right placed so that the bow cannot slip sideways. Place the heel of the left hand upon the upper limb of the bow, below the eye of the string. Now while the fingers and thumb of the left hand slide the eye towards the notch in the horn, and the heel pushes the limb away from the body, the right hand pulls the handle toward the person and thus resists the action of the left, by which the bow is bent, and at the same time the string is slipped into the nock, as the notch is termed. Take care to keep the three outer fingers free from the string, for if the bow should slip from the hand, and the string catch them, they will be severely pinched. In shooting in frosty weather, warm the bow before the fire or by friction with a woollen cloth. If the bow has been lying by for a long time, it should be well rubbed with boiled linseed oil before using it.

To unstring the bow hold it as in stringing, then press down the upper limb exactly as before, and as if you wished to place the eye of the string in a higher notch. This will loose the string and liberate the eye, when it must be lifted out of the notch by the forefinger, and suffered to slip down the limb.

Before using the bow hold it in a perpendicular direction, with the string toward you, and see if the line of the string cuts the middle of the bow. If not, shift the eye and noose of the string to either side, so as to make the two lines coincide. This precaution prevents a very common cause of defective shooting, which is the result of an uneven string throwing the arrow on one side. After using it unstring it, and at a large shooting-party unloose your bow after every round. Some bows get bent into very unmanageable shapes.

The general management of the bow should be on the principle that damp injures it, and that any loose floating ends interfere with its shooting. It should therefore be kept well varnished, and in a waterproof case, and it should be carefully dried after shooting in damp weather. If there are any ends hanging from the string cut them off close, and see that the whipping, in the middle of the string, is close and well-fitting. The case should be hung up against a dry, internal wall, not too near the fire. In selecting your bow be careful that it is not too strong for your power, and that you can draw the arrow to its head without any trembling of the hand. If this cannot be done after a little practice, the bow should be changed for a weaker one; for no arrow will go true, if it is discharged by a trembling hand. If an arrow has been shot into the target on the ground, be particularly careful to withdraw it by laying hold close to its head, and by twisting it around as it is withdrawn, in the direction of its axis. Without this precaution it may be easily bent or broken.

In shooting at the target the first thing is to nock the arrow, that is, to place it properly on the string. In order to effect this, take the bow in the left hand, with the string toward you, the upper limb being toward the right. Hold it horizontally while you take the arrow by the middle; pass it on the under side of the string and the upper side of the bow, till the head reaches two or three inches past the left hand. Hold it there with the forefinger or thumb, while you remove the right hand down to the neck; turn the arrow till the cock feather comes uppermost, then pass it down the bow, and fix it on the working part of the string. In doing this all contact with the feathers should be avoided, unless they are rubbed out of place, when they may be smoothed down by passing them through the hand.

The body should be at right angles with the target, but the face must be turned over the left shoulder, so as to be opposed to it. The feet must be flat on the ground, with the heels a little apart, the left foot turned toward the mark. The head and chest inclined a little forward so as to present a full bust, but not bent at all below the waist. Draw the arrow to the full length of the arm, till the hand touches the shoulder, then take aim. The loosing should be quick, and the string must leave the fingers smartly and steadily. The bow-head must be as firm as a vise, no trembling allowed.

The rules of an Archery Club are usually that a Lady Paramount be annually elected; that there be a President, Secretary, and Treasurer; that all members intending to shoot shall appear in the uniform of the club, and that a fine shall be imposed for non-attendance.

The Secretary sends out cards at least a week before each day of meeting, acquainting members with the place and hour.

There are generally four prizes for each meeting, two for each sex, the first for numbers, the second for hits. No person is allowed to take both on the same day. A certain sum of money is voted to the Lady Paramount, for prizes for each meeting.

In case of a tie for hits, numbers decide, and in case of a tie for numbers, hits decide. The decision of the Lady Paramount is final.

There is also a challenge prize, and a commemorative ornament is presented to the winner of this prize.

The distance for shooting is sixty or one hundred yards, and five-feet targets are used.

The dress or uniform of the club is decided by the Lady Paramount.

The expenses of archery are not great, about the same as lawn tennis, although a great many arrows are lost in the course of the season. Bows and other paraphernalia last a long time. The lady archers are apt to feel a little lame after the first two or three essays, but they should practise a short time every morning, and always in a loose waist or jacket. It will be found a very healthy and strengthening practice and pastime.

We must not judge of the merits of ancient bowmen from the practice of archery in the present day. There are no such distances now assigned for the marks as we find mentioned in old histories or poetic legends, nor such precision, even at short lengths, in the direction of the arrow. Few, if any, modern archers in long shooting reach four hundred yards; or in shooting at a mark exceed eighty or a hundred. Archery has been since the invention of gunpowder followed as a pastime only. It is decidedly the most graceful game that can be practised, and the legends of Sherwood Forest, of Maid Marion, Little John, Friar Tuck, and the Abbot carry us back into the fragrant heart of the forest, and bring back memories which are agreeable to all who have in them a drop of Saxon blood.

The usual dress is the Lincoln green of Robin Hood and his merry men, and at Auburn in New York they have a famous club and shooting ground, over the gate of which is painted this motto:—

"What is hit is history,
And what is missed is mystery."

The traveller still sees in the Alpine Tyrol, and in some parts of Switzerland, bands of archers who depend on the bow and arrow for their game. But there is not that skill or that poetry attached to the sport which made Locksley try conclusions with Hubert, in the presence of Prince John, as we read in the immortal pages of Ivanhoe.

The prize was to be a bugle horn mounted with silver, a silken baldric richly ornamented, having on it a medallion of Saint Hubert, the patron of sylvan sport. Had Robin Hood been beaten he would have yielded up bow, baldric, and quiver to the provost of the sports; as it was, however, he let fly his arrow, and it lighted upon that of his competitor, which it split to shivers.

THE SEASON, BALLS, AND RECEPTIONS.

"Good-night to the season! the dances,
The fillings of hot little rooms,
The glancings of rapturous glances,
The flarings of fancy costumes,
The pleasures which fashion makes duties,
The phrasings of fiddles and flutes,
The luxury of looking at beauties,
The tedium of talking to mutes,
The female diplomatists, planners
Of matches for Laura and Jane,
The ice of her Ladyship's manners!
The ice of his Lordship's champagne."

The season in London extends from May to August, often longer if Parliament is in session. In Paris it is from May to the *Grand Prix*, when it is supposed to end, about the 20th of June. In New York and Washington it is all winter, from November 1st to Lent, with good Episcopalians, and from November to May with the rest of mankind.

It then begins again in July, with the people who go to Newport and to Bar Harbor, and keeps up until September, when comes in Tuxedo and the gayety of Long Island, and the Hudson. Indeed, with the gayety of country-house life, hunting, lawn tennis and driving, it is hard to say when the American season ends.

There is one sort of entertainment which is a favourite everywhere and very convenient. It is the afternoon reception or party by daylight. The gas is lighted, the day excluded, the hostess and her guests are in beautiful toilets; their friends come in street dresses and bonnets; their male friends in frock coats. This is one of the anomalies of fashion. These entertainments are very large, and a splendid collation is served. The form of invitation is simply —

Mrs. Brownton at home
Thursday, from 3 to 6.

and unless an R. S. V. P. is appended, no reply is expected. These receptions are favourites with housekeepers, as they avoid the necessity of keeping the servants up at night.

The drawback to this reception is that, in our busy world of America, very few men can spare the time to call in the daytime, so the attendance is largely feminine.

On entering, the guest places a card on the table, or, if she cannot be present, she should send a card in an envelope.

After these entertainments, which are really parties, a lady should call. They are different things entirely from afternoon tea, after which no call is expected. If the reception is given to some distinguished person, the lady stands beside her guest to present all the company to him or her.

If on the card the word "Music" is added, the guests should be punctual, as, doubtless, they are to be seated, and that takes time. No lady who gives a *musicale* should invite more than she can seat comfortably; and she should have her rooms cool, and her lights soft and shaded.

People with weak eyes suffer dreadfully from a glare of gas, and when music is going on they cannot move to relieve themselves. The hostess should think of all this. Who can endure the mingled misery of a hot room, an uncomfortable seat, a glare of gas, and a pianoforte solo?

A very sensible reformation is now in progress in regard to the sending of invitations and the answering of the same. The post is now freely used as a safe and convenient medium, and no one feels offended if an invitation arrives with a two-cent stamp on the envelope. There is no loss of caste in sending an invitation by post.

Then comes the ball, or, as they always say in Europe, the dance, which is the gayest of all things for the *débutante*. The popular form for an invitation to an evening party is as follows:—

Mrs. Hammond

Requests the pleasure of

Mr. and Mrs. Norton's company

on Tuesday evening, December 23, at 9 o'clock.

R. S. V. P.   Dancing.

The card of the *débutante*, if the ball is given for one, is enclosed.

If a hostess gives her ball at some public place, like Delmonico's, she has but little trouble. The compliment is not the same as if she gave it in her own house, however. If there is room, a ball in a private house is much more agreeable, and a greater honour to the guest.

Gentlemen who have not an acquaintance should be presented to the young dancing set; but first, of course, to the *chaperon*. As, however, the hostess cannot leave her post while receiving, she should have two or three friends to help her. Great care should be taken that there be no wall-flowers, no neglected girls. The non-dancers in an American ball are like the non-Catholics in a highly doctrinal sermon: they are nowhere, pushed into a corner where there is perhaps a draught, and the smell of fried oysters. Such is the limbo of the woman of forty or over, who in Europe would be the belle, the person just beginning to have a career. For it is too true that the woman who has learned something, who is still beautiful, the woman who has maturity and experience, is pushed to the wall in America, while in Europe she is courted and admired. Society holds out all its attractive distractions and comforts to such a woman in Europe; in America it keeps everything, even its comforts, for the very young.

The fact that American ballrooms, or rather the parlours of our ordinary houses, are wholly disproportioned to the needs of society, has led to the giving of balls at Delmonico's and other public places. If these are under proper patronage there is no reason why they should not be as entertaining, as exclusive, and as respectable as a ball at home. Any hostess or group of managers should, if they give up a ball at home and use the large accommodations of Delmonico or the Assembly Rooms, certainly consider the claims of chaperons and mammas who must wearily sit through the German. It is to be feared that attention to the mamma is not yet a grace in which even her daughter excels. Young men who wish to marry mademoiselle had better pay her mother the compliment of getting her a seat, and social leaders should also show her the greatest attention, not alone from the selfish reason which the poet commemorates:—

> "Philosophy has got a charm,—
> I thought of Martin Tupper,—
> And offering mamma my arm,
> I took her down to supper.

> "I gave her Pommery, Côte d'Or,
> Which seethed in rosy bubbles;
> I called this fleeting life a bore,
> The world a sea of troubles."

It is to be feared that the life of a *chaperon* in America is not a bed of roses, even if softened by all these attentions.

Kept up late, pushed into a corner, the mother of a society girl becomes only a sort of head-chambermaid. Were she in Europe, she would be the person who would receive the compliments and the attention and be asked to dance in the German.

A competent critic of our manners spoke of this in the following sensible words:—

"The evils arising from the excessive liberty permitted to American girls cannot be cured by laws. If we ever root them out we must begin with the family life, which must be reformed. For young people, parental authority is the only sure guide. Coleridge well said that he who was not able to govern himself must be governed by others; and experience has shown us that the children of civilized parents are as little able to govern themselves as the children of savages. The liberty or license of our youth will have to be curtailed, as our society is becoming more complex and artificial, like older societies in Europe. The children will have to approximate to them in status, and parents will have to waken to a sense of their responsibilities, and subordinate their ambitions and their pleasures to their duties." Mothers should go out more with their daughters, join in their pleasures, and never permit themselves to be shelved.

Society is in a transition state in America. In one or more cities of the West and South it is considered proper for a young man to call for a young girl, and drive with her alone to a ball. In Northern cities this is considered very bad form. In Europe it would be considered a vulgar madness, and a girl's character compromised. Therefore it is better for the mother to keep her rightful place as guardian, *chaperon*, friend, no matter how she is treated.

Women are gifted with so much tact and so intuitive a faculty, that in the conduct of fashionable life they need but few hints.

The art of entertaining should be founded first, on good sense, a quiet considerateness, a good heart, a spirit of friendliness; next, a consideration of what is due to others and what is due to one's self. There is always a social conscience in one's organization, which will point aright; but the outward performance of conventional rules can never be thoroughly learned, unless the heart is well-bred.

Many ladies are now introducing dancing at crowded day receptions and teas. Where people are coming and going this is objectionable, as the hostess is expected to do too much, and the guests being in street dress, while the hostess and her dancers are in low evening dress, the appearance of the party is not ornamental.

Evening parties are far more formal, and require the most elaborate dress. Every lady who can wear a low-necked dress should do so. The great drawback in New York is now the ridiculous lateness of the hour—eleven or twelve—at which the guests arrive.

If a card is written,—

Mrs. Brown at home Tuesday evening,

some sticklers for etiquette say that she should not put R. S. V. P. on her card.

If she wishes an answer, she should say,—

Mrs. Brown
requests the pleasure of
Mr. and Mrs. Campbell's company.

R. S. V. P.

Perhaps the latter is better form. It is more respectful. The "At Home" can be used for large and informal receptions, where an individual acceptance is not required.

Garden parties are becoming very fashionable at watering-places, in rural cities, and at country houses which are accessible to a town. No doubt the garden party is a troublesome affair in a climate so capricious as ours. The hostess has to be prepared for a sudden shower, and to have two tables of refreshments. The effort to give the out-of-door plays in this country, as in England, has often been frustrated by a sudden shower, as at Mrs. Stevens' palace at Castle Point. It is curious that they can and do give them in England, where it always rains. However, these entertainments and hunting remain rather as visitors than as old and recognized institutions.

Americans all dance well, and are always glad to dance. Whether it be assembly, hunt ball, or private party, the German cotillion finishes the bail. It is an allegory of society in its complicated and bewildering complications, its winding and unwinding of the tangled chain.

In every large city a set arises whose aim is to be exclusive. Sometimes this privilege seems to be pushed too far. Often one is astonished at the black sheep who leap into the well-defended enclosures. In London, formerly, an autocratic set of ladies, well known as Almacks, turned out the Duke of Wellington because he came in a black cravat. In our republican country perpetual Almacks arise, offensive and defensive,—a state of things which has its advantages and disadvantages. It keeps up an interest in society. It is like the fire in the engine: it makes the train move, even if it sends out smoke and cinders which get into people's eyes and make them weep. It is a part of the inevitable friction which accompanies the best machinery; and if they have patience, those who are left out one winter will be the inside aristocrats of the next, and can leave somebody else out.

Quadrilles, the Lancers, and occasionally a Virginia Reel, are introduced to make the modern ball more interesting, and enable people who cannot bear the whirl of the waltz to dance. The elderly can dance a quadrille without loss of breath or dignity. Indeed, the Americans are the only people who relegate the dance to the young alone. In Europe the old gray-head, the old mustache, leads the German. Ambassadors and generals, princes and potentates, go spinning around with gray-haired ladies until they are seventy. Grandmothers dance with their grandsons. Socrates learned to dance. In Europe it is the elderly woman who receives the most flattering invitations to lead the German. An ambassadress of fifty would be very much astonished if the prince did not ask her to dance.

The saltatory art is like the flight of a butterfly,—hard to describe, impossible to follow. The *valse à deux temps* keeps its precedence in Europe as the favourite measure, varied with galop, polka, and polka mazourka. We add, in America, Dancing in the Barn, which is really a Spanish dance.

The *Pavanne* is worthy of study, and the *Minuet de la Cour* is a stately and beautiful thing, quite worthy of being learned, if it only teaches our women how to make a courtesy.

Each leader of the German is a potentate; he leads his troops through new evolutions, and into combinations so vast, varied, and changeful that it is impossible to do more than hint at them.

The proper name for a private ball is "a dance." In London one never talks of balls; it is always "a dance." Although supper is served generally at a buffet, yet some leaders, with large houses, are introducing little tables, which are more agreeable, but infinitely inconvenient. The comfort, however, of being able to sit while eating, and the fact that a party of four or six may enjoy their supper together would certainly determine the question as to its agreeableness. This is a London fashion, one set succeeding another at the same table. It can only be carried out, however, in a very large house or public place. The ball suppers in New York—indeed, all over America—are very "gorgeous feeds" compared with those one sees in Europe. The profusion of flowers, the hot oysters, boned turkey, terrapin, and canvas-back duck, the salmon, the game patties, salads, ices, jellies, and creams, all crowded in, sweetbreads and green peas, *filet de bœuf*, constant cups of *bouillon*,—one feels Carlyle's internal rat gnawing as one reads of them,—the champagne, the punch, the fine glass, choice china, the drapery of German looms, the Queen Anne silver, the porcelain of Sèvres and Dresden, the beauty of the women, the smart dressing, make the ball supper an elegant, an amazing, a princely sort of sight, saving that princes do not give such feasts,—only Americans.

WEDDINGS.

"Rice and slippers, slippers and rice!
Quaint old symbols of all that's nice
In a world made up of sugar and spice,
With a honeymoon always shining;
A world where the birds keep house by twos,
And the ring-dove calls, and the stock-dove coos,
And maids are many, and men may choose,
And never shall love go pining!"

If there were no weddings, there would be no art of entertaining. It is the key-note, the initial letter, the "open sesame," of the great business of society. Therefore certain general and very, perhaps, unnecessary hints as to the conduct of weddings in all countries may not be out of place here.

In London a wedding in high life—or, as the French call it, "higlif"—is a very sweeping affair. If we were to read the descriptions in the "Court Journal" of one wedding trousseau alone, furnished to a royal princess, or to Lady Gertrude Somebody, we should say with Fielding that "dress is the principal accomplishment of men and women." As for the wedding-cake which is built at Gunter's, it is a sight to see,—almost as big as Mont Blanc.

The importance of Gunter is assured by the "Epicure's Almanac," published in 1815; and for many years this firm supplied the royal family. When George III. was king, the royal dukes stopped to eat Gunter's pies, in gratitude for the sweet repasts furnished them in childhood; but now the Buzzards, of 197 Oxford Street, also are specialists in wedding-cakes.

Leigh Hunt, in one of his essays, described one Trumbull Walker as "the artist who confined himself to that denomination," meaning wedding-cake. His mantle fell on the Buzzards.

This enormous cake, and the equally enormous bouquet are the chief distinctive marks in which a London wedding differs from ours. To be legal, unless by special license, weddings in England must be celebrated before twelve o'clock. The reason given for this law is that before 1820 gentlemen were supposed to be drunk after that hour, and not responsible for what they promised at the altar.

In France, a singular difference of dress on the part of the groom exists. He always wears a dress-coat and white cravat, as do all his ushers and immediate friends. It looks very strange to English and American eyes.

How does a wedding begin? As for the premonitory symptoms, they are in the air for several weeks. It is whispered about amongst the bridesmaids; it gets into the papers. It would be easy to write a volume, and it would be a useful volume if it brought conviction to the hearts of the offenders, of the wrong done to young ladies by the newspapers who assume, without authority, to publish the news of an engagement. Many a match has been broken off by such a premature surmise, and the happiness of one or more persons injured for life.

Young people like to approach this most important event of their lives in a mutual confidence and secrecy; consequently society newspapers should be very careful how they either report an engagement, or declare that it is off. Sometimes rumors prejudicial to the gentleman are circulated without sufficient reason, and of course much ill-feeling is engendered.

The first intimation of an engagement should come from the bride's mother, and the young bride fixes the day of her wedding herself. Then the father and mother, or guardians, of the young lady issue cards, naming the day and hour of the wedding.

Brides often give the attendant maidens their dresses; or if they do not choose to do this, they suggest what they shall wear.

Six ushers generally precede the party into the church, after having seated the guests. These are generally followed by six bridesmaids, who walk two and two. No one wears a veil but the bride herself, who enters on her father's arm. Widows who marry again must not wear white, or veils. The fact that the bride is in white satin, and often with low neck and short sleeves, and the groom in full morning costume, is much criticised in France.

If the wedding occurs in the evening, the groom must wear a dress-coat and white tie.

The invitations to the wedding are very simple and explicit:—

General and Mrs. Brounlow
Request the pleasure of your company
at the marriage of their daughter
Exclairmonde
to
Mr. Gerald FitzGerald,
on Thursday, June 16th, at 12 o'clock,
St. Peter's Church.

In asking a young lady to be her bridesmaid, the bride is supposed to be prompted by claims of relationship or friendship, although fashion and wealth and other considerations often influence these invitations. As for the ushers, they must be unmarried men, and are expected to manage all matters at the church.

Music should play softly during the entrance of the family, before the service. The mother of the bride, and her nearest relatives, precede her into the church, and are seated before she enters, unless the mother be a widow and gives the bride away. The ceremony should be conducted with great dignity and composure on all sides; for exhibitions of feeling in public are in the worst possible taste. At the reception, the bride's mother yields her place as hostess for the nonce, and is addressed after the bride.

After two hours of receiving her friends, the young wife goes upstairs to put on her dress for the journey, which may be of any colour but black. Perhaps this is the time for a few tears, as she kisses mamma good-by. She comes down, with her mother and sisters, meets the groom in the hall, and dispenses the flowers of her bouquet to the smiling maidens, each of whom struggles for a flower.

The parents of the bride send announcement cards to persons not invited to the wedding.

Dinners to the young pair succeed each other in rapid succession. For the first three months the art of entertaining is stretched to its uttermost.

A widow, in marrying again, should not use the name or initials of her late husband. If she was Mary Steward, and had married Mr. Hamilton, and being his widow, wishes to marry James Constable, her cards should read:

MR. AND MRS. STEWARD
Request the pleasure of your company
at the marriage of their daughter
MARY STEWARD-HAMILTON
to
MR. JAMES CONSTABLE.

If she is alone, she can invite in her own name as Mrs. Mary Steward Hamilton; or better still, a friend sends out the cards in her own name, with simply the cards of Mrs. Mary Steward Hamilton, and of the gentleman whom she is to marry.

The custom of giving bridal presents has grown into an outrageous abuse of a good thing. There has grown up a rivalry between families; and the publicity of the whole thing, its notoriety and extravagance, ought to be well rebuked.

At the wedding refreshment-table, the bride sometimes cuts the cake and allows the young people to search for a ring, but this is rather bad for the gloves.

At a country wedding, if the day is fine, little tables are set out on the lawn. The ladies seat themselves, the gentlemen carry refreshments to them. The piazzas can be decorated with autumn boughs, evergreens, and flowers; the whole thing becomes a garden-party, and even the family dogs should have a wreath of white flowers around their necks.

Much ill feeling is apt to be engendered by the distinction which is inevitably made in leaving out the friends who feel that they were entitled to an invitation to the house. It is better to offend no one on so important an occasion.

Wedding-cards and wedding stationery should be simple, white without glaze, and with no attempt at ornamentation.

It is proper for the bride to have her left hand bare as she walks to the altar, as it saves her the trouble of taking off a long glove.

Child bridesmaids are very pretty and very much in favour. These charming children, covered with flowers and looking very grave and solemn, are the sweetest of heralds for a wedding procession.

There is not, however, much difficulty except when Protestant marries Catholic. Such a marriage cannot be celebrated at the High Altar; it leads to a house wedding which is in the minds of many much more agreeable, as saving the bride the journey to church. In this matter, one of individual preference of course, the large and liberal American mind can have a very wide choice.

In France the couple must go to the *Mairie*, where an official in a tricolour scarf, looking like Marat, marries them. This is especially the case if husband or wife is a divorced person, the Catholic church refusing to marry such. It is a curious fact, that in Catholic Italy a civil marriage is the only legal marriage; therefore good Catholics are all married twice. A mixed marriage in Catholic countries is very difficult; but in our country, alas! the wedding knot can be untied as easily as it is tied.

"This train waits twenty minutes for divorces" is a joke founded on fact.

"What do *divorcées* do with their wedding presents?" has been a favourite conundrum of late, especially with those sent by the friends of the husband.

If an evening wedding takes place in a church those who are asked to the house afterwards should go without bonnets. Catholic ladies, however, must always cover their heads in church; so they throw a light lace or mantilla over the head.

It is not often that the bride dances at her own wedding, but there is no reason why she should not.

"'Tis custom that makes cowards of us all." One brave girl was married on a Saturday in May, thus violating all the old saws and superstitions. She has been happy ever afterwards. Marriages in May used to be said to lead to poverty. It is the month of Mary, the Virgin, therefore Catholics object.

One still braver bride chose Friday; this is hangman's day, and also the day of the crucifixion, therefore considered unlucky by the larger portion of the human race.

However, marriage is lucky or unlucky as the blind goddess pleases; no foresight of ours can make it a certainty. Sometimes two very doubtful characters make each other better, and live happily; again two very fine characters but help to sublimate each other's misery. Perhaps no more hopeless picture of this failure was ever painted than the misery of Caroline and Robert Elsmere, in that masterly novel which led you nowhere.

There is a capital description of a French *bourgeoise* wedding in one of Daudet's novels:—

"The least details of this important day were forever engraved on Risler's mind.

"He saw himself at daybreak pacing his bachelor chamber, already shaved and dressed, with two pairs of white gloves in his pocket. Then came the gala carriages, and in the first one, the one with white horses, white reins, and a lining of yellow satin, his bride's veil floated like a cloud.

"Then the entrance to the church, two by two, with this white cloud always at their head, floating, light, gleaming; the organ, the verger, the sermon of the *curé*, the tapers twinkling like jewels, the spring toilets, and all the world in the sacristie—the little white cloud lost, engulfed, surrounded, embraced, while the groom shook hands with the representatives of the great Parisian firms assembled in his honour; and the grand swell of the organ at the end, more solemn because the doors of the church were wide open so that the whole quarter took part in the family ceremony; the noises of the street as the cortège passed out, the exclamations of the lookers-on,—a burnisher in a lustring apron crying aloud, 'The groom is not handsome, but the bride is stunning,'—all this is what makes one proud when he is a bridegroom.

"Then the breakfast at the works, in a room ornamented with hangings and flowers; the stroll in the Bois, a concession to the bride's mother, Madame Chèbe, who in her position as a Parisian *bourgeoise* would not have considered her daughter married without the round of the lake and a visit to the cascade; then the return for dinner just as the lights were appearing on the Boulevard, where every one turned to see the wedding party, a true, well-appointed party, as it passed in a procession of liveried carriages to the very steps of the Café Vefour.

"It was all like a dream.

"Now, dulled by fatigue and happiness, the worthy Risler looked dreamily at the great table of twenty-five covers, with a horseshoe at each end. Around it were well-known, smiling faces in whose eyes he seemed to see his own happiness reflected. Little waves of conversation from the different groups drifted across the table; faces were turned toward one another. You could see here the white cuffs of a black suit behind a basket of asclepias, here the laughing face of a girl above a dish of confections. The faces of the guests were half hidden behind the flowers and the dessert; all around the board were gayety, light, and colour.

"Yes, Risler was happy.

"Aside from his brother Franz, all whom he loved were there. First and foremost, facing him, was Sidonie,—yesterday the little Sidonie, to-day his wife. She had laid aside her veil for dinner, she had emerged from the white cloud.

"Now in her silken gown, white and simple, her charming face seemed more clear and sweet under the carefully arranged bridal wreath.

"By the side of Risler sat Madame Chèbe, the mother of the bride, who shone and glistened in a dress of green satin gleaming like a shield. Since morning all the thoughts of the good woman had been as brilliant as her robe. Every moment she had said to herself, 'My daughter is marrying Fremont and Risler,'—because in her mind it was not Risler whom her daughter married, but the whole establishment.

"All at once came that little movement among the guests that announces their leaving the table,—the rustle of silks, the noise of chairs, the last words of talk, laughter broken off. Then they all passed into the grand *salon*, where those invited were arriving in crowds, and, while the orchestra tuned their instruments, the men with glass in eye paraded before the young girls all dressed in white and impatient to begin."

HOW ROYALTY ENTERTAINS.

Stand back, and let the King go by.

—Old Play.

"Thrones, dominations, princedoms, virtues, powers."

When we approach the subject of royal entertainments, we cannot but feel that the best of us are at a disadvantage. Princes have palaces and retainers furnished for them. They have a purse which knows no end. They are either by the divine right, or by lucky chance, the personages of the hour! It is only when one of them loses his head, or is forced to abdicate, or falls by the assassin's dagger, that they approach at all our common humanity.

Doubtless to them, entertaining, being a perfunctory affair, becomes very tedious. Pomp is not an amusing circumstance and they get so tired of it all that when off duty kings and queens are usually the most plainly dressed and the most simple of mortals. The "age of strut" has passed away. No one cares to assume the puffiness of Louis XIV. or George IV.

Royal entertainments, however, have this advantage, they open to the observer the historical palace, and the pictures, gems of art, and interesting collections of which palaces are the great conservators.

It would seem that Louis XIV., called *le Grand Monarque*, Louis the Magnificent, was a master of the art of entertaining. Under him the science of giving banquets received, in common with the other sciences, a great progressive impulse. There still remains some memory of those festivals, which all Europe went to see, and those tournaments, where for the last time shone lances and knightly suits of armour. The festivals always ended with a sumptuous banquet, where were displayed huge centre-pieces of gold and silver, painting, sculpture, and enamel, all laudatory of the hero of the occasion.

This fashion made the fame of Benvenuto Cellini in the previous century. To-day, monarchs content themselves with having these centre-pieces made of cake, sugar, or ices. There will be no record of their great feasts for future ages.

Toward the end of the reign of Louis XIV., the cook, the *cordon bleu*, received favourable notice; his name was written beside that of his patron; he was called in after dinner. It is mentioned in some of the English memoirs that this fashion was not unknown so lately as fifty years ago in great houses in England, where the cook was called in, in his white cap and apron, publicly thanked for his efforts, and a glass of wine offered him by his master, all the company drinking his health. This must have had an excellent effect on the art of gastronomy.

Madame de Maintenon, whose gloomy sway over the old king reduced the gay court to the loneliness of an empty cathedral, threw a wet napkin on the science of good eating, and put out the kitchen fires for a season.

Queen Anne, however, was fond of good cheer, and consulted with her cook. Many cookery books have the qualification "after Queen Anne's fashion."

Under the Regent Orléans, a princely prince in spite of his faults, the art of good eating and entertaining was revived; and he has left a reputation for *piqués* of superlative delicacy, *matelots* of tempting quality, and turkeys superbly stuffed.

The reign of Louis XV. was equally favourable to the art of entertaining. Eighteen years of peace had made France rich, and a spirit of conviviality was diffused amongst all classes. The proper setting of the table, and order, neatness, and elegance, as essentials of a well-appointed meal, date from this reign. It is from this period that the history of the *petit soupers de Choisy* begins. We need hardly go in to that history of all that was reckless, witty, gay, and dissolute in the art of entertaining; but as one item, a floor was constructed so that the table and sideboard sank into the lower story after each course, to be immediately replaced by others which rose covered with a fresh course. From this we may imagine its luxury and detail.

Louis XV. was a proficient in the art of cookery; he also worked tapestry with his own hand. We should linger over his feasts with more pleasure had they not led on to the French Revolution, as a horrible dessert. His carving-knives later on became the guillotine.

Under Louis XVI. there was a constant improvement in all the "occupations which are required in the preparation of food" by cooks, *traiteurs*, pastry cooks, and confectioners. The art of preserving food, so that one could have the fruits of summer in the midst of winter, really began then, although the art of canning may safely be said to belong to our own much later time.

In the year 1740 a dinner was served in this order: Soup, followed by the *bouilli*, an *entrée* of veal cooked in its own gravy, as a side dish. Second course: A turkey, a dish of vegetables, a salad, and sometimes a cream. Dessert: Cheese, fruit and sweets. Plates were changed only thrice: after the soup, at the second course, and at dessert. Coffee was rarely served, but cherry brandy or some liqueur was passed.

Louis XVIII., who grew to be an immensely fat man, was a remarkable gastronome. Let any one read Victor Hugo's "Les Misérables," and an account of his reign, to get an idea of this magnificent entertainer. His most famous *maître d'hôtel* was the Duc d'Escars. When he and his royal master were closeted together to meditate a dish, the ministers of state were kept waiting in the antechamber, and the next day an official announcement was made, "Monsieur le Duc d'Escars a travaillé dans le cabinet."

How strangely would it affect the American people if President Harrison kept them waiting for his signature because he was discussing terrapin and Madeira sauce with his *chef*.

The king had invented the *truffles à la purée d'ortolans*, and invariably prepared it himself, assisted by the duke. On one occasion they jointly composed a dish of more than ordinary dimensions, and duly consumed the whole of it. In the night the duke was seized with a fit of indigestion, and his case was declared hopeless. Loyal to the last, he ordered an attendant to awake and inform the king, who might be exposed to a similar attack. His majesty was roused accordingly, and told that D'Escars was dying of his invention.

"Dying!" exclaimed the king: "well, I always said I had the better stomach of the two."

So much for the gratitude of kings. The Parisian restaurants, those world-renowned Edens of the gastronomer, were formed and founded on the theories of these cookery-loving kings. But political disturbances were to intervene in the year 1770. After the glorious days of Louis XIV. and the wild dissipation of the Regency, after the long tranquillity under the ministry of Fleury, travellers arriving in Paris found its resources very poor as to good cheer. But that soon mended itself.

It was not until about 1814 that the parent of Parisian restaurants, Beauvilliers, made himself a cosmopolitan reputation by feeding the allied armies. He learned to speak English, and in that way became most popular. He had a prodigious memory, and would recognize and welcome men who had dined at his house twenty years before. In this he was like General Grant and the Prince of Wales. It is a very popular faculty.

Beauvilliers, Méot, Robert, Rose Legacque, the Brothers Very, Hennevan, and Baleine, are the noble army of argonauts in discovering the Parisian restaurant; or rather, they founded it.

The Brothers Very, and the Trois Frères Prevenceaux, both in the Palais Royal, are still great names to compete with. When the allied monarchs held Paris, in 1814, the Brothers Very supplied their table for a daily charge of one hundred and twenty pounds, not including wine, and in Père-la-Chaise a magnificent monument is erected to one of them, declaring that his "whole life was consecrated to the useful arts," as it doubtless was.

From that day until 1890, what an advance there has been. There is now a restaurant in nearly every street in Paris, where one can get a good dinner. What a crowd of them in the Champs Élysées and out near the Bois.

A Parisian dinner is thoroughly cosmopolitan, and the best in the world, when it is good. Parisian cookery has declined of late in the matter of meats. They are not as good as they ought to be. But the sauces are so many and so fine that they have given rise to many proverbs. "The sauce is the ambassador of a king." "With such a sauce, a man could eat his grandfather."

Leaving France for other shores, for France has no monarch to entertain us now, let us see how two reigning monarchs entertain.

A presentation at the Court of St. James is a picturesque affair and worth seeing, although it is a fatiguing process. A lady must be dressed at eleven in the morning, in full court dress, which means low neck and short sleeves, with a train four yards long and three wide. She must wear a white veil and have three feathers in her hair so that they can be seen in front. White gloves are also *de rigueur*, and as they are seldom worn now, except at weddings, a lady must remember to buy a pair. The carriages approach Buckingham Palace in a long queue, and the lady waits an hour or more in line, exposed to the jeers of the populace, who look in at the carriage windows and make comments, laugh, and amuse themselves. One hopes that this may do these ragamuffins some good, for they look miserable enough.

Arriving in the noble quadrangle of Buckingham Palace, the music of the Guard's band enlivens one, and the silent, splendid figures of the household troops, the handsomest men in the world, sit like statues on their horses. No matter if the rain is pouring, as it generally is, neither man nor horse stirs.

Once inside the palace, the card of entrance is taken by one of the Queen's pages, some other official takes her cloak, and the lady wends her way up a magnificent staircase into another gallery, out of which open many fine rooms. Gentlemen of the Household in glittering uniforms, and with orders, stand about in picturesque groups.

The last room is filled with chairs, and is soon crowded with ladies and gentlemen, waiting for the summons to move on. The gentlemen are all in black velvet suits, with knee breeches and sword, silk stockings and low shoes.

A slight commotion at the little turnstile tells you to take your turn; you pass on with the others, your name is loudly called, you make three little courtesies to her Majesty, the Prince and Princess of Wales, you see a glittering line of royalties, you hear the words, "Your train, Madame," it is thrown over your arm by some cavalier behind, and all is over; except that you are amongst your friends, and see a glittering room full of people, and realize that nothing is so bad as you had feared. After about an hour, you find your carriage and drive home, or to your minister's for a cup of tea.

Then you receive, if you are fortunate, a great card from the Lord Chamberlain, with the Queen's command that you should be invited to a ball at Buckingham Palace. This ball is a sight to see, so splendid is the ball-room, so grand the elevated red sofas, with the duchesses and their jewels. Royalty enters about eleven o'clock, followed by all the ambassadors.

Of late years the Queen has relegated her place as hostess to the Princess of Wales, but during the jubilee year she kept it, and it was a beautiful sight to see the little woman all covered with jewels, with her royal brood around her.

The royal family go in to supper through a lane of guests. The supper-room is adorned with the gold plate bought by George IV., and many very fine pieces of plate given by other monarchs. The eatables and drinkables are what they would be at any great ball.

The prettiest entertainment of the jubilee year was, however, the Queen's garden-party. No one had seen that lovely park behind Buckingham Palace for eighteen years; then it was used for the garden-party given to the Khedive of Egypt. Now it was filled by a most picturesque group. The Indian princes with all their jewels, their turbans, their robes, their dark, handsome faces, stood at the foot of a grand staircase which runs from the palace to the green turf. Every other man was a king, a prince, a nobleman, a great soldier, a statesman, a diplomate, a somebody.

The women were all, of course, beautifully dressed in summer costume; and the grounds, full of ancient trees and fountains, artificial lakes with swans, marquees with refreshments, were as pretty as only a royal English park can be.

Presently we heard the sound of the bagpipes, and a procession headed by some dancing Scotchmen came along. It was the Queen, with all her children and grandchildren, ladies-in-waiting, and many monarchs, amongst whom marched Queen Kapiolani of the Sandwich Islands. The Queen walked with a cane, the Prince of Wales by her side. They all stopped repeatedly and spoke to their guests on either side; then the younger members of the family led the way to the refreshment tents, where a truly regal buffet was spread.

There was much talk, much music, much laughter, no stiffness. It was real hospitality. In one of the windows of the palace stood looking out the Crown Prince of Germany, later on to be the noble Emperor Frederic, even then feeling the pressure of that malady which in another year was to kill him. He who had been, in the procession of Princes on the great day, so important and so handsome a figure, was on this day a silent observer. The Queen after this gave an evening party to all the royalties, and the ambassadors, and many invited guests.

The hospitality of the Queen is, of course, regal, but her dinners must of a necessity be formal. General Grant mentioned his disappointment that he did not sit next her, when she invited him to Windsor, but she had one of her children on either side, and he came next to the Princess Beatrice.

The entertainments at Marlborough House are much less formal. The Prince of Wales, the most genial and hospitable of men, cannot always pen up his delightful cordiality behind the barriers of rank.

As for the King and Queen of Italy, they do not try to restrain their cordiality. The Court of Italy is most easy-going, democratic, and agreeable, in spite of its thousand years of grandeur. The favoured guest who is to be presented receives a card to the *cercle*, on a certain Monday evening. The card prescribes low-necked dress, and any colour but black. To drive to the Quirinal Palace on a moonlight night in Rome is not unpleasant.

The grand staircase, all covered with scarlet carpet, was lined with gigantic cuirassiers in scarlet, who stood as motionless as statues. We entered a grand hall frescoed by Domenichino. How small we felt under these giant figures. We passed on to another *salon*, frescoed by Julio Romano, so on to another where a handsome cavalier, the Prince Vicovara, received our cards, and opening a door, presented us to the Marchesa Villamarina, the Queen's dearest friend and favourite lady-in-waiting. We were arranged in rows around a long and handsome room. Presently a little movement at the door, and the deep courtesies of the Princess Brancaccio and the Princess Vicovara, both Americans, told us that the Queen had entered.

Truly she is a royal beauty, a wonder on a throne. An accomplished scholar, a thoughtful woman, Marguerite of Savoy is the rose of the nineteenth century; her smile keeps Italy together. She is the sweetest, the most beautiful of all the queens, and as she walks about accompanied by her ladies, who introduce every one, she speaks to each person in his or her own language; she is mistress of ten languages. After she had said a few gracious words, the Queen disappeared, and the Marchesa Villamarina asked us to take some refreshments, saying, "I hope we shall see you on Thursday."

The next day came an invitation to the grand court-ball. This is a very fine sight. The King and Queen enter and take their places on a high estrade covered with a crimson velvet baldaquin. Then the ladies and gentlemen of the household and the ambassadors enter.

The Count Gianotti, a very handsome Piedmontese, the favourite friend of the King, the prefect of the palace and master of ceremonies, declared the ball opened, and the Queen danced with the Baron Kendall. The royal quadrille over, dancing became general. The King stood about looking soldier-like, bored and silent; a patriot and brave man, he hates society. The Queen does all the social work, and she does it admirably.

What a company that was,—all the Roman nobility, the diplomatic corps, the visitors to Rome, S. P. Q. R., the senate and the Roman people. After the dancing, supper was announced. Royalty does not sup in public in Rome, as in England. The difference in etiquette is curious. The King and Queen retired. We went in as we pleased at ten o'clock, had seats, and supped gloriously; the excellent Italian cookery, of which we have spoken previously, was served admirably. The housekeeping at the Quirinal is excellent.

The Queen of Italy moves about amongst the ambassadors' wives, and summons any stranger to whom she may wish to speak, to her side. A presentation to her is more personal and gracious than a like honour at any other court.

A presentation at court resolves itself into two advantages. One sees the paraphernalia of royalty, always amusing and interesting to American eyes. Americans see its poetry, its almost vanished meaning, better than others. Power, even when it descends for a day on fresh Republican shoulders, is awe-inspiring. The boy who is a leader at school is more important than the boy who walks behind him. "A captain of thousands" was an old Greek term for leadership, dignity, and honour. Therefore it is not snobbery to desire to see these people on whom have fallen the ermine of power. It is snobbery to bow down before some unworthy bearer of a title; but when, as in the case of Marguerite of Savoy, there is a very good, a very gifted, a very wonderful woman behind it all, we are glad that she has been born to wear all these jewels.

We have in our minds one more scene, and a very picturesque one. In September, 1888, the Duc d'Aosta, brother to King Humbert, married his niece, Letitia Bonaparte, daughter of the Princess Clotilde and Prince Jerome Bonaparte. This marriage occurred at Turin. A fine week of autumn weather was devoted to this ceremony. It was a great gathering of all the family of Victor Emmanuel. The Pope had granted an especial dispensation to the nearly related couple. The degree of consanguinity so repellent to us, is not considered, however, as prejudicial to marriage in Spain, Italy, or Germany.

The King of Italy made this occasion of his brother's marriage, an open door for returning to the old Italian customs of past centuries, in the art of entertaining. The city of Turin was *en fête* for the week. At booths, in the open air, strolling companies were playing opera, tragedy, burlesque, and farce. At the King's charge, the streets were lined with gay decorations of pink and white silk, banners and escutcheons; music was heard everywhere, and at evening brilliant illuminations followed the river.

When the royal cortège appeared on their way to a public square they were preceded by six hundred young cavaliers in the dress of Prince Eugene, powdered hair, bright red and blue coats, each detachment escorting a royal carriage. First came the King and Queen, then the bridal pair.

They mounted a superb thing, like a basket of flowers, in the Piazza Vittorio Emmanuel, where all the royalties sat around the bride. Music and flags saluted them. The vast crowd sat and looked at them for two hours. A gayly decorated balloon, covered with roses, floated over the Queen's head, and finally, as the rosy light faded away, a gun from the fortress sounded the hour of departure. The glittering cavalcade drove back to the palace, and we foreigners knew that we had seen a real, mediæval Italian festa.

ENTERTAINING AT EASTER.

"There is a tender hue that tips the first young leaves of spring,
A trembling beauty in their notes when young birds learn to sing
A purer look when first on earth the gushing brook appears,
A liquid depth in infant eyes that fades with summer years."

In the early days of ecumenical councils it was a mooted point when Easter should be celebrated. The Christian Jews kept the feast on the same day as their Passover, the fourteenth of Nisan, the month corresponding to our March or April; but the Gentile church observed the first Sunday following this, because Christ rose from the dead on that day. It was not until the fourth century that the Council of Nice decided upon the first Sunday after the full moon which follows the twenty-first of March. The contest was waged long and heavily, but the Western churches were victorious; a vote settled it.

Perhaps this victory decided the later and more splendid religious ceremonials of Easter, which are much more observed in Rome and in all Catholic countries than those of Christmas. Constantine gratified his love of display by causing Easter to be celebrated with unusual pomp and parade. Vigils and night watches were instituted, people remaining all night in the churches in Rome, and carrying high wax tapers through the streets in processions.

People in the North, glad of an escape from four months of darkness, watch to see the sun dawn on an Easter morning. They have a superstitious feeling about this observance, which came originally from Egypt, and is akin to the legend that the statue of Memnon sings when the first ray of the sun touches it.

It is the queen of feasts in all Catholic churches, the world over. In early days, the fasting of Lent was restricted to one day, the Friday of Passion Week, Good Friday; then it extended to forty hours, then to forty days,—showing how much fashion, even in churchly affairs, has to do with these matters. One witty author says that, "people who do not believe in anything will observe Lent, for it is the fashion."

Certainly, the little dinners of Lent, in fashionable society, are amongst the most agreeable of all entertainments. The *crème d'écrevisse*, the oyster and clam soups, the newly arrived shad, the codfish *à la royale* and other tempting dainties are very good, and the dinner being small, and at eight o'clock, there is before it a long twilight for the drive in the Park.

A pope of Rome once offered a prize to the man who would invent one thousand ways of cooking eggs, for eggs can always be eaten in Lent, and let us hope that he found them. The greatest coxcomb of all cooks, Louis Ude, who was prone to demand a carriage and five thousand a year, was famous for his little Lenten *menus*, and could cook fish and eggs marvellously. The amusements of Lent have left one joke in New York. Roller skates were once a very fashionable amusement for Lenten afternoons, though now gone out, and a club had rented Irving Hall for their playground and chosen *Festina lente*, "Make haste slowly," for their motto. It was a very witty motto, but some wise Malaprop remarked, "What a very happy selection, 'Festivals of Lent!'"

However, Lent once passed, with its sewing circles and small whist-parties, then comes the brilliant Easter, with its splendid dinners, its weddings, its christenings and caudle parties, its ladies' lunches, its Meadow Brook hunt, its asparagus parties, and the chickens of gayety which are hatched out of Easter eggs. It is a great day for the confectioner. In Paris, that city full of gold and misery, the splendour and luxury of the Easter egg *bonbonnière* is fabulous. A few years since a Paris house furnished an Easter egg for a Spanish infanta, which cost eight hundred pounds sterling.

Easter dinners can be made delightful. They are simple, less heavy, hot, and stuffy, than those of mid-winter. That enemy of the feminine complexion, the furnace, is put out. It no longer sends up its direful sirocco behind one's back. Spring lamb and mint sauce, asparagus and fresh dandelion salad, replace the heavy joint and the canned vegetables. A foreigner said of us that we have everything canned, even the canvas-back duck and the American opera. Everything should be fresh. The ice-cream man devises allegorical allusions in his forms, and there are white dinners for young brides, and roseate dinners for *débutantes*.

For a gorgeous ladies' lunch, behold a *menu*. This is for Easter Monday:—

Little Neck clams.

Chablis.   Beef tea or *consommé* in cups.

Côtelettes de cervelles à la cardinal.   Cucumbers.

Little ducks with fresh mushrooms.

Champagne.   Artichokes.

Sweetbread à la *Richelieu.*

Asparagus, Hollandaise sauce.

Claret.   Roman punch.

Pâté de foie gras.

Roast snipe.

Tomato salad, lettuce.

Liqueur.   Ice-creams, in form of nightin-gales' nests.

Strawberries, sugared fruit, nougat cakes.

Coffee.

Of course, a season of such rejoicing, when "Christians stand praying, each in an exalted attitude, with outstretched hands and uplifted faces, expressing joy and gladness," is thought to be very propitious for marriage. There is generally a wedding every day, excepting Friday, during Easter week. A favourite spring travelling-dress for an Easter bride is fawn coloured cashmere, with a little round hat and bunch of primroses.

For a number of choir boys to sing an epithalamium, walking up the aisle before the bride, is a new and very beautiful Easter fashion.

A favourite entertainment for Easter is a christening. Christening parties are becoming very important functions in the art of entertaining. Many Roman Catholics are so anxious for the salvation of the little new soul, that they have their children baptized as soon as possible, but others put off this important ceremony until mamma can go to church, when little master is five weeks old. Then friends are invited to the ceremony very much in this fashion:—

> Mr. and Mrs. Hamilton request the pleasure of your company at the baptism of their infant daughter at the Cathedral, Monday, March 30, at 12 o'clock. At home, after the ceremony, 14 W. Ellicott Square.

Many wealthy Roman Catholics have private chapels where the ceremony may be performed earlier.

Presents are sent to the mamma, of flowers and bonbonnières shaped like an altar, a cradle, a powder-box; and there may be gold tea-scoops, pap-spoons and a caudle-cup. Gifts of old Dutch silver and the inevitable posy or couplet are very favourite gifts for the baby and mamma on these auspicious occasions.

Caudle is a very succulent porridge made of oatmeal, raisins, spices, and rum, all boiled together for several days until it becomes a jelly gruel. It is very much sweetened, and is served hot in cups. The caudle-cup designed by Albrecht Dürer for some member of the family of Maximilian is still shown. Caudle cards are very often stamped with a cameo resemblance of these cups, and the invitation reads:—

> Mrs. James Hamilton,
> at Home,
> Thursday, March 30, from three to six.
> Caudle.

These do not require an answer.

Very pretty tea-gowns are worn by mamma and the ladies of her family for this entertainment, but the guests come in bonnets and street dresses. There is no objection to having the afternoon tea-table with its silver tea-kettle, alcohol-lamp, pretty silver tea-set, plates of bread and butter, and little cakes ready for those ladies who prefer tea. Caudle is sometimes added to the teas of a winter afternoon, by the remnants of old Dutch families, even when there is no little master as a raison d'être, and delicious it is.

There is a pretty account of the marriage of Marguerite of Austria with Philibert, the handsome Duke of Savoy. It is called Mariage aux œufs. She had come to the

Castle of Brae, in the charming district of Bresse lying on the western slopes of the Alps. Here the rich princess kept open house, and Philibert, who was hunting in the neighbourhood, came to pay his court to her. It was Easter Monday, and high and low danced together on the green. The old men drew their bows on a barrel filled with wine, and when one succeeded in planting his arrow firmly in it he was privileged to drink as much as he pleased *jusqu'à merci.*

A hundred eggs were scattered in a level place, covered with sand, and a lad and lass, holding each other by the hand, came forward to execute a dance of the country. According to the ancient custom, if they succeeded in finishing the *branle* without breaking a single egg they became affianced, and even the will of their parents might not avail to break their union. Three couples had already tried it unsuccessfully and shouts of laughter derided their attempts, when the sound of a horn was heard, and Philibert of Savoy, radiant with youth and happiness, appeared on the scene. He bent his knees before the noble *châtelaine* and besought her hospitality. He proposed to her to try the egg fortune. She accepted. Their grace and beauty charmed the lookers-on and they succeeded, without a single crash, in treading the perilous maze.

"Savoy and Austria!" shouted the crowd. And she said, "Let us adopt the custom of Bresse."

They were married, and enjoyed a few years of exquisite happiness; then the beloved husband died. Marguerite survived him long, but never forgot him. She built in his memory a beautiful church. Travellers go to-day to see their magnificent tomb.

The egg has been in all ages and in all countries the subject of infinite mystery, legend, and history. The ancient Finns believed that a mystic bird laid an egg in the lap of Vaimainon, who hatched it in his bosom. He let it fall in the water, and it broke. The lower portion of the shell formed the earth, the upper the sky, the liquid white became the sun, the yolk the moon, while little bits of egg-shells became the stars.

Old English and Irish nurses instruct the children, when they have eaten a boiled egg, to push the spoon through the bottom of the shell to hinder the witches from making a boat of it.

It is difficult to ascertain the precise origin of the custom of offering eggs at the festival of Easter. The Persians, the Russians, and the Jews all follow it.

Amongst the Romans the year began at Easter, as it did amongst the Franks under the Capets. Many presents are exchanged, and as an egg is the beginning of all things, nothing better could be found as an offering. Its symbolic meaning is striking. We offer our friends all the blessings contained under that fragile shell, whose fragility represents that of happiness here below. The Romans commenced their repasts with an egg; hence the proverbial phrase, *"ab ovo usque ad mala,"* or, as we still say, "beginning *ab ovo.*"

Another reason given for the Easter egg is that, about the fourth century, the Church forbade the use of eggs in Lent. But as the heretical hens would go on laying, the eggs accumulated to such a degree that they were boiled hard and given away. They were given to the children for playthings, and they dyed them of gay colours. In certain churches in Belgium the priests, at the beginning of a glad anthem, threw the eggs at the choristers who threw them back again, dancing to the music whilst catching the frail eggs that they might not break.

In Germany, where means are more limited than in France, the Easter egg *bonbonnière* is rare. There are none of the eight-hundred-pound kind, which was made of enamel, and which on its inside had engraved the gospel for the day, while by an ingenious mechanism a little bird, lodged in this pretty cage, sang twelve airs from as many operas.

But in Germany, to make up for this poverty, they have transformed the hare into an oviparous animal, and in the pastry cook's windows one sees this species of hen sitting upright in a nest surrounded by eggs. I have often wondered if that inexplicable saying "a mare's nest," might not have been "a hare's nest." As a *lucus a non lucendo* it would have done as well. When a German child, at any season of the year, sees a hare run across the field, he says, "Hare, good little hare, lay plenty of eggs for me on Easter day." It is the custom of German families, on Easter eve, to place sugar-eggs and real eggs, the former filled with sugar plums, in a nest, and then to conceal it with dried leaves in the garden that the joyous children may hunt for them on Easter morning.

It is a superstition all over the world that we should wear new clothes on Easter Day. Bad luck will follow if there is not at least one article which is new.

HOW TO ENTERTAIN CHILDREN.

From the realms of old-world story
There beckons a lily hand,
That calls up the sweetness, the glory,
The sounds of a magic land.

Ah, many a time in my dreaming
Through that blessed region I roam!
Then the morning sun comes with its beaming
And scatters it all like foam!

Heine.

In the life of Madame Swetchine we read the following account of the amusements of a clever child:—

"The occupation of a courtier did not prevent Monsieur Soymonof from bestowing the most assiduous care on the education of a daughter, who for six years was his only child. He was struck by the progress of her young intellect. She showed an aptitude for languages, music, and drawing, while she developed firmness of character,—a rare quality in a child.

"She desired a watch with an ardour which transpired in all her movements, and her father had promised her one. The watch came and was worn with the keenest enjoyment; but suddenly a new thought seized upon the little Sophia. She reflected that there was something better than a watch. To relinquish it of her own accord, she hurried to her father and restored to him the object of her passionate desires, acknowledging the motive. Her father looked at her, took the watch, shut it up in a bureau drawer, and said no more about it.

"M. Soymonof's rooms were adorned with bronzes, medals, and costly marbles. Sophia was on terms of intimacy with these personages of fable and history; but she felt an unconquerable repugnance to a cabinet full of mummies. The poor child blushed for her weakness, and one day, when alone, opened the terrible door, ran straight to the nearest mummy, took it up, and embraced it till her strength and courage gave away, and she fell down in a swoon. At the noise of her fall, her father hastened in, raised her in his arms, and obtained from her, not without difficulty, an avowal of the terrors which she had hitherto concealed from him. But this supreme effort was as good for her as a victory. From that day the mummies were to her only common objects of interest and curiosity.

"Studious as was her education, M. Soymonof did not banish dolls. His daughter loved them as friends and preserved this taste beyond her childish years, but elevated it by the admixture of an intellectual and often dramatic interest. Her dolls were generally of the largest size. She gave them each a name and part to act, established connected relations between the different individuals, and kept up animated dialogues which occupied her imagination vividly, and became a means of instruction. Playing dolls was for her an introduction to ethics and a knowledge of the world.

"Catherine's court was a succession of continual *fêtes*. The fairy pantomimes performed at the Hermitage were the first to strike the imagination of the child, who as yet could not relish the tragedies of Voltaire. She composed a *ballet* which she called 'The Faithful Shepherdess and the Fickle Shepherdess.' She writes in her sixtieth year: 'One of the liveliest pleasures of my childhood was to compose festive decorations which I loved to light up and arrange upon the white marble chimney-piece of my schoolroom. The ardour which I threw into designing, cutting out, and painting transparencies, and finding emblems and mottoes for them was something incredible. My heart beat high while the preparations were in progress but the moment my illumination began to fade an ineffable devouring melancholy seized me.'"

This extract is invaluable not only for its historic importance, but for the key-note which it sounds to a child's nature. The noble little Russian girl at the court of Catherine of Russia found only those pleasures lasting which came from herself, and when she could invest the fairy pantomime with her own personality.

A fairy pantomime is possible to the poorest child if some superior intelligence, an older sister or aunt, will lend her help. The fairies can all be of pasteboard, with strings as the motive power. There can be no cheaper *corps de ballet*, nor any so amusing.

"You have done much for your child" is an expression we often hear. "You have had a nurse, a nursery governess, a fine pony for your boy, you take your children often to the play and give them dancing parties, and yet they are not happy." It is the sincere regret of many a mamma that she cannot make her children happy. Yet in a large town, in a house shut up from our cold winter blasts, what can she do? A good dog and a kind-hearted set of servants will solve the problem better than all the intellect in the world. Grandmamma brings a doll to the little girl, who looks it over and says: "The dolly cannot be undressed, I do not want it." It is the dressing and the undressing which are the delights of her heart.

A boy wants to make a noise, first of all things. Let him have a large upper room, a drum, a tambourine, a ball, and there he should be allowed to kick out the effervescence of early manhood. Do not follow him with all manner of prohibitions. Constant nagging and fault-finding is an offence against a child's paradise. Put him in a room for certain hours of the day where no one need say, "Get down! don't do that! don't make so much noise!" Let him roar, and shout, and climb over chairs and tables, and tear his gown, and work off his exuberance, and then he will be very glad to have his hands and face washed and listen to a story, or come down to meet papa with a smiling countenance.

Children should be allowed to have pet birds, kittens, dogs, and as much live stock as the house will hold; it develops their sympathies. When a bird dies, and the floodgates of the poor little heart are opened, sympathize with it. It is cruel to laugh at childish woe. Never refuse a child sympathy in joy or sorrow. This lack of sympathy has made more criminals than anything else.

Children should never be deceived either in the taking of medicine or the administration of knowledge. One witty writer a few years ago spoke of the bad influence of good books. He declared that reading "that Tommy was a good boy and kept his pinafore clean and rose to affluence, while Harry flung stones and told fibs and was carried off by robbers," developed his sympathies for Harry; and that although he was naturally a good boy he went, for pure hatred of the virtuous Tommy, to the river's brink and helped a bad boy to drown his aunt's cat, and then went home and wrote a prize composition called "Frank the Friendless, or Honesty is Best." All this was because the boy saw that Tommy was a prig, that his virtue was of that kind mentioned in Jane Eyre, in which the charity child was asked whether she would rather learn a hymn or receive a cake; she said "Learn a hymn," whereupon she received "two cakes as a reward for her infant piety." Children cannot be humbugged; they can be made into hypocrites, however, by too many good books.

The best entertainment for children is to let them play at being useful. Let the little girl get papa's slippers, brush his hat, even if the wrong way, find his walking stick, hold the yarn for grandma's knitting, or rock her brother's cradle, and she will be happy. Give the boy a printing-press or some safe tools, let him make a garden, feed his chickens, or clean out the cage of his pet robin, and he will be happy. Try to make them think and decide for themselves. A little girl says, "I don't know which dress to put on my dolly, Mamma, which shall I?" The mamma will be wise if she says, "You must decide, you know dolly best."

When a child is ill or nervous, the great hour of despair comes to the mamma. A person without nerves, generally a good coloured mammy, is the best playmate, and a dog is invaluable. It is touching to see the smile come to the poor bloodless lips in a hospital ward, as a great, big, kindly dog puts his cold nose out to reach a little feverish hand. There is a sympathy in nature which intellect loses.

Madame Swetchine's fear of the mummies has another lesson in it. Children are born with pet aversions, as well as with that terrible fear which is so much bigger than they are. The first of their rights to be respected is that they shall not be frightened, and shall not be too seriously blamed for their aversions. Buffalo Bill, who knows more about horses than most people, says that no horse is born bad; that he is made a bucking horse, a skittish horse, or a stumbling horse by being badly trained,—misunderstood when he was young. How true this is of human nature! How many villains are developed by an unhappy childhood! How many scoundrels does the boys' hall turn out! We must try to find these skeletons in the closet, this imprisoned spectre which haunts the imaginative child, and lay the ghost by sympathy and by common-sense. Cultivating the imagination, not over-feeding it or starving it, would seem to be the right way.

Perhaps there are no better ways of entertaining children than by a juggler, the magic lantern, and simple scientific experiments. We use the term advisedly. Jugglery was the oldest of the sciences. Aaron and Moses tried it. One of the most valuable solaces for an invalid child—one with a broken leg, or some complaint which necessitates bed and quiet—is an experiment in natural magic.

One of these simple tricks is called "The Balanced Coin." Procure a bottle, cork it, and in the cork place a needle. Take another cork, and cut a slit in it, so that the edge of a dollar will fit into it; then put two forks into the upper cork. Place the edge of the coin, which holds the upper cork and forks, on the point of the needle, and it will revolve without falling. This will amuse an imprisoned boy all the afternoon.

The revolving image is a most amusing gentleman. Let poor Harry make this himself. Cut a little man out of a thin bit of wood, making him end in one leg, like a peg-top, instead of in two. Give him a pair of long arms, shaped like oars. Then place him on the tip of your finger, and blow; he will stand there and rotate, like an undecided politician.

The Spanish dancer is another nice experiment. Cut a figure out of pasteboard, and gum one foot on the inverted side of a watch-glass; then place the watch-glass on a Japan waiter or a clean plate. Hold the plate slanting, and they will slide down; but drop a little water on the waiter or plate, and instead of the watch-glass sliding, it will begin to revolve, and continue to revolve with increased velocity as the experimentalist chooses. This is in consequence of the cohesion of water to the two surfaces, by which a new force is introduced. These experiments are endless, and will serve a variety of purposes, the principal being that of entertaining.

To take children to the pantomime at Christmas is the universal law in England. We have seldom the pantomime here. We have the circus, the menagerie, and the play. A real play is better for children than a burlesque, and it is astonishing to see how soon a child can understand even Hamlet.

To allow children to play themselves in a fairy tale, such as "Cinderella," is a doubtful practice. The exposure, the excitement, the late hours, the rehearsals, are all bad for young nerves; but they can play at home if it is in the daytime.

When boys and girls get old enough for dancing-parties, nothing can be more amusing than the sight of the youthful followers of Terpsichore. It is a healthy amusement, and if kept within proper hours, and followed by a light supper only, is the most fitting of all children's amusements. Do not, however, make little men and women of them too soon. That is lamentable.

As for ruses and catch-games like "The Slave Despoiled," "The Pigeon Flies," "The Sorcerer behind the Screen," "The Knight of the Whistle," "The Witch," "The Tombola," one should buy one of the cheap manuals of games found at any bookstore, and a clever boy should read up, and put himself in touch with this very easy way of passing an evening.

The games requiring wit and intelligence are many; as "The Bouquet," "The Fool's Discourse," which has a resemblance to "Cross Questions," "The Secretary," "The Culprit's Seat." All these need a good memory and a ready wit. All mistakes are to be redeemed by forfeit.

Of the games to be played with pencil and paper, none is funnier than "The Narrative," in which the leader decides on the title, and gives it out to the company. It may be called "The Fortunate and Unfortunate Adventures of Miss Palmer." The words to be used may be "history," "reading," "railway accident," "nourishment," "pleasures," "four-in-hand," etc. The paper has a line written, and is folded and handed thus to the next,—each writer giving Miss Palmer whatever adventures he pleases, only bringing in the desired word. The result is incoherent, but amusing, and Miss Palmer becomes a heroine of romance.

There are some children, as there are some grown people, who have a natural talent for games. It is a great help in entertaining children to get hold of a born leader.

The game called "The Language of Animals" is one for philosophers. Each player takes his pencil and paper, and describes the feelings, emotions, and passions of an animal as if he were one. As, for instance, the dog would say: "I feel anger, like a human being. I am sometimes vindictive, but generally forgiving. I suffer terribly from jealousy. My envy leads me to eat more than I want, because I do not wish Tray to get it. Gluttony is my easily besetting sin, but I never got drunk in my life. I love my master better than any one; and if he dies, I mourn him till death. My worst sorrow is being lost; but my delights are never chilled by expectation, so I never lose the edge of my enjoyments by over-raised hopes. I want to run twenty miles a day, but I like to be with my master in the evening. I love children dearly, and would die for any boy: I would save him from drowning. I cannot wag my tongue, but I can wag my tail to express my emotion."

The cat says: "I am a natural diplomatist, and I carry on a great secret service so that nobody knows anything about it. I do not care for my master or mistress, but for the house and the hearth-rug. I am very frugal, and have very little appetite. I kill mice because I dislike them, not that I like them for food. Oh, no! give me the cream-jug for that. I am always ready to do any mischief on the sly; and so if any one else does anything, always say, 'It was the cat.' I have no heart, by which I escape much misery. I have a great advantage over the dog, as he lives but a few years and has but one life. I have a long life, and nine of them; but why the number nine is always connected with me, I do not know. Why 'cat-o-nine-tails?' Why 'A cat has nine lives,' etc.?"

Thus, for children's entertaining we have the same necessities as for grown people. Some one must begin; some one must suggest; some one must tell how. All society needs a leader. It may be for that reason our own grown-up society is a little chaotic.

Perhaps the story of Madame Swetchine and her watch conveys a needed moral. Do not deluge children with costly gifts. Do not thus deprive them of the pleasures of hope. Anticipation is the dearest part of a child's life, and an overfed child, suffering from the pangs of dyspepsia, is no more to be pitied than the poor little gorged, overburdened child, who has more books than he can read and more toys than he can ever play with. Remember, too, "Dr. Blimber's Young Gentlemen," and their longing jealousy of the boy in the gutter.

CHRISTMAS AND CHILDREN.

"Then I stooped for a bunch of holly
Which had fallen on the floor,
And there fell to the ground as I lifted it
A berry—or something more;
And after it fell my eyes could see
More clearly than before!
But oh! for the red Christingle
That never was missing of yore,
And oh! for the red Christingle
That I miss forever more!"

Christingles are not much known in this country. They are made by piercing a hole in an orange, putting a piece of quill three or four inches long, set upright, in the hole, and usually a second piece inside this. Each quill is divided into several slips, each one of which is loaded with a raisin. The weight of the raisins bends down the little boughs, giving two circles of pendants. A coloured taper is placed in the upper quill and lighted on Christmas Eve. The custom is a German one.

The harbinger of Christmas, in Holland, is a Star of Bethlehem carried along through the cities by the young men who pick up alms for the poor. They gather much money, for all come to welcome this symbol of peace. They then betake themselves to the head burgomaster of the town, who is bound to give them a good meal.

The little Russian, amid the snows, looks for the red candle and the Christmas Tree, and the ice is all alight with gay illuminations. The little Roman boy watches with delight the preparation for the *Beffana* in the public squares of Rome. For the *Beffana* is the witch who rides on a broomstick; she is a female Santa Claus, who brings presents to a good child and a bunch of rods to a bad one. Her worship is celebrated on Christmas Eve to the sound of trumpets and all manner of unearthly noises. Then the boy goes to the Church of the Augustins, to see the little Jesus Child lying in the lap of his Holy Mother. He hears the most charming music, and singing choristers swing the censer before the Host. Above his head Saint Michael fights with the dragon. He sees the splendid procession of the cardinals in their gorgeous red and white robes, and as he goes down the broad marble steps, on each side of which beautiful statues stand in niches, his mother, poor Dominica, peasant of the Campagna, kneels and makes the sign of the cross, and tells her boy that this is Christmas, the day on which the Jesus Child was born to take his sins away. Again he wanders with her through the market-place; every one gives him playthings, fruits, and cakes; a rich foreigner tosses him a coin. The little Antonio asks why, and his mother tells him it is Christmas, but not so gay as when she was a little girl, for then the *pifferari*, the shepherds from the mountains, came, in their short cloaks with ribbons around their pointed hats, to play on their bagpipes before every image of the Virgin. Then they go again to the Church, the beautiful Church of Ara Coeli, to hear the angel girls make Christmas speeches to welcome the little Christ-child, and as he looks at the image of the Madonna, all hung with jewels, he wishes it were Christmas all the year round.

The Christmas tree dates back to the Druids, but seems to have disappeared from England for several centuries. Meantime, it blossomed in Germany, where, under the tender and soft Scandinavian influence which has such an admirable and ameliorating effect on homely German life, it has continued to bear its fruit for six hundred years. It came back to England in the days of Queen Charlotte, who, true to her German associations, had a tree dressed at Kew Palace in the rooms of her German attendant. It was hung, writes the Hon. Amelia Murray, with gifts for the children, "who were invited to see it; and I remember," she says, "what a pleasure it was to hunt for one's name."

The "Mayflower," which brought much else that was good, forgot the Christmas tree. It was not until the beginning of the present century that one could be seen near Plymouth Rock. Men and women now living can remember when Washington Irving's "Sketch-book" told to them the first story of an English Christmas, and some brave women determined to hang a few boughs and red berries around the cold, barren church.

Then the tree began to bud and burgeon with gifts, and the rare glories of colour crept in upon the snows of winter. The red fire on the hearth, the red berries on the mantel, brought in the light which grew pale in winter, the hospitality and the cheer of the turkey and plum-pudding went around, and Christmas carols began to be sung by men of Puritan antecedents. Old Christmas, frightened away at first by a few fanatics, came at last to America to stay, and the mistletoe, prettiest, most weird, most artistic of parasites, was removed from dreary Druidical associations, and no longer assists at human sacrifices, — unless some misogynist may so consider the getting of husbands.

The English Christmas is the typical one in the art of entertaining. In every country neighbourhood, public county balls are conducted with great pomp during the twelve days of Christmas. From all the great houses within ten or fifteen miles come large parties, dressed in the latest London fashions, among them the most distinguished lights of the London world. Country residents are also conspicuous, and for people who live altogether in the country this is the chosen occasion for the first introduction of a daughter into society. The town hall or any other convenient building is beautifully dressed with holly and mistletoe. The band is at the upper end and the different sets form exclusive groups about the room, seldom mixing even in the Virginia Reel and other country dances.

The private festivities of Christmas consist of a dinner to the tenantry and a large one to the family, all of whose members are expected. The mistletoe is hung conspicuously from the great lantern in the hall, or over the stag's head at the door. The rooms are wreathed with holly, each picture is framed in it, and the ladies put the red berries in their hair and all over their dresses. The customary turkey, a mighty bird, enters, making an event at the dinner, while later on, a plum-pudding, all ablaze, with a sprig of holly in the midst, makes another sensation. Mince-pies are set on fire with the aid of a little alcohol, which is poured over them from a small silver ladle. After the dinner, is passed the loving cup, a silver cup with two handles, containing a hot, spiced, sweetened ale. It has two mouths, and as it is lifted its weight requires both hands.

In England, Christmas and New Year's still keep some of the mediæval village customs. Men go about in motley, imitating quacks and fortune-tellers, and there is much noise and tooting of horns. These mummers are sent to the servants' hall, where a plentiful supper and horns of ale await them. The waits, or carol singers, are another remnant of old Christmas. In remote parts of England the stables are lighted, to prove that man has not forgotten the Child born and laid in a manger. As for the parish festivities, in which the hall has so prominent a part, the school feasts, the blankets for the poor, the clothing-club meetings at Martinmas, all has been told us in novels, which have also given us many a picture of comfortable and stately English life.

The modern English squire does not, however, eat, drink, and make merry for twelve days, as he used. The wassail-bowl is broken at the fountain, and mince-pies and goose-pies and yule-cakes are thought to be heavy for modern digestion. But the good cheer remains.

The noblest as well as the humblest of all English houses, especially in Yorkshire, keep up the old superstition of lighting the Yule log, "the ponderous ashen fagot from the yard," and great ill-luck is foretold if its flame dies out before Twelfth Night. Frumenty, which is a porridge boiled with milk, sugar, wine, spices, and raisins, is served. It was in a cup of frumenty, as every conscientious reader of fairy stories will remember, that Tom Thumb was dropped by his careless nurse. The Christmas pie of Yorkshire, is a "brae goose-pie" which Herrick in one of his delightful verses thus defends:

> "Come guard this night the Christmas pie,
> That the thiefe, though ne'er so slie,
> With his fleshhooks, don't come nie
> To catch it.

> "From him who all alone sits there,
> Having his eyes still in his eare,
> And a deale of nightly feare
> To watch it."

In America, the young people are utilizing Christmas day as they do in England, if there is no frost, to go a-hunting. Afternoon tea, under the mistletoe in the hall of a country house, is generally taken in a riding habit.

In most families it is a purely domestic festival; although, as the tree has been enjoyed the night before, when Santa Claus, the great German sprite, has held his revels, there is no reason why a grand dinner to one's friends should not be given. And let us plead that the turkey, our great national bird, may not be cooked by gas. He is so much better roasted before a wood fire.

There are some difficulties in giving a Christmas dinner in a large city, as nearly all the waiters are sure to be drunk, and the cook has also, perhaps, been at the frumenty. Being a religious as well as a social festival, it is apt to bring about a confusion of ideas. But, everything else apart, it is Children's Day; it is the day when, as Dickens says, we should remember the time when its great Founder was a child Himself. It is especially the day for the friendless young, the children in hospitals, the lame, the sick, the weary, the blind. No child should be left alone on Christmas Day, for loneliness with children means brooding. A child growing up with no child friend is not a child at all, but a premature man or woman.

The best Christmas present to a boy is a box of tools, the best to a girl any number of dolls. After dressing and undressing them, giving them a bath, taking them through a fit of sickness, punishing them, and giving them an airing in the park,—for little maidens begin to imitate mamma at a very early age,—the next best amusement is to manufacture a doll's house. The brother must plane the box,—an old wine box will do,—and fit in it four compartments, each of which must be elaborately papered. Then a "real carpet" must be nailed down and pictures hung on the wall. These bits, framed with gold paper, usually require mamma's help. The kitchen must be fitted up with tins, which perhaps had better be bought, but after the *batterie de cuisine* is finished, then the chairs and beds should be made at home. Cardboard boxes can be cut into excellent doll's beds. Pillows, bolsters, mattress, sheets, pillow-cases, will keep little fingers busy for many days.

When they get older, and can write letters, a post-office is a delightful boon. These are to be bought, but they are far more amusing if made at home. Any good-sized card-box will do for this purpose. The lid should be fastened to it so that when it stands up it will open like a door. A slit must be cut out about an inch wide, and from five to six inches long, so as to allow the postage of small parcels, yet not large enough even to admit the smallest hand. Children should learn to respect the inviolate character of the post from the earliest age.

On the door should be written the times of the post. Most children are fond of writing letters to one another, and this will of course give rise to a grand manufacture of note paper, envelopes, and post-cards, and will call forth ingenuity in designing and colouring monograms and crests, for their note paper and envelopes. An envelope must be taken carefully to pieces, to form a flat pattern. Then those cut from it have to be folded, gummed together, a touch of gum put on the flap and the monogram made to correspond. It is wonderful what occupation this gives for weeks. A paint-box should be also amongst the Christmas gifts.

Capital scrap-books can be made by children. Old railway guides may be the foundation, and every illustrated paper the magazine of art. A paste-pot, next to a paint-box, is a most serviceable toy.

Children like to imitate their elders. A little boy of two years enjoys smoking a pipe as he sees grandpapa smoke, and knocks out imaginary ashes, as he does, against the door.

Hobby horses are profitable steeds, and can be made to go through any amount of paces. But mechanical toys are more amusing to his elders than to the child, who wishes to do his own mechanism. A boy can be amused by turning him out of the house, giving him a ball or a kite, or letting him dig in the ground for the unhappy mole. Little girls, who must be kept in, on a rainy day, or invalid children, are very hard to amuse and recourse must be had to story-telling, to the dear delightful thousand and one books now written for children, of which "Alice in Wonderland" is the flower and perfection.

For communities of children, as in asylums and schools, there is nothing like music, songs, and marches; anything to keep them in time and tune. It removes for a moment that institutionized look which has so unhappy an effect.

Happy is the child who has inherited a garret full of old trunks, old furniture, old pictures, any kind of old things. It is a precious inheritance. Given the dramatic instinct and a garret, and a family of quick-witted boys and girls will have amusement long after the Christmas holidays are passed.

It would be a great amusement for weeks before Christmas, if children were taught to make the ornaments for the tree, as is done in economical Germany. Here the ideas of secrecy and mystery are so associated with Santa Claus that such an idea would be rejected. But a thing is twice as interesting if we put ourselves into it.

At Christmas time let us invoke the fairies. They, the gentry, the wee people, the good people, are very dear to the real little wee people, who see the fun and do not believe too much in them. The fairies who make their homes under old trees and resort to toadstools for shelter, and who make invisible excursions into farmhouses have afforded the Irish nurse no end of legends. An old nurse once held a magnificent position in the nursery because she had seen a fairy.

The Christmas green was once the home of the peace-loving wood-sprite. Christmas evergreens and red berries make the most effective interior decorations, their delightful fragrance, their splendid colour renders the palace more beautiful, and the humble house attractive. Before Twelfth Night, January 6, they must all be taken down. The festivities of this great day were much celebrated in mediæval times, and the picture by Rubens, "The King Drinks," recalls the splendour of these feasts. It is called Kings' Day to commemorate the three kings of Orient, who paid their visit to the humble manger, bringing those first Christmas gifts of which we have any account.

The negroes from Africa, who were brought as slaves to the West Indian Islands, always celebrate this day with queer and fetich rites. It is in honour of the black king Melchior whom we see in the pictures "from Afric's sunny fountains."

The Twelfth-Night cake, crowned with candles, is cut and eaten with many ceremonies on this occasion. The universality of Christmas is its most remarkable feature. Trace it as one will to the ancient Saturnalia, this universality is still inexplicable. It long antedates the Christian era. The distinctly modern customs are the giving of gifts, and the good eating, which, if followed back, we find to have been gluttony among the Norsemen.

To the older members of the family the day is a sad one. The little verse at the head of the chapter recalls the fact that for every child gone back to heaven, there is one Christingle less. But if it will bring the rich to the poor, if it will not forget a single legend or grace, if the holly and evergreen will breathe the sweetest and highest significance, if we can remember that every simple festival at Christmas which makes the hearth-stone brighter is a tribute to the highest wisdom, if we connect Christmas and humanity, then shall we keep it aright. For the world unlocks its heart on every Christmas Day as it has done for eighteen Christian centuries. The cairn of Christmas memories rises higher and higher as the dear procession of children, those constantly arriving, precious pilgrims from the unknown world, halts by the majestic mountain to receive gifts, giving more than they take. For what would Christmas be without the children?

CERTAIN PRACTICAL SUGGESTIONS.

The rules laid down in books of etiquette may seem preposterously elaborate and absurd to the denizens of cities, and to those who have had the manual of society at their fingers' ends from childhood, but they may be like the grammar of an unknown tongue to the youth or maiden whose life has been spent in seclusion or a rustic neighbourhood. As it is the aim of this unpretending volume to assist such young people, a few hints to young men coming fresh from life on the plains, or from an Eastern or Western college, from any life which has separated them from the society of ladies, may not be considered impertinent.

A young man on coming into a great city, or into a new place where he is not known, should try to bring a few letters of introduction. If he can bring such a letter to any lady of good social position, he has nothing further to do but deliver it, and if she takes him up and introduces him, his social position is made. But this good fortune cannot always be commanded. Young men often pass through a lonely life in a great city, never finding that desired opportunity.

To some it comes through a friendship on the tennis ground, at the clubs, or through business. If a friend says to some ladies that Tilden is a good fellow, Tilden will be sought out and invited. It is hardly creditable to any young man to live in a great city without knowing the best ladies' society. He should seek to do so, and perhaps the simplest way would be for him to ask some friend to take him about and to introduce him. Once introduced, Tilden should be particular not to transcend the delicate outlines of social suffrance. He must not immediately rush into an intimacy.

A call should never be too long. A woman of the world says that one hour is all that should be granted to a caller. This rule is a good one for an evening visit. It is much better to have one's hostess wishing for a longer visit than to have her sigh that you should go. In a first visit, a gentleman should always send in his card. After that he may dispense with that ceremony.

A gentleman, for an evening visit, should always be in evening dress, black cloth dress-coat, waistcoat, and trousers, faultless linen and white cravat, silk stockings, and polished low shoes. A black cravat is permissible, but it is not full dress. He should carry a crush hat in his hand, and a cane if he likes. For a dinner-party a white cravat is indispensable; a man must wear it then. No jewelry of any kind is fashionable, excepting rings. Men hide their watch chains, in evening dress.

The hands should be especially cared for, the nails carefully cut and trimmed. No matter how big or how red the hand is, the more masculine the better. Women like men to look manly, as if they could drive, row, play ball, cricket, perhaps even handle the gloves.

A gentleman's dress should be so quiet and so perfect that it will not excite remark or attention. Thackeray used to advise that a watering-pot should be applied to a new hat to take off the gloss. The suspicion of being dressed up defeats an otherwise good toilet.

We will suppose that Tilden becomes sufficiently well acquainted to be asked to join a theatre party. He must be punctual at the rendezvous, and take as a partner whomever the hostess may assign him, but in the East he must not offer to send a carriage; that must come from the giver of the party. In this, Eastern and Western etiquette are at variance, for in certain cities in the West and South a gentleman is expected to call in a carriage, and take a young lady to a party. To do this would be social ruin in Europe, nor is it allowed in Boston or New York. If, however, Tilden wishes to give a theatre party, he must furnish everything. He first asks a lady to *chaperon* his party. He must arrange that all meet at his room, or a friend's house. He must charter an omnibus or send carriages for the whole party; he must buy the tickets. He is then expected to invite his party to sup with him after the theatre, making the feast as handsome as his means allow. This is a favourite and proper manner for a young man to return the civilities offered him. It is indispensable that he should have the mother of one of the young ladies present. The custom of having such a party with only a very young *chaperon* has fallen, properly, into disrepute. And it seems almost unnecessary to say so, except that the offence has been committed.

A man should never force himself into any society, or go anywhere unasked. Of course, if he be taken by a lady, she assumes the responsibility, and it is an understood thing that a leader of society can take a young man anywhere. She is his sponsor.

In the early morning a young man should wear the heavy, loosely fitting English clothes now so fashionable, but for an afternoon promenade with a lady, or for a reception, a frock coat tightly buttoned, gray trousers, a neat tie, and plain gold pin is very good form. This dress is allowed at a small dinner in the country, or for a Sunday tea.

If men are in the Adirondacks, if flannel is the only wear, there is no dressing for dinner; but in a country house, where there are guests, it is better to make a full evening toilet, unless the hostess gives absolution. There should always be some change, and clean linen, a fresh coat, fresh shoes, etc., donned even in the quiet retirement of one's own home. Neatness, a cold bath every morning, and much exercise in the open air are among the admirable customs of young gentlemen of the present day. If every one of them, no matter how busy, how hard-worked, could come home and dress for dinner, it would be a good habit. Indeed, if all American men, like all English men, would show this attention to their wives, society would be far more elegant. A man always expects his wife to dress for him; why should he not dress for her? He is then ready for evening visits, operas, parties, theatres, wherever he may wish to go. No man should sit down to a seven o'clock dinner unless freshly dressed.

If Tilden can afford to keep a tilbury, or a dog-cart, and fine horses, so much the better for him. He can take a young girl to drive, if her mamma consents; but a servant should sit behind; that is indispensable. The livery and the whole turnout should be elegant, but not flashy, if Tilden would succeed. As true refinement comes from within, let him read the noble description of Thackeray:—

"What is it to be a gentleman? Is it to be honest, to be gentle, to be generous, to be true, to be brave, to be wise, and possessing all these qualities to exercise them in the most gentle manner? Ought a gentleman to be a loyal son, a true husband, and honest father? Ought his life to be decent, his bills to be paid, his tastes to be high and elegant? Yes, a thousand times yes!"

Young men who come to a great city to live are sometimes led astray by the success of gaudy adventurers who do not fall within the lines of the above description, men who get on by means of enormous impudence, self-assurance, audacity, and plausible ways. But if they have patience and hold to the right, the gentleman will succeed, and the adventurer will fail. No such man lasts long. Give him rope enough, and he will soon hang himself.

It is not necessary here to refer to the etiquette of clubs. They are self-protecting. A man soon learns their rules and limitations. A man of honesty and character seldom gets into difficulty at his club. If his club rejects or pronounces against him, however, it is a social stigma which it is hard to wipe out.

A young man should lose no opportunity of improving himself. Works of art are a fine means of instruction. He should read and study in his leisure hours, and frequent picture galleries and museums. A young man becomes the most agreeable of companions if he brings a keen fresh intelligence, refined tastes, and a desire to be agreeable into society. Success in society is like electricity,—it makes itself felt, and yet is unseen and indescribable.

It is a nice thing if a man has some accomplishment, such as music or elocution, and to be a good dancer is almost indispensable. Yet many a man gets on without any of these.

It is a work-a-day world that we live in, and the whole formation of our society betrays it. Then dress plainly, simply, and without display. A gentleman's servants often dress better than their master, and yet nothing is so distinctive as the dress of a gentleman. It is as much a costume of nobility as if it were the velvet coat which Sir Walter Raleigh threw down before Queen Elizabeth.

It may not be inappropriate here to say a word or two on minor points. In addressing a note to a lady, whom he does not know well, Tilden should use the third person, as follows:—

> Mr. Tilden presents his compliments to Mrs. Montgomery and begs to know if she and Miss Montgomery will honor him with their company at a theatre party in the evening of April 3d, at the Chestnut Street Theatre.

R. S. V. P.   117 South Market Place.

This note should be sealed with wax, impressed with the writer's coat of arms or some favourite device, and delivered by a private messenger who should wait for an answer. In addressing a letter to a gentleman, the full title should be used,—"Walter Tilden, Esq.," or, first name not known, "— — Tilden, Esq.," never, "Mr. Walter Tilden." If it be an invitation, it is not etiquette to say "Mister."

In writing in the first person, Tilden must not be too familiar. He must make no elisions or contractions, but fill out every word and line, as if it were a pleasure.

It is urged against us by foreigners, that the manners of men toward women partake of the freedom of the age; that they are not sufficiently respectful. But, if careless in manner, American men are the most chivalrous at heart.

At a ball a young man can ask a friend to present him to a lady who is chaperoning a young girl, and through her he can be presented to the young girl. No man should, however, introduce another man without permission. If he is presented and asks the girl to dance, a short walk is permitted before he returns his partner to the side of the *chaperon*. But it is bad manners for the young couple to disappear for a long time. No man should go into a supper-room alone, or help himself while ladies remain unhelped.

To get on in society involves so much that can never be written down that any manual is of course imperfect; for no one can predict who will succeed and who will fail. Bold and arrogant people—"cheeky" people—succeed at first, modest ones in the long run. It is a melancholy fact that the most objectionable persons do get into fashionable society. It is to be feared that the possession of wealth is more desired than the possession of any other attribute; that much is forgiven in the rich man which would be rank heresy in the poor one.

We would not, however, advise Tilden to choose his friends from the worldly point simply, either of fashion or wealth. He should try to find those who are well bred, good, true, honourable, and generous. Wherever they are, such people are always good society.

In the ranks of society we find sometimes the ideal gentleman. Society may not have produced so good a crop as it should have done; yet its false aims have not yet dazzled all men out of the true, the ideal breeding. There are many clubs; but there are some admirable Crichtons,—men who can think, read, study, work, and still be fashionable.

A man should go through the fierce fires of social competition, and yet not be scorched. All men have not had that fine, repressive training, which makes our navy and army men such gentlemen. The breeding of the young men of fashion is not what their grandfathers would have called good. They sometimes have a severe and bored expression when called on to give up a selfish pleasure. One asks, "Where are their manners?"

Breeding, cultivation, manners, must start from the heart. The old saying that it takes three generations to make a gentleman makes us ask, How many does it take to unmake one? Some young and well-born men seem to be undoing the work of the three generations, and to have inherited nothing of a great ancestor but his bad manners. An American should have the best manners. He has had nothing to crush him; he is unacquainted with patronage, which in its way makes snobs, and no one loves a snob, least of all the man whom the snob cultivates.

The word "gentleman" although one of the best in the language, should not be used too much. Be a gentleman, but talk about a man. A man avoids display and cultivates simplicity, neatness, and fitness of things, if he is both a man and a gentleman.

COMPARATIVE MERITS OF AMERICAN AND FOREIGN MODES OF ENTERTAINING.

There is no better old saw in existence than that comparisons are odious; they are not only odious, but they are nearly if not quite impossible. For instance, if we compare a dinner in London with a dinner in New York, we must say, Whose dinner? What dinner? If we compare New York with Paris, we must say, What Paris? Shall we take the old Catholic aristocracy of the Faubourg St. Germain, or the upstart social spheres of the Faubourg St. Honoré and the Chaussée d'Antin? Or shall we take *Tout Paris*, with its thousand ramifications, with its literary and artistic salons, the *Tout Paris mondain*, the *Tout Paris artiste*, the *Tout Paris des Premières*, and all the rest of that heterogeneous crowd, any fragment of which could swallow up the "four hundred," and all its works?

Shall we attempt to compare New York or Washington with London, with its four millions, its Prince of Wales set, its old and sober aristocracy of cultivated people, whose ideas of refinement, culture, and of all the traditions of good society date back a thousand years? Would it be fair, either, to attempt to say which part of this vast congeries should be taken as the sample end, and which part of America with its new civilization should be compared with any or all of these?

Therefore any thoughts which follow must be merely apologized for, as the rapid observations of a traveller, who, in seeing many countries, has loved her own the best, and who puts down these fleeting impressions, merely with a hope to benefit her own, even if sometimes criticising it.

Twenty years ago, Justin McCarthy, than whom there has been no better international critic, wrote an immortal paper called, "English and American Women Compared." It was perhaps the most complimentary, and we are therefore bound to say the fairest, description of our women ever given to the world. It came at a time when the American girl was being served up by Ouida, the American senator by Anthony Trollope, and the American *divorcée* by Victorien Sardou, in "L'Oncle Sam." There was never a moment when the American needed a friend more.

In that gentle, yet pungent paper, Mr. McCarthy refers to our extravagance, our love of display, our superficial criticisms of the merits of English literary women, judged from the standpoint of dress, and of a singular underlying snobbery which he observed in a few, who wished that the days of titles and of aristocratic customs could come back to the land where Thomas Jefferson tied his horse to the Capitol palings, when he went up to take the Presidential oath. Since that paper was written what a flood of prosperity has deluged the land; what a stride has been made in all the arts of entertaining! What houses we possess; what dinners we give!

What would Horace Walpole say, could he see the collections of some of our really poor people, not to mention those of our billionnaires? Should he go out to dinner in New York, the master of Strawberry Hill and the first great collector could see more curious old furniture, more hawthorn vases, more antique teapots, more rare silver, and more *chiffons* than he had ever dreamed of; he could see the power which a young, vigorous nation possesses when it takes a kangaroo trick of leaping backward into antiquity, or forward into strange countries, and what it can bring home from its constant globe-trotting, in exchange for some of its own silver and gold. He would also see the power which art has possessed over a nation so suddenly rich that one reads with alarm the axiom of Taine, "When a nation has reached its highest point of prosperity, and begins to decay, then blossoms the consummate flower of art."

We need not go so far back as Horace Walpole; it even astonishes the collector of last year to find that he must come to New York to buy back his Japanese bronzes, and his Capo di Monte, his Majolica and peach-blow vase. We may say that we have the oldest of arts, that of entertaining, wrested from the hands of the oldest of nations, and placed almost recklessly in the hands of the youngest,—as one would take a delicate musical instrument from the hands of a master and put it in the hands of a child. What wonder if in the first essay some chords are missed, some discords struck? Then we must remember that modern life is passing, slowly but decidedly, through a great revolution, now nearly achieved. The relation of equality is gradually eclipsing every other,—that of inequality, where it does survive, taking on its least noble form, as most things do in their decay. In Europe there is still deference to title, although the real power of feudalism was broken by Louis XI. Its shadow remains even in republican France, where if a man has not a title he is apt to buy or to steal one. On this side of the Atlantic there is a deference paid to wealth, however obtained. This is a much greater strain upon character, a more vulgar form of snobbery than the reverence for title; for a title means that sometime, no matter how long ago, some one lived nobly and won his spurs.

We may therefore assume that the great necromancer Prosperity, with his wand, luxury, has suddenly placed our new nation, if not on a footing with the old, certainly as a new knight in the field, whose prowess deserves that he should be mentioned. Or, to change the metaphor, we can imagine some spread-eagle orator comparing us to a David who with his smooth stones from the brook, dug up in California and Nevada, is giving all modern Goliaths a crack in the forehead. When we come to make a comparison, however, let us narrow this down to the giving of a dinner in London, in distinction to giving a dinner in any city in America, and see what our giant can do.

London possesses a regular system of society, a social citadel, around which rally those whose birth, title, and character are all well-known. It is conscious of an identity of interest, which compacts its members, with the force of cement, into a single corporation.

The queen and her drawing-room, the Prince of Wales and his set, the royal family, the nobility and gentry, what is called the aristocracy form a core to this apple, and this central idea goes through all its juices.

Think what it must mean to a man to read that he is descended from Harry Hotspur, Bolingbroke, Clarendon, Sidney, Spenser, Cecil. Imagine what it must have been to have known the men who daily gathered around the tables of the famous dinner-givers. Imagine what the dinners at Holland House were, and then compare such a dinner with one which any American could give. And yet, improbable as it may seem, the American dinner might be the more amusing. The American dinner would have far more flowers; it would be in a brighter room; it would be more "talky," perhaps,—but it could not be so well worth going to. In England, in the greater as well as in the simpler houses, there is a respect for intellect, for intelligence, that we have not. It is the fashion to invite the man or the woman who has done something to meet the most worshipful company, and the young countess just beginning to entertain would receive from her grandmother, who entertained Lord Byron, this advice, "My dear, always have a literary man, or an artist in your set."

The humblest literary man who has done anything well is immediately sought out and is asked to dinner; and the artist of merit, in music, painting, architecture, literature, is sure of recognition in London. One is almost always sure to see, at a grand dinner in London, some quiet elderly woman, who receives the attention of the most distinguished guests, and one learns that she is Mrs. So-and-So, who has written a story, or a few hymns.

In this respect for the best part of us, our brains, the London dinner-giver has shown his thousand years of civilization; he is playing the harp like a master.

To return for a moment to the criticism of Justin McCarthy. He says in it, that while he admired the American taste in dress, he could not admire a certain confusion of mind, by which an otherwise kindly and well-informed American woman misjudged a person who preferred to go plain, or shabby, if you will. In fact, he stood up for the right which every English woman will claim as her own, "to be dowdy," if she will. The Queen has taught her this. While the Princess of Wales, the younger daughters of the Queen, and much of the fashion of London dresses itself in Paris, and is consequently very smart, there is still a class who look down on clothes and consider them a small matter. Perhaps that is the reason why such stringent regulations are laid down for the court dress.

Magnificent, stately, and well-ordered, are the dinners of London,—a countess at the head of the table, a footman behind each chair, in great houses a very fine dinner, and splendid pieces of plate, some old china, pictures on the wall from the pencils of Rembrandt, Rubens, Van Dyck, Gainsborough, and Sir Joshua. Sweet, low-voiced, and well-bred are the women, with beautiful necks, and shoulders, and fine heads. The men are they who are doing the work of the world in the House of Lords, the House of Commons, in India, in Egypt, in the Soudan; there is a multiplicity of topics of conversation. No English stiffness exists at the dinner, and there is always present some literary man or woman, some famous artist as the *pièce de resistance*; such are the dinners of London.

The luncheons are simpler, and here one is sure to meet men advanced in thought, and women of ideas, and there is no question as to the rent-roll. Wealth has absolutely nothing to do with society success in London.

We might mention many a literary and artistic *salon*, over which charming and fascinating, young and fashionable women preside with the mingled grace, which adds a beauty and a meaning to Emerson's famous *mot* that "fashion is funded politeness." We might mention many a literary or artistic man or woman of London, who is the favoured friend of these great ladies, who would, if an American, never be asked to a luncheon at Newport, or admitted to a ball at Delmonico's, because he was not fashionable. It would not occur to the gay entertainers to think that such a person would be desirable.

Paris, as the land of the *mot* and the epigram, has always had a great attraction for literary people. Carlyle said of England that it was composed of sixty millions of people, mostly fools. His own experience as a favoured guest at Lady Ashburton's, and other great houses, ought to have modified his decision. In America, the Carlyles would have been called "queer," and probably left out. In England, it is a recommendation to be "queer," original, thoughtful. In that bubble which rises to the top, to which Mr. McAllister has given the name "the four hundred," it is not a recommendation to be queer, original, or thoughtful.

That some men and women of genius have commanded success in society only proves the rule; that some people of fashion have become writers, and painters, and poets, and have still kept their foothold, is only the exception.

Charles Astor Bristed, born to fortune and fashion, declared that what he gained in prestige in England by becoming an author, he lost in America. What woman of fashion goes out of her way to find the man of letters who writes the striking editorials in a morning paper in New York? In London, a dozen coroneted notes await such a lucky fellow. Perhaps the most curious instance of the awkward handling of that rare and valuable instrument, which we call the art of entertaining in America, is the deliberate ignoring of the best element of a dinner party, — the hitherto unknown, or the well-known man of brains. This distinguishes our entertaining from that of foreigners.

The best society we have in America is that at Washington; the President's house is the palace. He and his ministers, and the judges of the Supreme Court, the officers of the army and navy, are our aristocracy, — a simple, unpretending one, but as real in its social laws and organization as any in the world. And there intellect reigns. The dinners at Washington, having a kind of precedence, reinforced by intelligence, independent of wealth, and regardless of the arbitrary rules of a self-elected leadership, are the most agreeable in this country, if not in the world. We have said there are many sorts of Paris, and so there are many sorts of America. It must not be supposed that clever people do not get together, and that there are not dinners of the brightest and the best. Outside the "four hundred" there is a group of fifty thousand or more, who have travelled, thought, and read, experienced, and learned how to give a good dinner, — a witty dinner.

I use the term "four hundred" as a convenient alias for that for which Americans have no other name; that is, the particular reigning set in every city, every small village. In Paris, republic as it is, there is still a very decided aristocracy. There is the Duchesse Rochefaucauld Bisaccia, and the eccentric Duchesse d'Uzes, and so on, who are decidedly the four hundred. There are the very wealthy Jews, like the Rothschilds, who are much to be commended for their recognition of the supremacy of art and letters. They have become the protectors of these classes commercially, and their intelligent wives have made their *salons* delightful, by bringing in men of culture and talent. On Sundays the Comtesse Potocka, who wears the best pearls in Paris, tries to revive the traditions of the Hotel Rambouillet, in her beautiful hôtel in the Avenue Friedland. Her guests are De Maupassant, Ratisbonne, Coquelin, the painter Bérand, and other men of wit. The Baroness de Poilly has a tendency to refine Bohemianism and is an indefatigable pleasure seeker. The only people she will not receive are the financiers and the heavy-witted. The Comtesse de Beaumont says that the key to her house is "wit and intellect without regard to party, caste, or school." Carolus Duran, Alphonse Daudet, the painters, whoever is at the head of music, literature, or the dramatic art, is welcomed there.

The princes of the House of Orléans, are most prominent in their attentions to people of talent. The Princesse Mathilde has a house in the Rue de Berri full of exquisite pictures by the old masters, and a few of the modern school. Her *salon* is a model of comfort and refined elegance, and at her Sunday receptions, where one meets the world, are men distinguished in diplomacy, art, and letters.

But what simple dinners, as to meat and drink, do any of these great people give, compared to the dinners which are given constantly in New York,—dinners which are banquets, but to which the young *littérateur* or painter would not be invited! That is to say, in London and in Paris the fashionable woman who would make her party more fashionable, courts the literary and artistic guild; as a guild, the fashionable woman in America does not court them.

It may be said that this is an unfair presentation of the case, because in London there may be patronage on one side, while in America there is perfect equality, and the literary man is a greater aristocrat than the fashionable woman who gives the party. This is in one sense true, for the professions have all the honour here. The journalists are often the men who give the party. The witty lawyer is the most honoured guest everywhere; so are certain *littérateurs*.

People who have become rich suddenly, who wish to be leaders, to have gay, young, well-dressed guests at their dinners, do not desire the company of any but their own kind. Yet they try to emulate the dinners of London, and are surprised when some English critic finds their entertainments dull, flat, and unprofitable, overloaded and vulgar. The same young, gay, rich dancing set in London would have asked Robert Browning to the dinner, merely as a matter of fashion. And it is this fashion which is commendable. It improves society.

The social recognition of the dramatic profession is not here what it is in England or France. There is no Lady Burdett Coutts to take Mr. Irving off on her yacht. No actor here has the social position which Mr. Irving has in London. Who ever heard of society running after Mr. John Gilbert, one of the most respectable men of his profession, as well as a consummate actor?

In London, duchesses and countesses run after Mr. Toole; he is a darling of society. Mr. and Mrs. Bancroft have done much to help their profession and themselves by taking the initiative, and giving delightful little evenings. But it is vastly more common, to see many of the leading actors and actresses in society in London than in New York. Indeed, it is the custom abroad to ask, "what has he done, what can he do?" rather than, "how much is he worth?" The actor is valued for what he is doing. Perhaps our system of equality is somewhat to blame for this, and the woman of fashion may wait for the dramatic artist to take the initiative and call on her. But we know that any one who should urge this would be talking nonsense. In our system of entertaining in a gay city, it is the richest who reigns, and although there are some people who can still boast a grandfather, it is the new-comer who is the arbiter of fashion. Such a person could, in London or Paris or Rome, merely as a fashionable fad, invite the artist or the writer to make her party complete. In America she would not do it, unless the man of genius were a lion, a foreigner, a novelty. Then she would do so, and perhaps run after him too much.

And now, as we have been treating of a very small, unimportant, and to the great American world, unknown quantity, the reigning set in any city, let us look at the matter from within. Have we individually considered the merits of the festive plenty which crowns our table, relatively to the selection of the company which is gathered around it?

Have we in any of our cities those *déjeuners d'esprit*, as in Paris, where certain witty women invite other witty women to come and talk of the last new novel? Have we counted on that possible Utopia where men and women meet and talk, to contribute of their best thought to the entertaining? Have we many houses to which we are asked to a banquet of wit? Are there many opulent people who can say, The key to my house is wit and intellect, and character, without regard to party, caste or school? If such a house can be found, its owner has, all other things being equal, conquered the art of entertaining.

Now, all people of talent are not personages of society. To be that, one must have good manners, know how to dress one's self and respect the usages of society. We should not like to meet Dr. Johnson at a ball, but it is very rare to find people nowadays, however learned, however retired, however gifted, who have discarded as he did, the decencies of deportment. The far greater evil of depriving society of its backbone should be balanced against this lesser danger.

There are literary and artistic and academic *salons* in Paris, which are the most interesting places to the foreigner, which might be copied in every university town of America, to the infinite advantage of society. A fashionable young woman of Paris never misses these, or the lectures, or her Thursday at the Comédie Française where she hears the classic plays of Molière and even Shakspeare. It makes her a very agreeable talker, although her culture may not be very deep. She is not a bit less particular as to the number of buttons on her gloves, or the becomingness of her dress, because she has given a few hours to her mental development. In America, we have thoughtful women, gifted women, brilliant women, but we rarely have the combination which we see in France, of all this with fashion.

When this young and fashionable hostess gives a dinner, or an evening, she invites Coquelin and some of his witty compeers, and she talks over Molière with the men who understand him best.

It is possible that French *littérateurs* care more for society than their American brothers. They go into it more, and at splendid dinners in Paris I remember the writers for the "Figaro," as most desirable guests. The presence of members of the French Academy, for instance, is much courted, and as feminine influence plays a considerable *rôle* in the Academy elections, it is advisable for playwrights, novelists, and aspiring writers generally to cultivate influential relations with a view to the future. However this may be, literature and art are more highly honoured socially in Paris than in America, and men of letters lead a very joyous existence, dining and being dined, and making a dinner delightfully brilliant.

The artists of Paris have become such magnates, living in sumptuous houses and giving splendid fêtes, that it is hardly possible to speak of their being left out; they are mostly agreeable men, — Carolus Duran and Bonnat especially. But painters, especially portrait painters, are always favourites in all fashionable society.

The French women talk much about being in the "movement" which to the American ear may be translated the "swim." They follow every picture exhibition, can quote from the "Figaro" what is going on, they criticise the last play, the last new novel, they do much hard work, but they seek out and honour the man of brains, known or unknown, who has made a fine play or novel.

Every woman in America may take a lesson in entertaining from the old world, and strive to combine this respect for both conditions, the luxury which feeds, and the brain which illuminates. A house should be at once a pleasure and a force, — a force to sustain the struggling, as well as a pleasure to the prosperous.

A merely sumptuous buffet, a check sent to Delmonico for a "heavy feed" does not master that great art, which has illuminated the noblest chapters in the history of our race, and led to the most complete improvement in the continuous development of mankind. Without each other we become savages, with the conquering of the art of entertaining we reach the highest triumphs of civilization.

It is a progressive art, while those that we have worshipped stand still. No architect of our day, even when revealing the inner conceit which cynics say possesses all minds, would hope to surpass the builders of the Parthenon, no carver of marble hopes to reach Phidias, no painter dares to measure his brush with Raphael, Titian, or Velasquez. "In Asia art has been declining for ages; the Moor of Fez would hardly recognize what his race did in Granada; the Indian Mussulman gazes at the Pearl Mosque as if the genii had built it; the Persians buy their own old carpets; and the Japanese confess, with a sigh, that their own old ceramic work cannot be equalled now." In all art there is "despair of advance," except in the art of entertaining.

That is always new and always progressive; there is no end to the originality which may be brought to bear upon it. This rule should be constantly enforced. A hostess must take pains and trouble to give her house a colour, an originality, and a type of its own. She must put brains into her entertaining.

We have begun this little book, somewhat bumptiously perhaps, with an account of our physical resources. Let us pursue the same strain as to our mental wealth. We have not only witty after-dinner speakers — in that, let no country hope to rival us — amongst our lawyers, journalists, and literary men, but we have our clergy. It would be difficult to find any hamlet in the United States where there is not one agreeable clergyman, more often three or four.

The best addition to a company is an accomplished divine, who knows that his mission is for two worlds. He need not be any the less the ambassador to the next, of which we know so little, because he is a pleasant resident and improver of this world, of which many of us feel that we know quite enough. The position of a popular clergyman is a peculiar and a dangerous one, for he is expected to be merry with one, and sad with another, at all hours of the day. Next to the doctor, we confide in him, and the call on his sympathies might well make a man doubtful whether any of his emotions are his own.

But the scholarship, the communing with high ideas, the relationship to his flock, all tend to the formation of that type of man which we call the agreeable, and America is extremely rich in this eminent aid to the art of entertaining. As a Roman Catholic bishop once observed, "As a part of my duty, I must make myself agreeable in society;" and so must every clergyman.

And to say truth, we have few examples of a disagreeable clergyman. While his cloth surrounds him with reverence and respect, his fertile brain, ready wit, and cheerful co-operation in the pleasure of the moment, will be like a finer education and a purifying atmosphere. From the days of Chrysostom to Sydney Smith the clergy should be known as the golden-mouthed. The American mind, brilliant, rapid, and clear, the American speech, voluble, ready, and replete, the talent for repartee, rapier-like with so many of our orators, and the quick wit which seems to be born of our oxygen, all this, added to the remarkable beauty and tact of our women, of which all the world is talking, and which the young aristocrats of the old world seem to be quite willing to appropriate, makes splendid provision for a dinner, a reception, an afternoon tea, or a ball.

We sometimes hear complaints of the insufficiency of society, and that our best men will not go into it. If there is such an insufficiency, it is because we have too much sufficiency, we are struggling with the overplus, often as great an embarrassment as the too little. It is somebody's fault if we have not learned to play on this "harp of a thousand strings."

We need not heed the criticism of the world, snobbishly; we are a great nation, and can afford to make our own laws. But we should ask of ourselves the question, whether or not we are too lavish, too fond of display, too much given to overfeeding, too fond of dress, too much concerned with the outside of things; we should take the best ideas of all nations in regard to the progressive art, the art of entertaining.

Lector House believes that a society develops through a two-fold approach of continuous learning and adaptation, which is derived from the study of classic literary works spread across the historic timeline of literature records. Therefore, we aim at reviving, repairing and redeveloping all those inaccessible or damaged but historically as well as culturally important literature across subjects so that the future generations may have an opportunity to study and learn from past works to embark upon a journey of creating a better future.

This book is a result of an effort made by Lector House towards making a contribution to the preservation and repair of original ancient works which might hold historical significance to the approach of continuous learning across subjects.

HAPPY READING & LEARNING!

LECTOR HOUSE LLP
E-MAIL: lectorpublishing@gmail.com

9 789390 215058

Lightning Source UK Ltd.
Milton Keynes UK
UKHW011823190620
365269UK00006B/1377